I0800976

With Christ in the Voting Booth

Casting Down Imaginations *Before* Casting Your Vote

David J. Shedlock

CALVARY PRESS PUBLISHING
1-855-2-CALVARY (855-222-5827)
www.calvarypress.com
PRINTED IN THE USA

With Christ in the Voting Booth
Casting Down Imaginations Before Casting Your Vote
by David J. Shedlock

Printed in the United States of America

ISBN 978-1-879737-96-9

Unless otherwise indicated, Bible quotations are taken from the King James Version of the Bible.

Cover Design by Michelle R. Stam.

More information about the book may be found at www.calvarypress.com.

The author may be reached at djshedlock@gmail.com.

www.calvarypress.com

Foundational principles, seminal truths and central ideas derived from the Scripture, applied to all of life, are the substance of a God-centered Christian world and life view. This includes the political arena. David Shedlock, in his work, With Christ in the Voting Booth, sheds the light of God's Word upon the subject of politics, which he weaves in with his own depth of insight and wisdom gleaned from years of experience, aiming especially at the foundational level. As his pastor, I am very pleased to recommend his work as an engaging read for those desiring to be salt and light. The apostle Paul was not unfamiliar with the political situation of his day, nor was he averse to making his appeal to Caesar. Thus, like him, we would seek to have the mind of Christ in our dealings with our fellow man. With Christ in the Voting Booth will be a great benefit to Christ's people.

Mike Ericson
Pastor
Trinity Presbyterian Reformed Church
Johnston, Iowa

Proverbs 27:17 says, "Iron sharpeneth iron; so a man sharpeneth the countenance of his friend." David has helped to sharpen me, challenge me, make me reconsider arguments and even at times frustrated me. In the end though, I know that it has helped me to be certain what I espouse at Caffeinated Thoughts is coming from a Biblical worldview.

Not that we always get it right. We are not perfect, and neither are our politicians. Thankfully, we don't go into the voting booth alone; Christ goes with us. So, what are we to do when faced with two bad choices in the voting booth? David calls all those who claim Christ as Savior to filter their politics through what Scripture teaches. It isn't always black and white, but there is guidance available from Scripture. Readers will benefit from not only David's handling of Scripture, but also a wealth of experience in standing up for life, even when it means sacrifice.
You won't put Christ in the Voting Booth down without being challenged—and sharpened.

Shane Vander Hart
Editor-in-Chief
Caffeinated Thoughts
Des Moines, Iowa

In his book, "With Christ in the Voting Booth," David Shedlock explores the many challenges facing the Christian voter in our current highly politicized environment. David is certainly not timid about wrestling with arduous issues and always seeks for honest and Scriptural solutions. Obviously, Jesus did not come as a social reformer or political deliverer, even though His ministry took place in the midst of a very difficult social and political atmosphere. His primary objective and Divine calling was to rescue the lost souls of individual men and women from sin and eternal separation from God through the saving power of the Gospel and transforming work of the Holy Spirit.

But you'll discover as a reader of Shedlock's book, that even though in reality the moral, social, and political state of a people may be irrelevant to the advance of the Gospel—Christians still have the privilege to "occupy till He comes" while using the voting booth. One quote I found particularly instructive was "This does not mean that Christians shouldn't do politics; it is that politics shouldn't do them in."

I found this to be a good reminder not to fall into the trap of thinking we must devote all of our time, energy, money, and strategy into putting a facade of morality on our nation - or the "appearance of righteousness" over our governmental and political institutions--thus confusing our real role as Christians in a spiritually lost world. I would encourage every voter, regardless of your faith or political preference to read this thoughtful and well researched book.

Randy Davis
Drawing Closer Ministries
Ottumwa, Iowa

Acknowledgements

To Michelle Stam: I can only hope people will judge this book by its cover. Thank you.

To Shane Vander Hart: Thanks for permission to reprint portions of posts made earlier on the websites, *Caffeinated Thoughts* and *Caffeinated Theology*. Your support of Sarah Palin while I was supporting Mike Huckabee reminded me to make sure I get my facts straight.

To Christopher Levi, one of my ruling elders, who is also my friend and fearless editor: Your honest critique on the big things and attention to detail made this book more readable, yea (yeah!), more Biblical. Your passion to see the book say what is right without being obnoxious kept me from being myself, for which I am also thankful. I cannot repay you for the hours you spent working on this book—unless it becomes a New York Times bestseller, so I suggest that you get a-promotin'.

To my sister Shirley, with whom I have debated and discussed the most important things in life for over 35 years: Though we usually disagree on the basics, I have never felt unloved by you. Your reasonable criticism has encouraged me to make my thoughts clearer and fairer.

To Governor Mike Huckabee: Your belief in this work from the beginning made it possible, and your bold witness for Christ gave me hope that Christians can rule in a way that is pleasing to Him.

To the staff and faculty at Marshalltown Community College (Linda Moore, Molly Mauer, Jason Poock, Katie Kothenbeutel and Joanne Carpenter) whose encouragement, research, critiques and ideas made this book more professional and helped give me the "ummph" needed to finish: Thank you.

To my friends and members of my family whose proofreading skills put to shame this English instructor: Thank you, Mrs. Edward F. Hills,

Lynn Ericson, Breanne Hammett, Sheryl Stam, Barb Heki, Sanne Guyer and Michael Herrick for your kind words and help.

To my boss, Tamara Davisson, and the rest of the staff at Woodward Academy, many who stayed up all night just to make sure I was working and not sleeping: I couldn't have done it without you.

Finally, to Pastor Ericson and my other elders, Brian Myers and Stephen Stam, whose gracious, firm and thoroughly Spiritual advice both now and through the years has seeped through my work here.

Special Acknowledgement

The year goes wrong,
And tares grow strong,
Hope starves without a crumb;
But God's time is our harvest time,
And that is sure to come.

Lewis J. Bates

To my wife, Judy, whom the Lord has graciously made my helpmate in life: You know what a sinner I am, and love me, still. When I am tempted to pursue the meaningless or harmful, you pull me to safety. You are primarily responsible for what is not in this book: the trivial, the mundane, the temporal. You kept me focused on the eternal Son of God and His Lordship, rather than political fads.

We talked through every page of this book and though your lovely fingerprints are invisible to the dear reader, I can see them everywhere. I love you.

Dedication

By faith Joseph, when he died, made mention of the departing of the children of Israel; and gave commandment concerning his bones.

Hebrews 11:21

And Joseph took an oath of the children of Israel, saying, God will surely visit you, and ye shall carry up my bones from hence. So Joseph died, being an hundred and ten years old: and they embalmed him, and he was put in a coffin in Egypt.

Genesis 50:25f

And the bones of Joseph, which the children of Israel brought up out of Egypt, buried they in Shechem, in a parcel of ground which Jacob bought of the sons of Hamor the father of Shechem for an hundred pieces of silver: and it became the inheritance of the children of Joseph.

Joshua 24:32

This is dedicated to the memory of my father, Clarence Joseph Shedlock, who by faith made promise from his hospital bed that when he got out of the hospital he would attend church, even if he had to be wheeled inside the doors.

Just as the bones of Joseph were taken in a coffin to a place symbolic of eternal life, my own father's body was wheeled in a casket to a place symbolic of eternal fellowship with the saints of God, an Assembly of God church in little Byesville, Ohio.

May this work remind us to join these two men in looking, not for a temporal city made by the hands of man, but the Eternal City, whose builder and maker is God.

Author's Preface

Theologian Frances Turretin wrote, "We give to the Scriptures such a sufficiency and perfection as is immediate and explicit. There is no need to have recourse to any tradition independent of them."

I have tried to abide by this principle in this book. I believe every word in the Bible is infallible, and that none of the words that have come from my own imagination are infallible. Readers should examine each of my claims against the Scriptures, chewing on the meat and throwing away the bones.

I have quoted or cited many sources. This does not mean I endorse the viewpoints of those sources. Some of them are professing unbelievers (even some of our nation's founders), so I won't try to make them into something they consciously rejected. On the other hand, just because I have major differences with Christians on some issues, does not mean I think they are not Christians. The exemplary lives of many have put mine to shame.

I never try to prove to others the Bible is true. I simply assert that it is. The Christian agrees and already believes it to be so. The unbeliever never will be convinced by logic alone that the Bible is true; that is the work of the Holy Spirit. The Bible is also very clear that every man knows God exists, and was born with a conscience sufficient to prove to him that he is a sinner. For those that insist upon labels, that makes me a presuppositionalist. Of course, this does not mean that I do not marshal other arguments to support my ideas, but that they are primarily used to illustrate my points, not prove them.

If you do not know Christ, I hope you will get a glimpse of Him here. I've tried not to hide the truth nor play games with serious matters, but I have also tried to make the book non-partisan. The issues here are more spiritual than political. Without any apologies, this book is written for the

Christian. My hope is that this book will be fodder for further discussion among them, and result in better understanding of what it means to be *With Christ in the Voting Booth*.

Foreword by Mike Huckabee

In polite company, one avoids discussing three highly controversial subjects. David Shedlock bluntly writes about two of them here: Religion and Politics. *With Christ in the Voting Booth* leaves no question he thinks religion, or specifically "faith in God", is the more important of the two. But he's not afraid to mix it up. Utilizing the Bible, history, logic and lots of original sources, David is not so much interested in the religious character of the people of the U.S. (that's a given!), nor our Christian heritage, but rather emphasizes the need for ethical, truth-based politics and governance today.

When I began my service as the governor of Arkansas, some were skeptical that as a former Baptist pastor I could resist shoving my personal theology down everyone's throat. When I finished my terms 10½ years later, few people still held that fear. It can be done. In this book, David warns against two extremes every Christian voter and politician faces: putting too much faith in the government, and developing a rebellious attitude toward government, an institution ordained by God.

He writes:

> Because we are sinners, we need government. But what kind of government is needed to restrain wicked men? ... Government-too-big tends to dehumanize us, making us more like numbers to be counted than people to be served.
>
> Some people do not see the government as the God-ordained means for protecting society from those who would destroy it. On this basis, Ayn Rand libertarianism refuses to protect us against attacks on life and marriage; thus it is godless government, or government-too-small.

> Some detractors have frantically warned us that politicians like George W. Bush, Mike Huckabee, Rick Santorum, Ron Paul and Michele Bachmann are theocrats, people who believe that God will or should rule in the civil realm via the church or clergy. These naysayers are hyperventilating.... There is not one shred of evidence that any of the candidates listed above has ever been a theocrat or a theonomist.

With Christ in the Voting Booth is not a dated Voter's Guide that promotes certain candidates and after the election becomes as useful as day-old toast. Instead, Shedlock has written a book that addresses issues that crop up in every election. What if the candidate isn't fully pro-life? What if he or she wants to raise my taxes? Does God care who wins the presidency and my local mayor's race? Can I vote for a liberal candidate like Barack Obama? Should gender, race or religion enter my decision? What about third parties, or sitting it out altogether?

I have watched David regularly tackle tough issues like these in his blog posts at Caffeinated Thoughts. He does his homework and genuinely seeks to tell the truth. While I may not always agree with him, thoughtful Christians shouldn't ignore the advice he gives when they go to the ballot box or when they decide to run for office themselves. His strategy is simple: explain the principles, philosophy and process of politics from a Biblical perspective, and apply each of these elements to actual decisions voters make in the voting booth, and politicians must make every day in Washington, in state capitals all across the country, and in city halls everywhere.

Every primary season and general election is important. We ought to get it right this time.

Table of Contents

With Christ in the Voting Booth

Casting Down Imaginations *Before Casting Your Vote*

For the weapons of our warfare are not carnal, but mighty through God to the pulling down of strong holds; Casting down imaginations, and every high thing that exalteth itself against the knowledge of God, and bringing into captivity every thought to the obedience of Christ.

II Corinthians 10:4-5

Introduction

Knowing who to vote for doesn't always come easy for the Christian. No unambiguous voice from heaven whispers: "This is my candidate, vote for him." Even though almost every candidate in America claims to be a Christian, most of us know a few Christians we wouldn't trust with a loaded BB gun, let alone access to the launch button of the world's largest cache of nuclear weapons.

Thankfully, God has given us His Word, "the ultimate voter's guide." Using the Bible, *With Christ in the Voting Booth* provides tools to resist Government Too Small and Government Too Big, while embracing Government Just Right, not based upon false promises and "Christian" utopian fantasies, but rather the most important political success story of all: The Voter and Governor Who Please God.

I know politics isn't everything. It isn't even the main thing. Christians, who believe in heaven and want to escape hell, recognize that here, there is no continuing city (Heb. 13:14) and are looking for a country where the Righteous One dwells (Heb. 11:14-16). Some Christians even suggest that it is foolish to concern themselves with politics, likening it to polishing brass on a sinking ship. Yet every four years, many of those same Christians vote during the primary season, and most of them vote for president the following November. Nevertheless, they aren't activists, they have never been to a Tea Party, and they don't blog about government. They don't want a bailout. They don't want a handout. They just want to be left alone to raise their families as they see fit.

If this is you, don't worry. I am not out to create political activists or political junkies, I only hope that together we will begin to think Biblically before we vote. It is not enough to vote Republican or support "conservative" candidates. While there may not be a specific Bible verse that directly addresses every policy decision a mayor or senator has to make, God's Word is not silent on the whole process of governing righteously.

I do not claim to know who will be in the running for all the major political offices in 2016, let alone in the years beyond. Although I have no personal insight into the will of God, I know there is no secret ballot. God sees every box we check. Jesus goes with us into the voting booth, and God requires that whatever we do, we do to the glory of God (1Co. 10:31). I can say with confidence that He requires that if a Christian votes, he or she votes in obedience to the Word of God and in faith, leaving the results to Him. He has promised to never leave His people:

> But if from thence thou shalt seek the LORD thy God, thou shalt find him, if thou seek him with all thy heart and with all thy soul. When thou art in tribulation ... if thou turn to the LORD thy God, and shalt be obedient unto his voice; (For the LORD thy God is a merciful God); he will not forsake thee, neither destroy thee, nor forget the covenant of thy fathers which he sware unto them.
>
> Deuteronomy 4:29-31

Brief History of the Modern Christian Right

> There is nothing vainer than the idea that we can restore a nation, rebuild our once great country, and leave Christ out. That's the whole conservative movement in a nutshell. It's been apart from Christ.[1]

Without much fanfare, Evangelicalism and conservative politics got married in the 1970s.[2] Its progeny, the Christian Right,[3] was conceived in the shadows of Roe v. Wade (1973) and saw the light of day in the release of Francis Schaeffer's books[4] and films *How Should We Then Live* (1976)

---

[1] John Lofton, quoted in Gregg Jackson and Steve Deace (2011) *We Won't Get Fooled Again*, JAJ Publishing

[2] For a discussion of earlier influences on the Christian Right, see Steve Wolfgang, *Millennialism and The American Political Dream* Guardian of Truth XXVI: 4, pp. 54-58.

[3] Politics also had a sister who got married to liberal Christianity and helped spawn the religious left.

[4] Schaeffer's books have been cited by both Mike Huckabee and Michele Bachmann as having a profound impact on their lives. See

and *Whatever Happened to the Human Race* (1979); the ascendancy of James Dobson's Focus on the Family radio broadcasts (starting in 1977); and the founding of the Moral Majority by Jerry Falwell and Paul Weyrich (1979).

Political foundations for the evangelical surge were built a bit earlier when Phyllis Schlafly started the Eagle Forum in 1972, which eventually led to her successful fight against the Equal Rights Amendment. Though a Catholic, she could be called the midwife of the Evangelical Right.

Many evangelicals voted for the "Born Again[5]" Baptist Sunday School teacher Jimmy Carter in 1976, but Ronald Reagan wooed them to the Republican Party in 1980 and 1984 with his strong pro-life message and book, *The Conscience of a Nation.*

The growing movement did not generate a candidate of its own until 1988, when Christian Broadcasting Network and 700 Club founder and broadcaster Pat Robertson finished a strong second in the Iowa caucuses behind Bob Dole. Robertson's campaign rather quickly fizzled not long after he finished fifth in the New Hampshire primary. From 1992 to 2000, evangelicals split their support among many candidates during Republican primaries, including Pat Buchanan, Alan Keyes, Orrin Hatch, John Ashcroft and Gary Bauer, but they also helped propel George W. Bush to the White House. For many evangelicals, Bush had given a credible testimony of his personal conver-sion and faith in Christ during the primary season leading up to the 2000 election.

For over 30 years then, politically-minded evangelicals worked mostly through the Republican Party, arguably seeing little progress[6]. For years we played second-fiddle to other conservative interests, most of which we whole-heartedly agreed with: lower taxes and less regulation, strong defense, home-grown energy and free markets. We have been strong advocates of the Constitution, whether the 2nd Amendment right to

---

http://caffeinatedthoughts.com/2011/03/mike-huckabee-five-books-he-recommends

http://www.charismamag.com/index.php/online-exclusives/1594-novemeber-2011/31984-michele-bachmann

[5] Newsweek, October 25, 1976, cover story, "Born Again—Evangelicals".

[6] Other than the G. W. Bush appointment of two assumed pro-life Catholics to the US Supreme Court (John Roberts and Samuel Alito), the religious right has seen little progress. See *Blinded by Might: Can the Religious Right Save America*? Cal Thomas and Ed Dobson (1999) Zondervan: Grand Rapids, and also John MacArthur, *Why Government Can't Save You: An Alternative to Political Activism* by John MacArthur (2000) Word: Nashville

bear arms or the 10th Amendment limits to the power of the federal government. Questions remain. Have we been wasting our time seeking political solutions to what are essentially spiritual problems? Or have we been going about politics the wrong way all along? Are evangelicals gaining influence in the Republican Party and the country? If so, is this a good or bad thing?

In the chapters that follow, I will try to provide an antidote to our political ills, which I believe are a symptom of *spiritual* ills. And I will demonstrate that the problems do not come from too little political involvement, but rather from lack of knowledge concerning who God is and what He requires in the political process. Bright ideas, hard work and lofty goals, as important as they are, can never replace the blessing of the Maker of Heaven and Earth.

Few Christians today look to the Bible for guidance on the question of who to vote for or what government is supposed to look like. We've been hoodwinked or browbeaten into thinking that it is illegal or unethical to mix church and state, politics and religion. We have had a vague sense that we have a duty to vote for candidates who advocate prevailing conservative notions about abortion or homosexual marriage, but, sadly, this sense of duty is fading in the face of "more pressing problems."

In 2008, 24% of professing *Evangelical* Christians voted for Barack Obama,[7] even though as a politician he had never lifted a finger to protect any unborn children[8] nor protected any of those that mercifully managed to escape the hand of the abortionist.[9] It should have been apparent where he would take the country. He strongly supported homosexual marriage[10] and the agenda of the gay, lesbian, bisexual and transgender (LGBT) movement,[11] though his public stand seemed more moderated.

Other believers think the Bible doesn't address issues specifically enough to be helpful in our modern society, or they don't want to offend someone by taking a stand on controversial issues lest they lose the opportunity to share Jesus with them later. These are some of our ills.

---

[7] New York Times, 11/07/2008, *Obama Made Gains Among Younger Evangelical Voters, Data Show* by Laurie Goodstein (online edition)

[8] http://www.issues2000.org/social/Barack_Obama_Abortion.htm

[9] http://www.factcheck.org/2008/08/obama-and-infanticide

[10] http://www.calitics.com/showDiary.do?diaryId=6307

[11] http://obama.3cdn.net/36ddd2f5daac41cb21_rym6bxaax.pdf

2008: A Case Study

For more than three decades evangelicals had been praying for a presidential candidate they could support whole-heartedly. For a few months in the last election cycle, it looked like their prayers might be answered. Mike Huckabee, a Baptist preacher-turned-Governor, offered himself at the Values Voter Summit in October of 2007, "not as one who comes to you, but as one who comes *from* you." Huckabee would go on to become a top contender for the Republican nomination for President.

The same month Governor Huckabee spoke at the Values Voter Summit, however, a Wall Street Journal article by John Fund[12] portrayed him as "harsh" and "hard-right" on social issues, but a fiscal liberal.[13] It was a potshot heard around the world that would eventually be republished over four thousand times on the internet. The contrast could hardly have been clearer. Here is a guy that holds your views on the social issues (but is way too strident about them) and none of your views on anything else. It was supported with critical quotes from conservative stalwart Phyllis Schlafly. I believe this hit piece, more than any other, planted the seeds of confusion in the minds of many Christians. It created a template that Governor Huckabee could not overcome and prevented him from gaining the traction needed to win the Republican nomination.

Perhaps this is one reason well-known evangelical Christian leaders also went AWOL. In November of 2007, Pat Robertson endorsed Rudy Giuliani, who was possibly the most pro-abortion candidate to ever run for President of the United States on the Republican ticket. Can you imagine any prominent evangelical endorsing such a pro-abortion candidate when Robertson himself ran for president in 1988? I cannot. This shows how far the mighty Robertson has fallen in 25 years. This endorsement gave tacit permission for Christians to vote for candidates who were not pro-life, including Barack Obama. Meanwhile, James Dobson waited until after Super Tuesday to endorse Governor Huckabee when it was too little, too late.

A few evangelical leaders, like the late Paul Weyrich, one of the founders of the Moral Majority, later regretted not joining the Huckabee campaign. Here is a first-hand description of a post-election meeting of

---

[12] http://forums.gunboards.com/archive/index.php/t-9144.html?s=0dbf22f150cce5026256cd4960d49e86

[13] This was totally unfair, but Governor Huckabee was unable to change the impression. See Rod Martin, The Daily Caller: *The Huckabee You Should Have Known* (5/23/2011)

evangelicals that included Weyrich and Michael Farris, a homeschooling advocate and leading Huckabee supporter:

> "The room—which had been taken over by argument and side conversations—became suddenly quiet. Weyrich, a Romney supporter and one of those Farris had chastised for not supporting Huckabee, steered his wheelchair to the front of the room and slowly turned to face his compatriots. In a voice barely above a whisper, he said, 'Friends, before all of you and before almighty God, I want to say I was wrong.'
>
> "In a quiet, brief, but passionate speech,Weyrich essentially confessed that he and the other leaders should have backed Huckabee, a candidate who shared their values more fully than any other candidate in a generation. He agreed with Farris that many conservative leaders had blown it. By chasing other candidates with greater visibility, they failed to see what many of their supporters in the trenches saw clearly: Huckabee was their guy."[14]

Not all of the rank and file on the religious right backed Governor Huckabee, either. To show how important this was, consider the South Carolina primary. Huckabee only got 40% of the evangelical vote and finished 15,000 votes behind John McCain, a candidate who back in 2000 had insulted some evangelicals by calling Pat Robertson and Jerry Falwell "agents of intolerance." Despite that fact, McCain was able to split the remaining 60% of the evangelical vote with Fred Thompson and Mitt Romney. Had Huckabee been able to persuade even 10% of the evangelicals who voted for other candidates in South Carolina to support him, he would have won South Carolina and *might* be President today instead of Barack Obama.

It should be noted here, however, that even endorsement of a candidate by leaders of the religious right might not make much difference. In 2012, shortly before the South Carolina primary, many evangelical leaders endorsed Rick Santorum, who is Catholic. Nevertheless, he still finished third in that state behind Newt Gingrich and Mitt Romney.

Governor Huckabee's candidacy raises several questions. How do the people of God sift through all the choices? Is there a "perfect" candidate for the Christian? Are moderates right when they tell us the general elec-

[14] http://conservativetimes.org/?p=1815

torate won't vote for social conservatives? What should Christians do if we are faced with someone who is right on abortion and the meaning of marriage, but differs with us on other issues? How important is it that a candidate be a Christian at all?

With Christ in the Voting Booth will offer a view of the relation of Christianity and State that is a needed corrective to bad habits practiced by Christian pundits and politicians, as well as the Christian who only considers politics near election time.

This book is mostly about principles and philosophy, with a little process and pragmatism thrown in for good measure. Most of the principles apply to the election of mayors, governors and legislators, as well as presidents. It is also about hope, though not the false, utopian kind of hope Barack Obama promised, nor the "take back the country" kind of hope argued for by so many on the right. It cannot come from an inherent trust in our governors[15] or the promises they make. Real hope for the Christian is found in God and His works. Psalm 78:5-7 offers this multi-generational benediction, presented here from God's Hymnbook:

> His testimony and his law
> in Isr'el he did place,
> And charg'd our fathers it to show
> to their succeeding race;
> That so the race which was to come
> might well them learn and know;
> And sons unborn, who should arise,
> might to their sons them show:
> That they might set their hope in God,
> and suffer not to fall
> His mighty works out of their mind,
> but keep his precepts all[16]

[15] Frequently I will use the single word "governors" in place of government officials. It is a synonym for the word "magistrate" as used by many theologians. I believe the Bible speaks much more about those who govern than the institution of government itself because people can be held accountable, "governments" can't. Governors then means office-bearers at all levels of government, not just the heads of the jurisdiction called a "state", such as Iowa.

[16] Scottish Metrical Psalter of 1650

SECTION ONE

EVERLASTING PRINCIPLES

Chapter One

Our President: Elected or Selected?

One Little Word Shall Fell Him

It was 1971. Over 150,000 hamstrung American soldiers continued to battle bravely against the Communists of North Vietnam and the Viet Cong, while many of their comrades returned home and faced humiliation from some of their own countrymen. Instead of getting a pat on the back and a warm handshake, they got the cold shoulder and spit in the eye. Deserving merry welcome-home celebrations, they found themselves denounced at the airport as traitors and baby-killers.

In the spring of that year, God would use the keen ears of a lonely captive in the Hanoi Hilton[17] and the mumblemouth of a future Senator from Boston as agents to carry out His plan to keep a Republican President in the White House.[18]

The dispassionate voice blaring through the PA system at the Vietnamese concentration camp seemed unreal to Prisoner-of-War, Navy Commander Paul Galanti. What he heard was purported to be a former Navy Lieutenant, who had returned home from Vietnam and was now speaking to Congress.[19] Galanti had spent about 5 years as a POW and wished he too could go and build a happy and peaceful home with the woman who had become his wife shortly before he was taken captive by the North Vietnamese. Now he was forced to listen to this prevaricator on a loudspeaker telling made-up stories about American troops, suggesting they had routinely done awful and unthinkable things, from bombing villages of innocent civilians to shooting at them like sport. He was portraying his compadres as vicious and sadistic. In short, the man's testimony was being broadcast into Galanti's ears to demoralize him and his fellow POWs by getting them to believe they were serving an evil regime or to confess to war crimes they did not commit.

The gist of what Galanti heard that day would stay in the forefront of his thinking, even after his joyous return home upon his release in 1973. But one seemingly insignificant detail from that speech would be buried in his memory, only to return on the day of God's choosing thirty years later.

In 2003, Galanti was invited to a meeting of veterans to discuss the possible candidacy of Senator John Kerry, a Democrat from Massachusetts, who was seeking to oust President George W. Bush. Someone at the meeting offered to play a few audio clips from Kerry's past anti-war days, including Kerry's Winter Soldier testimony before Congress. Galanti had understood there were many hearings, many testimonies and many false claims being made against American soldiers while he was a POW, so he took no special note of Kerry's involvement. There was no reason for him

---

[17] This was the name given in irony to a prison camp holding captured U.S. military personnel, which was nothing like a luxury hotel. Our enemies had frequently used torture and inhumane treatment to brutalize Paul Galanti, John McCain and many, many others captured during the war.

[18] *Nixon* would be reelected the next year, but that is not who I am referring to.

[19] http://weblog.theviewfromthecore.com/2004_03/ind_003274.html

to think this was the anti-war speaker he heard back when he was a prisoner, until the following clip was played:

> They told the stories at times they had personally raped, cut off ears, cut off heads, taped wires from portable telephones to human genitals and turned up the power, cut off limbs, blown up bodies, randomly shot at civilians, razed villages in a fashion reminiscent of *Genghis Khan*.... (emphasis mine)[20]

Kerry had mispronounced the name of that barbarian as "jen-jus" Khan rather than "geng-us". When Galanti heard this tape played, the memories of his mental torture flooded back. He immediately knew this was the man whose voice was used to torment him and his fellow soldiers. He had never heard anyone else pronounce that name in that way. Galanti immediately volunteered to do anything he could to oppose Kerry's candidacy. Knowing nothing else about him, it was enough. This wasn't just any anti-war protester. This was THE traitor, as Galanti saw it. *This* was personal.

After this meeting, Paul Galanti and others formed a 527 organization called Swift Boat Veterans for Truth. They would eventually run millions of dollars' worth of television and radio ads, including one ad which featured Galanti. These helped ignite opposition to Kerry and kept him on the defensive the rest of his campaign. It blunted the effect of a decorated veteran's opposition to the Iraq War which might have been a winning issue for him otherwise (just as the American people were starting to grow weary of the war). Instead, questions about Kerry's anti-war protests and the legitimacy of his medals were *the* issues that dominated the campaign. I am not arguing for the truth or falsity of the ad campaigns,[21] rather, I am pointing out how one mispronounced word may have cost Kerry the election. Certainly the Swift Boat campaign made a profound impact:

> The single most effective ad campaign of the election cycle has thus far cost only about $500,000: the campaign launched at the beginning of this month by the new anti-Kerry group, Swiftboat Veterans for Truth.

---

[20] http://www.vvaw.org/commentary/?id=399

[21] http://www.factcheck.org/swift_boat_veterans_anti-kerry_ad_he_betrayed.html

> Within less than a week, polls found that half of all registered voters had heard about the Swiftboat vets' advertisements. Close to half, 44%, of all independent voters surveyed say they find the ads "credible." In the two weeks since the ads first aired, Kerry's support among veterans has collapsed by some 19 points: President Bush has now gained a 55-37 lead in this group.
>
> According to some reports, the Swiftboat vets' site is now drawing more traffic than the official Kerry-Edwards Web site, and the little group's servers have been overwhelmed.
>
> Why has this one group drawn so much notice—especially as compared to groups like MoveOn.org, which have outspent them by 20 or more to one?
>
> In their devastating second ad, "Sellout"[22], they first air tape of a young John Kerry alleging that U.S. forces in Vietnam committed atrocities "reminiscent of Ghengis [sic] Khan." They intersperse his voice with clips of men like Paul Galanti, an officer who spent seven years in a POW camp. Galanti says: "John Kerry gave the enemy for free what I and many of my comrades in the prison camps of North Vietnam took torture to avoid saying."[23]

Senator John Kerry of Massachusetts wanted to be president of the United States. God opposed it, so it didn't happen. I've got a long list of people God didn't want to be president. Let's start with Mike Huckabee. I don't know why God didn't want one of His own preachers to be president in 2008; I certainly did. The Lord raised up Barack Obama to be president instead.

It was not because I had a vision from God or a visit from angels that I can say that God selected Obama, I got it from the Bible. No, I didn't crack the code (there is no code). I don't have a special set of magical reading glasses, nor did I twist some difficult-to-understand prophecy to fit my own preconceived notions. I did what any political prognosticator could do: I read and applied a simple passage of Scripture. Here it is:

"He removeth kings, and setteth up kings" (Dan. 2:21).

---

[22] http://www.swiftvets.com/index.php?topic=Ads

[23] David Frum, 8/24/2004, National Post: *The ad that worked,* pg. A16

John Calvin's theology had an enormous influence on Western thought and the views of some of the founders of our nation. He addressed this passage in Daniel and spoke specifically of God setting up kings:

> We naturally fancy that they acquire their power by their own talents, or by hereditary right, or by fortuitous accident. Meanwhile, all thought of God is excluded when the industry, or valor, or success, or any other quality of man is extolled! Hence it is said in the Psalms, neither from the east nor the west, but God alone is the judge (Ps. 75:6f). The Prophet there derides the discourses of those who call themselves Wise, and who gather up reasons from all sides to show how power is assigned to man, by either his own counsel and valor, or by good fortune, or other human and inferior instruments. Look round, says he, wherever you please, from the rising to the setting of the sun, and you will find no reason why one man becomes lord of his fellow-creatures rather than another.

We should not presume to know who Jesus *would* vote for[24], but I can tell you with 100% certainty who God wanted to be president *after* the 1980 elections. It was Ronald Reagan. He even gave the Gipper another four more years, just like he did Richard Nixon (well, actually God gave Nixon only about two more years). Bill Clinton got a full eight, but it seemed to be touch and go there for a while.

If it is true that God picks our presidents, couldn't God just pick one without us even voting on him? In fact, He did just that very thing, *once*. On August 9th, 1974, Gerald Ford was installed as our 38th president having never received a single vote as a presidential or vice-presidential candidate. While serving as minority leader of the U.S. House of Representatives, Ford was *appointed* vice-president after Richard Nixon's VP, Spiro Agnew, resigned under federal investigation for tax evasion. When Nixon subsequently resigned during the Watergate scandal, Ford became president.

[24] D. James Kennedy wrote "So can anyone be so bold as to say how Jesus would vote? I think the answer is yes." *How Would Jesus Vote? A Christian Perspective on the Issues* by D. James Kennedy and Jerry Newcombe (2008) Waterbrook: Colorado Springs, p. 81
See also W. H. Carney (2006) *How Would Jesus Vote? A Biblical Perspective on Today's Hot Political Issues*, Creation House.
I disagree with both Kennedy and Carney. The focus should be on what God commands us to do, not speculate on what Jesus would do.

President Ford, himself, seemed to recognize his dependency on God when during his first speech in office he stated that

> I am acutely aware that you have not elected me as your president by your ballots, and so I ask you to confirm me as your president with your prayers. And I hope that such prayers will also be the first of many.[25]

After two years, when the voters finally did have an opportunity to vote on Ford, they voted him out. So did the people thwart the will of God by voting in Jimmy Carter, instead of God's pick, Gerald Ford? No, they did not. It was God who raised up Ford *and* put him down again. He also lifted up Carter in 1976 and set him aside in 1980. And so it was with our first 45 presidents. And so it will be for the 46th, and so on, as long as the Republic lasts.

The idea that God sets up kings (and presidents) and takes them down again is not new with me, nor limited to the one passage above. It is a truth that is dispersed throughout the whole Bible. Before we look at some more examples from both Scripture and history, I must address an objection that might immediately come to mind: "If God picks our presidents, why even vote?"

This challenge is similar to the one offered to Calvinists who believe God chooses who He is going to save. Why, these objectors ask, pray for the lost or even preach[26] if God determines who is going to get saved? J.I. Packer, however, argued

> You acknowledge that God is sovereign in salvation. You pray for the conversion of others. In what terms, now, do you intercede for them? Do you limit yourself to asking that God will bring them to a point where they can save themselves, independently of Him? I do not think you do. I think that what you do is to pray in categorical terms that God will, quite simply and decisively, save them: that He will open the eyes of their understanding, soften their hard hearts, renew their natures, and move their wills to receive the Saviour. You ask God to work in them everything necessary

---

[25] http://www.americanrhetoric.com/speeches/geraldfordpresidentialoath.html

[26] We preach and share Jesus because we are commanded to. I believe that no such explicit command exists to vote, though there may be some compelling reasons we should.

> for their salvation. You would not dream of making it a point in your prayer that you are not asking God actually to bring them to faith, because you recognize that that is something He cannot do. Nothing of the sort! When you pray for unconverted people, you do so on the assumption that it is in God's power to bring them to faith.[27]

In other words, Packer changes "Why pray if God does the saving?" to "Why *even* pray if God *doesn't* do the saving?" Prayer is part of the *means* God may use to save someone.

In the same way, we pray and vote because God is sovereign in determining our leaders *and* lets us have a part in choosing our presidents. Usually the guy with the most votes becomes President, though not always. In 2000, Al Gore got more votes than George W. Bush but he still didn't become president. Is it because the U.S. Supreme Court stole the election on behalf of Bush? No. Although there was a dispute over the ballots and votes in Florida,[28] the essential reason Gore lost was because the founders of this country decided to award the presidency to whoever wins the electoral vote (which is determined by a tally of electors chosen in a state-by-state, winner-take-all system[29]) rather than the popular vote. From the uproar the decision caused in 2000, one might think this had never happened before. But much to the chagrin of Gore supporters, it had actually happened two other times in U.S. history. First, when Rutherford B. Hayes was elected in 1876 and second, when Benjamin Harrison was elected in 1888.[30] Speaking of President Harrison, another time the will of the people

---

[27] Packer, J.I., *Evangelism and the Sovereignty of God*, 1961, Inter-Varsity Press: Downers Grove, p. 21

[28] Attorney for the Landmark Foundation, Mark Levin (who thought *Bush v. Gore* was decidedly wrong and wrongly decided) makes a convincing case that Bush would have won under every conceivable scenario even if the Supreme Court had sided with Vice-President Al Gore in *Bush v Gore*. See *Men in Black: How the Supreme Court is Destroying America* (2005) Regnery: Washington DC, pp. 170-173

[29] "There are 48 states that have a winner-takes-all rule for the Electoral College. In these states, whichever candidate receives a majority of the vote, or a plurality of the popular vote (less than 50 percent but more than any other candidate) takes all of the state's electoral votes. Only two states, Nebraska and Maine, do not follow the winner-takes-all rule." http://www.archives.gov/federal-register/electoral-college/faq.html#takeall

[30] http://usgovinfo.about.com/od/thepoliticalsystem/a/electcollege_2.htm

was thwarted was when President William Henry Harrison died in office only one month after his inauguration. A common cold turned into pneumonia and Vice-President John Tyler became the new president, though his detractors called him "His Accidency"[31]

In light of God's sovereignty, we might be tempted to just sit back and wait to see what happens. However, let us return to the simple fact that God often uses the actions of people to accomplish His will in choosing their civil leaders (Jdg. 9:6). Christians should not believe their actions are without consequences. God can use his obedient people to change history. Joseph rescued Egypt from famine by his God-given wisdom and purity. The actions of Hebrew mid-wives not only saved many Israelite babies, but saved Moses, who himself would be used by God to lead the Israelites out of the slavery of Egypt. The lesson here is not "don't do anything." It is trust God, and then *do* what is right. God can send slimepits (Gen. 14:10), insanity (Dan. 4:30-32, 5:21) or worms (Acts 12:21-23) to humble rulers when they fail to acknowledge that He is sovereign, or He can send voters to raise up whomever He wills to be president. Here are some relevant passages:

> And the vale of Siddim was full of slimepits; and the kings of Sodom and Gomorrah fled, and fell there; and they that remained fled to the mountain.
>
> Genesis 14:10

> The king spake, and said, Is not this great Babylon, that I have built for the house of the kingdom by the might of my power, and for the honour of my majesty? While the word was in the king's mouth, there fell a voice from heaven, saying, O king Nebuchadnezzar, to thee it is spoken; The kingdom is departed from thee. And they shall drive thee from men, and thy dwelling shall be with the beasts of the field: they shall make thee to eat grass as oxen, and seven times shall pass over thee, until thou know that the most High ruleth in the kingdom of men, and giveth it to whomsoever he will.
>
> Daniel 4:30-32

> And he was driven from the sons of men; and his heart was made like the beasts, and his dwelling was with the wild asses: they fed

[31] http://www.whitehouse.gov/about/presidents/johntyler

> him with grass like oxen, and his body was wet with the dew of heaven; till he knew that the most high God ruled in the kingdom of men, and that he appointeth over it whomsoever he will.
>
> Daniel 5:21

> And upon a set day Herod, arrayed in royal apparel, sat upon his throne, and made an oration unto them. And the people gave a shout, saying, It is the voice of a god, and not of a man. And immediately the angel of the Lord smote him, because he gave not God the glory: and he was eaten of worms, and gave up the ghost.
>
> Acts 12:21-23

Our campaigning may be the means he will use to bring about His will; nevertheless, God commands us to pray for our leaders.

> I exhort therefore, that, first of all, supplications, prayers, intercessions, and giving of thanks, be made for all men; For kings, and for all that are in authority; that we may lead a quiet and peaceable life in all godliness and honesty.
>
> I Timothy 2:1-2

How we fret and agitate, vote and campaign, call our congressmen and petition for redress, but oh(!) that we would only pray to live a quiet and peaceable life. Because He is both sovereign over kings and gracious, He hears *and* answers such a prayer. Hear this and be hopeful: "The king's heart is in the hand of the LORD, as the rivers of water: he turneth it whithersoever he will" (Prov. 21:1). And for the Christian, we have the added promise "that all things work together for good to them that love God, to them who are the called according to his purpose." (Rom. 8:28).

Insomnia Saved the Day, with a Little Help from Arrogance

The book of Esther is an unusual book in the canon of Scripture. God's name is not mentioned even once. Yet, His guiding hand is there at every stage: at one time, turning hearts; at another, changing circumstances. Envy had motivated Haman to conceive a two-fold plan that would cause the king to hang righteous Mordecai on the gallows he built, and destroy God's people with a mischievous decree. But God would not allow Haman's plans to bear fruit. I quote this at length because nearly every detail displays the Providence of God:

> On that night could not the king sleep, and he commanded to bring the book of records of the chronicles; and they were read before the king. And it was found written, that Mordecai had told of Bigthana and Teresh, two of the king's chamberlains, the keepers of the door, who sought to lay hand on the king Ahasuerus. And the king said, "What honour and dignity hath been done to Mordecai for this?" Then said the king's servants that ministered unto him, "There is nothing done for him." And the king said, "Who is in the court?" Now Haman was come into the outward court of the king's house, to speak unto the king to hang Mordecai on the gallows that he had prepared for him. And the king's servants said unto him, "Behold, Haman standeth in the court." And the king said, "Let him come in." So Haman came in. And the king said unto him, "What shall be done unto the man whom the king delighteth to honour?"
>
> Now Haman thought in his heart, *To whom would the king delight to do honour more than to myself*? And Haman answered the king, "For the man whom the king delighteth to honour, Let the royal apparel be brought which the king useth to wear, and the horse that the king rideth upon, and the crown royal which is set upon his head: And let this apparel and horse be delivered to the hand of one of the king's most noble princes, that they may array the man withal whom the king delighteth to honour, and bring him on horseback through the street of the city, and proclaim before him, Thus shall it be done to the man whom the king delighteth to honour." Then the king said to Haman, "Make haste, and take the apparel and the horse, as thou hast said, and *do even so to Mordecai the Jew*, that sitteth at the king's gate: *let nothing fail of all that thou hast spoken*."
>
> Then took Haman the apparel and the horse, and arrayed Mordecai, and brought him on horseback through the street of the city, and proclaimed before him, "Thus shall it be done unto the man whom the king delighteth to honour." And Mordecai came again to the king's gate. But Haman hasted to his house mourning, and having his head covered. And Haman told Zeresh his wife and all

> his friends everything that had befallen him. Then said his wise men and Zeresh his wife unto him, If Mordecai be of the seed of the Jews, before whom thou hast begun to fall, thou shalt not prevail against him, but shalt surely fall before him.
>
> Esther 6:1-13

It is not necessary that God be mentioned in this book to know that His hand is present. Every word oozes with the wisdom and justice of God. When later in the book we are told Haman was hanged in the noose he had prepared for Mordecai (Est. 7:9,10), it is according to what the Scripture says elsewhere in Psalm 7:15-16: "He made a pit, and digged it, and is fallen into the ditch which he made. His mischief shall return upon his own head, and his violent dealing shall come down upon his own pate."

Just in case we missed the point, God also turned the blessing Haman had intended for himself, into a blessing for Mordecai. The greater the hutzpah Haman displayed in being so arrogant and extravagant in desiring his own honor, the greater the blessing redounded to Mordecai.

Application in the Voting Booth

First, we must confess that it is God who picks our presidents, not us. This will keep us and our leaders humble before God.

> Lift not up your horn on high: speak not with a stiff neck. For promotion cometh neither from the east, nor from the west, nor from the south. But God is the judge: he putteth down one, and setteth up another.
>
> Psalm 75:5-7

Second, Christian candidates and their supporters should be careful not to promise more than they can deliver. Our political history is littered with single-term politicians who made campaign promises they could not or did not keep. Do you remember when George H.W. Bush said "Read my lips, no new taxes!"? When he reneged, the voters said "bye-bye." It wasn't just that Bush raised taxes; it was that he couldn't be trusted to be a man of his word.

Third, since God uses means, it behooves us then to recognize that God has given those of us who live in a democratic republic a great privilege and responsibility to vote in a way that is pleasing to God:

> As the servants of Christ, doing the will of God from the heart; with good will doing service, as to the Lord, and not to men: knowing that whatsoever good thing any man doeth, the same shall he receive of the Lord.
>
> Ephesians 6:6b-8

If we vote, we must vote in a way that honors God and shows His character (1Co. 10:31). We will return to this theme again in later chapters and determine if a Christian is required to vote.

Fourth, we should be careful not to presume upon the future. Be wary of anybody who says they absolutely know their favorite candidate will win. No, they don't. God's sovereignty is brought before us again in the following passage:

> Go to now, ye that say, Today or tomorrow we will go into such a city, and continue there a year, and buy and sell, and get gain: Whereas ye know not what shall be on the morrow. For what is your life? It is even a vapour, that appeareth for a little time, and then vanisheth away. For that ye ought to say, If the Lord will, we shall live, and do this, or that. But now ye rejoice in your boastings: all such rejoicing is evil.
>
> James 4:13-16

In recent decades, several candidates who seemed to have great potential for high office ended up making other plans because a scandal, a gaffe or some incident from their past derailed their candidacy. One candidate brags about his faithfulness to his wife to the press, and shortly afterward the same press published what appeared to be unseemly pictures of himself with another woman on a private yacht.[32] Another discovers that the mere accusation of crying due to a slight against his wife can cause the voters to turn against him.[33] One ill-spoken word or unveiled secret from the past can help determine who our leaders will *not* be.[34]

Fifth, the sovereignty of God is not to be acknowledged only during election seasons. Even *as* leaders reign, the Word describes the Lord's ruling *through* them and their accountability *to* Him. Psalm 2 requires that kings, just like everybody else, bow the knee to Jesus. One major premise

---

[32] Gary Hart

[33] Edmund Muskie

[34] George Allen, Thomas Eagleton, Herman Cain, etc.

of Samuel Rutherford's *Lex Rex* (or *The Law and the Prince)* was that kings do not stand above the law. It is said in our culture that we believe in the rule of law. We should, therefore, be suspicious of Congress when it exempts itself from laws pertaining to insurance, banking rules or insider trading.

> And it shall be, when he sitteth upon the throne of his kingdom, that he shall write him a copy of this law in a book out of that which is before the priests the Levites: And it shall be with him, and he shall read therein all the days of his life: that he may learn to fear the LORD his God, to keep all the words of this law and these statutes, to do them: *That his heart be not lifted up above his brethren*. (emphasis mine)
>
> Deuteronomy 17:18-20a

Last, we must admit that God's purposes are not the same as ours. He may intend to judge a nation or to chastise the church. Or it may even be to bless her in some way. Scriptures show that God even raises pagans such as Pharaoh, Cyrus and Darius for His own glory or the protection of God's people (Rom. 9:17, 2Ch. 36:22-23, Ezra 6:7-12).

Chapter Two

Man Is Fallen and He Can't Get Up

When we learn that a public official, celebrity, minister or other prominent citizen uses racist language, cheats on a spouse, steals huge sums of money or does things much worse, it's called a scandal. Actor Mel Gibson, football player O.J. Simpson, Governor Mark Sanford, Senator John Edwards, golfer Tiger Woods, televangelist Jimmy Swaggart and even President Bill Clinton, all blighted their own reputations when their bad behaviors became publicly known.

Politicians, in particular, are subject to have their lives scrutinized to the point where some misdeed from their own past could come back to haunt them at any time. Even their family members will be closely examined for potential blemishes and warts. At times, we seem obsessed with scandal.

Scandal is not to be confused with sin, however. Scandal is the public face of sin. It is said that for every cockroach you see, 200 lurk behind the walls. In the same way, only a small portion of the sins of mankind ever reach the eyes of the public and become scandals. But if sin really is so rampant, why are we shocked[35] when government officials are caught in a sin? Why do we talk so much about scandal and so little about sin? The answers involve some very bad news and the *Good News*.

---

[35] We are like the Captain Renault character in the movie *Casablanca* who said he was "shocked, shocked" to find gambling going on in a casino (right before thanking a clerk for handing him his winnings). www.youtube.com/watch?v=-Gf8NK1WAOc

The Bad News is That We Are *All* Morally Blind

We can't properly see our own sins or fairly evaluate the sins of others because human pride tends to make our own sins appear small, while making the sins of others appear large. This is perhaps why God warns us against judging unfairly:

> Judge not, that ye be not judged. For with what judgment ye judge, ye shall be judged: and with what measure ye mete, it shall be measured to you again. And why beholdest thou the mote that is in thy brother's eye, but considerest not the beam that is in thine own eye? Or how wilt thou say to thy brother, Let me pull out the mote out of thine eye; and, behold, a beam is in thine own eye? Thou hypocrite, first cast out the beam out of thine own eye; and then shalt thou see clearly to cast out the mote out of thy brother's eye.
>
> Matthew 7:1-5

C.S. Lewis describes how God sees the people in our lives who trouble us with all of their glaring faults, people who are so hard to live with, who have fatal flaws that drive us crazy, who refuse to listen to us when we try to help them. But then Lewis adds this further observation:

> He [God] sees one more person of the same kind—the one you never do see. I mean, of course, yourself. That is the next great step in wisdom—to realize that you also are just that sort of person....
>
> It is important to realize that there is some really fatal flaw in you: something which gives others the same feeling of despair which their flaws give you. And it is almost certainly something you don't know about—like what the advertisements call "halitosis", which everyone notices except the person who has it. But why, you ask, don't the others tell me? Believe me; they have tried to tell you over and over and over again. And you just couldn't "take it". Perhaps a good deal of what you call their "nagging" or "bad temper" are just their attempts to make you see the truth. And even the faults you do know you don't know fully. You say, "I admit I lost my temper last night"; but the others know that you're always doing it, that you are a bad-tempered person. You say, "I admit I drank too much last Saturday"; but everyone else knows that you are a habitual drunkard.

Not everybody agrees on this point, of course. Some people go so far as to deny the depravity of mankind altogether and instead assert that our basic nature is good. But who determines what good is? God or man? If sin has distorted our view, how can we know our opinions on these things are valid? The situation is similar to the problem of insanity. The insane man does not know he is insane; neither does the unconverted sinner begin to grasp the enormity of his sin.

The Good News is That God Has Not Left Us in the Dark

We do not have to rely upon our own biased opinions on these issues. Jesus routinely opens the eyes of those who acknowledge they are blind. "For thou art my lamp, O LORD: and the LORD will lighten my darkness." (2Sa. 22:29)

Jesus Himself is the Light of the World. Furthermore, just as he led His people Israel by light in the wilderness (Neh. 9:12), so He will lead his people today by His Word (Ps. 43:3, Lk. 1:79). Since this book is not a theological treatise on sin, in this chapter I will only touch on a few Biblical lessons concerning sin, which I will refer back to from time to time in the remainder of the book as they apply to politics.

Lesson #1 We Have All Sinned

Lesson #2 We Are All Sinners

Sin isn't just limited to politicians and public figures. You could certainly arrive at the idea that sin is prevalent in American culture just by reading advice or gossip columns or by browsing through crime reports in the local newspaper. Check-kiting, drunk driving, petty theft and child abuse all indicate *something* is wrong with the human heart. Moreover, our daily lives are filled with lies, gossip, fits of anger and perverse thoughts that never reach the level needed to call the police. Nevertheless, I don't hold strongly to these ideas about sin because of what I find in the news or even from what I see with my own eyes. I am convinced *from the Word of God* that these lessons are true: As a Christian, this is where I begin.

> If we say that we have no sin, we deceive ourselves, and the truth is not in us. If we confess our sins, he is faithful and just to forgive us our sins, and to cleanse us from all unrighteousness. If we say that we have not sinned, we make him a liar, and his word is not in us.
>
> I John 1:8-10

> As it is written, There is *none* righteous, *no, not one*: There is *none* that understandeth, there is *none that seeketh after God*. They are *all* gone out of the way, they are together become unprofitable; there is *none that doeth good, no, not one*. Their throat is an open sepulchre; with their tongues they have used deceit; the poison of asps is under their lips: Whose mouth is full of cursing and bitterness: Their feet are swift to shed blood: Destruction and misery are in their ways: And the way of peace have they not known: *There is no fear of God before their eyes*.... For *all* have sinned, and come short of the glory of God.
>
> Romans 3:10-18, 23

Lesson #1 indicates that all of us have committed acts that were forbidden by God, and failed to do everything He has commanded. Most people who believe in the existence of God will grant that they have sinned. They will say "I'm not perfect" or "I am only human." This admission, however, does not mean they understand the import of the doctrine. To sin does not simply mean we occasionally make some mistakes. "Missing the mark" is a good definition for sin only if "missing a flight" is what Islamic terrorists did on 9/11. Our sins are not accidents. They are intentional acts of treason against a merciful and holy God.

At first glance it might appear that saying "I have sinned" and saying "I am a sinner" is saying the same thing, but it is not. I have taken a few hikes in my day, but that does not make me a hiker. Sometimes you may sing in the shower or while the car radio blares "I Write the Songs", but crooning the tunes does not make you Barry Manilow.

Lesson #2 shows that it isn't just that we sin. It's that we *are sinners*. We do indeed *choose* to sin, but that sin comes out of the cesspool of our filthy hearts:

> And he said, that which *cometh out of the man*, that defileth the man. For *from within, out of the heart of men*, proceed evil thoughts, adulteries, fornications, murders, thefts, covetousness,

> wickedness, deceit, lasciviousness, an evil eye, blasphemy, pride, foolishness: *All these evil things come from within, and defile the man*. (emphasis mine)
>
> Matthew 7:20-23

Sin is embedded into who we are, into our fallen natures. By "fallen", I mean that Adam's sinful nature was passed on to all of his descendants, even though mankind was *created* upright and good (Ecc. 7:9). This is the meaning of the phrase "original sin" and was included as the first line in the New England Primer: "In Adams Fall, We Sinned All."

Thinking the problem is just what we *do* and not what we *are* promotes the illusion that we could cure ourselves if we could just get treatment for our bad habits. Men in prison often delude themselves and think they have had a religious conversion because they have repented of the particular sin that put them in the slammer or the contributing vices such as taking drugs, gambling, drinking or engaging in sexual immorality. But they have not met the physician who came to give them a new heart and redeem them from their individual sins *and* their condition.

> When Jesus heard it, he saith unto them, They that are whole have no need of the physician, but they that are sick: I came not to call the righteous, but sinners to repentance.
>
> Mark 2:17

"Sinner" is a description of *who* we are. It is our identity apart from Christ. It is why the Romans passage above not only tells us we sin; it also says we are incapable of doing anything good in our unbelieving state. The latter doctrine is offensive to us because we are tempted to measure our goodness by the works we do that benefit other people, not by the standard of God's Law which requires that every act be done to the Glory of God and with perfect motive.

Lesson #3 Man is Not Perfectible, Nor Can He Save Himself

> Can the Ethiopian change his skin, or the leopard his spots? Then may ye also do good, that are accustomed to do evil.
>
> Jeremiah 13:23

> But we are all as an unclean thing, and all our righteousnesses are as filthy rags; and we all do fade as a leaf; and our iniquities, like the wind, have taken us away. And there is none that calleth upon thy name, that stirreth up himself to take hold of thee: for thou hast hid thy face from us, and hast consumed us, because of our iniquities.
>
> Isaiah 64:6f

Because we are sinners, we cannot save our own souls by good works. It is not only the things we have done that keep us from serving God, it is because of who we are and what we are like. We cannot change ourselves. Those who have already committed acts of treason cannot put themselves in good graces with the king simply because they start acting like good subjects. Many Nazi war criminals tried to blend in with society after WWII. Those discovered decades after the close of WWII were held accountable, no matter how much they seemed to be model citizens at the time of their discovery.[36]

This inability to save ourselves is why we need a Savior (rather than just a good example), why we need grace and why we need to have our eyes opened. The Bible describes our condition as "dead in trespasses and sins" (Eph. 2:1).

What Can the Justice System Do?

The American system regularly goes through changes as our leaders and the people themselves seem to look at the world through different eyes. Our Supreme Court struck down the use of the death penalty in 1972; then just 5 years later overturned its own ruling, granting states "permission" to carry out capital punishment. Mass murderer Gary Gilmore was the first person executed in the new era.

What is the purpose of the criminal justice system? The names we use tell us what we think. A penitentiary implies that the goal is to have a prisoner repent for the things they have done wrong. A correctional facility is intended to correct the criminal behavior. A reformatory is supposed to reform the behavior. However, when prisoners are released and resume committing crimes, it shows that outward conformity to the strictures of prison life does not necessarily indicate a change of heart.

[36] New York Times, 2/04/09, Uncovering Lost Path of the Most Wanted Nazi by Souad Mekhennet and Nicholas Kulish

Governor Mike Huckabee's view of the criminal justice system came under scrutiny particularly because of clemencies he granted while he was governor of Arkansas to two high-profile criminals: Wayne Dumond and Maurice Clemmons. The latter went on to murder four police officers in cold blood after being released by Washington State's justice system.[37] Huckabee's position is that he could not know what Clemmons would do in the future, and that Clemmons' original sentence was way out of line compared to others who had committed similar crimes.[38] These cases, nevertheless, raise legitimate questions. How should governors and presidents use pardon and clemency power? To correct an injustice? To reward good behavior? When a prisoner has been converted to Jesus?[39]

Lesson #4 Misery is Sin's Company

It is important to see the difference between a sin and the results of that sin. The two main results of sin in this life are misery and scandal, the latter which I discussed at the beginning of this chapter. Misery includes the guilt feelings or personal shame that accompanies sin (Gen. 3:8), the "natural" consequences to sin, the breach that corrupts all of our relationships, the physical pain, suffering and temporal curses[40] for our own sins, and finally, death and eternal punishment (2Th. 1:6-10).

Much of our time in society is spent dealing with the misery of our sins: Poverty, divorce, sickness and disease, miscommunication, the ravages of nature and wild animals, and death itself are a result of sin in the world. Almost all of the discussions and debates about the right size and best kind of government center on problems caused by sin: the death penalty, fighting terrorism, racism, etc.

---

[37] For a balanced and Christian view of the role of retribution in our system, read Joe Carter's Huckabee and the Limits of Compassion at First Things Blog.

[38] The current Governor of Arkansas, Mike Beebe and the Washington justice system had a greater culpability in the Clemmons case, according to Caleb Hannan (Seattle Weekly, October 21, 2010).

[39] Jerry Falwell and Pat Robertson failed in their efforts to persuade then Governor George Bush of Texas to stop the execution of Karla Faye Tucker, who had committed a brutal murder in 1983 but later become a model prisoner after accepting Christ. She was put to death in 1998.

[40] The word "curses" seems medieval to our ears. I am not referring to the practice of people putting hexes on each other, or other things associated with witchcraft. But rather, I am referring to God's just acts of punishing sin in this life (sometimes as a means of discipline).

Mike Huckabee has pointed out that we cannot separate the economic issues in our country from the moral ones: "People say this is not a year where we ought to be talking about social issues.... [but] we need to understand there is a direct correlation between the stability of families and the stability of our economy." [41] Welfare exists, in part, because of the breakdown of the family due to divorce and abandonment, for example.

Lesson #5 The List of Sins is Long

I have been hinting all along that we are tempted to see sins only when they are associated with particular results. But the fact that we *are* sinners suggests that every aspect of our lives is tainted with sin. Sin is more than crime, vice or scandal. Many of our sins are invisible to the human eye, though the consequences of those sins change our lives every day. The so-called "Seven Deadly Sins"[42] (lust, gluttony, greed, sloth, wrath, envy and pride) are just some of the sins of the heart that destroy us inwardly and sometimes break out into scandal.

Christians recognize that the Ten Commandments were published on two tablets. Sometimes we focus solely on the Second Table of the Law (sins against men) and ignore the First Table (sins against God). This is a form of humanism we must reject. God requires devotion to Him in His Person and prohibits idolatry, profanity and Sabbath-breaking. We are commanded to not only love our neighbors as ourselves but to love God with all our heart, soul, mind and strength, Though many of these sins are not forbidden as part of our criminal or civil law; nevertheless, we may consider them when examining the fruit of the politicians who would lead our country.

Just as we began this chapter talking about scandal and politics, so we conclude it by discussing the relevancy of how sin is dealt with in the public arena. President Clinton's defenders suggested that sexual sins are nobody's business though they are lied about under oath, while Governor Sanford of South Carolina appeared to glory in adultery, rather than repent of it.[43] During the Nixon years, it became an axiom that it is not the crime

---

[41] http://www.cbsnews.com/8300-503544_162-503544-3.html?keyword=Huckabee#ixzz1fypvqJY9

[42] Every sin is deadly: "For the wages of sin is death; but the gift of God is eternal life through Jesus Christ our Lord." (Rom. 6:23)

[43] In a press conference, Sanford called the other woman his "soulmate" and said it was more than an affair, it was a "love story." New York Daily News, 6/30/09

that brings politicians down, it is the cover up. How we deal with sin is as important as the sin itself.

Lesson #6 The Wages of Sin is Death, But the Gift of God is Eternal Life

Sin is ugly and deadly from the very beginning. It is an affront to our Maker. Every sin is worthy of death in the sight of God. God says "the soul that sinneth, it shall die" (Eze. 18:20, see also Gen. 2:17) and "the wages of sin is death" (Rom. 3:23).

Thankfully, God has not treated Christians as our sins deserve. By God's grace we repent. By God's grace we are also forgiven. Jesus made the great exchange. The Sinless One took upon himself our sins and paid the penalty for them, and by grace gave us sinners His righteousness.

He paid a debt He did not owe;
I owed a debt I could not pay;
I needed someone to wash my sins away.
And, now, I sing a brand new song:
"Amazing Grace".
Christ Jesus paid a debt that I could never pay.[44]

Hope and Change You Can Believe In

> If in this life only we have *hope in Christ*, we are of all men most miserable. But now is Christ risen from the dead, and become the firstfruits of them that slept. For since by man came death, by man came also the resurrection of the dead. For as in Adam all die, even so in Christ shall all be made alive.... Behold, I shew you a mystery; We shall not all sleep, but we shall all be *changed*, In a moment, in the twinkling of an eye, at the last trump: for the trumpet shall sound, and the dead shall be raised incorruptible, and we shall be *changed*. (emphasis mine)
>
> I Corinthians 15:19-22, 51-52

In a world full of sin and misery, there is only one source of hope and change that you can count on. People will fail you. You will fail yourself. Governments and politicians are doomed to fail both you and your family.

---

[44] Lyrics by Ellis J. Crum

Perhaps you find yourself "most miserable" as the text above explains. Let me assure you that Christ has come to redeem you, both for this life *and the life to come*. He is someone trustworthy to whom you can attach your hopes.

SECTION TWO

GOVERNMENT OF THE SINNER, BY THE SINNER, FOR THE SINNER

Chapter Three

Whenever I Kill Somebody, It's Not My Fault!

America's bloodiest crime against students wasn't committed by white teenagers in black trench coats,[45] tired of being bullied. Nor was it carried out by an angry Chinese graduate student disappointed that a rival claimed an academic honor he was hoping for.[46] It wasn't a gangster, a preppie, a nerd or a geek.

No. It was none of these. It was 55-year old school board member and building maintenance man, Andrew Kehoe of Bath, Michigan.[47] Sometime, perhaps a day or two before May 18, 1927, Kehoe bludgeoned to death his weak and chronically ill wife. Then on the morning of the 18th he set his whole farm on fire, tying up his animals so even they couldn't escape the flames of his rage. While the fire trucks from town headed towards his farm, an elaborate time bomb he had concocted and concealed in the floors at the elementary school exploded, killing dozens of children and teachers. Not yet finished, he then drove to the school and blew up three more victims and himself, apparently firing a shot gun into the back of his dynamite and shrapnel-filled car. All told, 45 souls were murdered by Kehoe.

---

[45] http://www.cnn.com/SPECIALS/2000/columbine.cd/Pages/MAFIA_TEXT.htm

[46] New York Times, 3/27/07, A Tale of Power and Intrigue in the Lab, Based on Real Life by Dennis Overbye

[47] http://www.biography.com/people/andrew-kehoe-235986

The only thing Kehoe left behind was a homemade sign attached to a fence near his burned-down home that read "CRIMINALS ARE MADE, NOT BORN", showing that Kehoe, about to become one of the most blood-thirsty murderers in U.S. history, believed it was not his fault. Evidently he was so angered that his own taxes had been raised to fund the building of the new school, he destroyed it. And like all unrepentant sinners, he blamed others for his sins: from the superintendent who supported the school bond issue, to the children who gained from his loss, to the teachers who taught them. He killed them all. Or at least he tried. Half of the explosive devices he secreted into the school during his year-long plot didn't ignite or the body count would have been much higher.

If criminals are made, not born, then we *can* blame society for everything Kehoe did.

If criminals are made, not born, then paranoid conspiracy theorists, disgruntled postal workers, jilted and jealous lovers and control-freak cult leaders can't be blamed when they go on rampages, killing family members, coworkers and strangers in malls, restaurants, churches and grocery stores.

But criminals *are* born.[48] But before we celebrate too quickly that we are not like Kehoe, take note. We are all born for a life of crime. Give us a little encouragement or provocation, refuse to restrain our selfish impulses, give us the ideas and opportunity, and we would all be criminals. As sons of our father Adam, we are prone to be tax cheats, child molesters, shoplifters and drunk drivers. I don't say these things to prove we are sinners,[49] but I say them to illustrate what the Bible teaches: unrestrained sin leads to crimes. Not every sin is a crime. But every crime is a sin in action. Cain's envy led him to kill Abel. Joseph's own brothers were driven by jealousy to kidnap and sell him. David lusted and committed adultery, then committed murder to cover up his other sins.

Author Mark Gado remembers the bloody deeds of Kehoe this way: "A day when one man's strange obsession was transformed into hate and hate transformed into murder."[50] While Kehoe's deadly deeds seemed to happen suddenly, James 1:14-15 suggests it is not so simple. Sin goes through stages: "But every man is tempted, when he is drawn away of his

---

[48] As well as made, see Chapter 5 on restraint.

[49] It would be self-evident that we are sinners if our sin did not blind us to the fact!

[50] http://www.trutv.com/library/crime/serial_killers/history/bath/bath_6.html

own lust, and enticed. Then when lust hath conceived, it bringeth forth sin: and sin, when it is finished, bringeth forth death."

"Little" Sins Grow Into Big Crimes

So, when does a thief become a thief? When he pilfers with his hands? No, it is before that. It is before he plans his theft. It is before he stares at the object and covets it. His sin began the moment his heart inclined him to steal. Governors, on the other hand, can only punish the thief when he is caught with the goods, not when his heart inclines him the wrong way or he thinks about stealing. The purpose of government is not then to convert sinners, but instead, help restrain them from carrying out what their hearts would incline them to *do*. That is the reason we have governors in the first place.

We now know that Jared Lee Loughner, mass murderer and would-be assassin of Democratic Congresswoman Gabrielle Giffords, was not a Tea Party member, a Rush Limbaugh dittohead, a Sarah Palin campaign worker or a subscriber to Glenn Beck's *Fusion* magazine.[51] Though almost everyone seems to think Loughner is crazy, he probably isn't. If the accusations are true, he is depraved: morally bad or debased; corrupt; perverted. Regrettably, the American people have bought the lie that people don't really commit acts of unspeakable violence; they are mentally ill.

Kenneth Ward shot Clay Sanner to death at a Mormon church in Visalia, California. Ward was later killed in a shootout with police. One relative of Ward told the press "Mental illness killed my brother and Mr. Sanner."[52] In other words, Ward wasn't really responsible, his sickness was. I realize that such thoughts can be a source of comfort for relatives of the perpetrators who can't fathom the idea their loved ones did something that was just evil. But how does that make sense when relatives or friends of the *victim* use such language?

Teenager Zahid Makda of Standerton, Mpumalanga (South Africa) was accused of having his own parents murdered because they refused to give him money to go out. He allegedly hired a classmate and another man to stab them to death. A close family friend and guardian of the couple's

---

[51] When we are not blaming the culture at large or a killer's family, we sometimes seek reasons in the political realm to explain the crime. Conveniently, it is better if you can prove the other party is at fault!

[52] San Diego Union Tribune 8/30/2010, Olivia Munoz, Suspect in Mormon church attack was former member.

children said "He must have snapped. No one in his real frame of mind is going to do a thing like that."[53]

Rio Grande City, Texas was the site of a triple murder and suicide. The murders were committed by Francisco Pinal who was apparently having marital problems with his wife Lydia, whom he killed along with his mother-in-law and another woman. He later murdered himself. Ricardo Gonzalez, the nephew of Lydia, told police that Francisco used to threaten people with a gun. "I guess he was heartbroken and that can drive people to do crazy things."[54]

And who can forget that Nadil Hasan, the shooter who went on a rampage at Fort Hood, killing over a dozen American soldiers was immediately branded a victim of post-traumatic stress disorder. Charles Krauthammer recognized the problem with all of this and labeled it "medicalizing mass murder."[55]

But was Hasan sick? No. We try to cure the sick; or if incurable, we have pity on them. We certainly don't punish people when they are sick. In a perversion of right and wrong, the more heinous the crime, the more likely someone besides the perpetrator will be blamed. Now that is crazy. The fact that people are capable of *great* evil is what we tend to deny. Christians and especially governors and judges must view murder differently, however.

This empathy for perpetrators leads to strange ideas. When I was a youth pastor, I told the youth group about a man in St Louis who had murdered his wife by throwing her off the top of a roller coaster. They responded that *she* must have been a very bad person. *She!?* Have we really come to the place where the victim of a violent crime is assumed to be the evil one? We must regain a sense of right and wrong or electing "good" public officials will not stem the decay of our cultural glue.

Can you imagine Adam and Eve suggesting that Cain had just snapped and that is why he struck his brother with a heavy blunt object? Or perhaps King David just lost it when he found out Bathsheba was pregnant with his child and then ordered her husband murdered on the battlefield. No, there is a sin called murder. The shedding of innocent blood—whether it be in the womb with a surgical weapon or by starving to death an elderly or sick family member—is cold blooded murder. We should offer no excuses, no justification, no blaming someone else. The same goes for those who kill

[53] http://m.iol.co.za/article/view/s/11/a/20369

[54] Boston.com (9/01/10) *Police: South Texas Man Killed 3 Women, Self*

[55] New York Daily News, Charles Krauthammer, 11/13/2009, online edition

a spouse, child, parent, neighbor or the clerk behind a convenience store counter. Let's stop calling the people who do these things "sick", no matter how bloody or how shocking the massacre. Let's call them what they are: Evil. Wicked. Wrong.

Before we address the relationship between sinful mankind and its governors, there are two more aspects to sin that are relevant. First, the idea of mutiny (Chapter 4), followed by a discussion of how sin is restrained (Chapter 5).

Chapter Four

Anarchy: The Rule of a Thousand Tyrants

Adam and Eve's sin in the Garden of Eden was not just a single act of wrongdoing. It was the first blast of man's rebellion against his Creator and Ruler. One of Satan's temptations was that Adam and Eve would be like God if they ate what God said not to eat. From that moment on, man's offspring—*rogues* who want to be ruled by nobody and *busybodies* who want to rule over everybody—became mutineers. Rejecting God as ruler of the Universe (a violation of the First Commandment), the hearts of these men erected an idol in His place (a violation of the Second Commandment). One of the strangest paradoxes in the world is that Anarchist and Tyrant, Libertine and Legalist, Sadducee and Pharisee, natural enemies all, will unite in agreement: God must go.

Mutiny is not only carried out by rulers and religious leaders; we can see it carried out in our everyday lives, from the grade-school bully who demands that his subjects turn over their candy to the ne'er-do-well who can't wait to write graffiti on the bathroom walls. At work, the boss wants to rule over everyone's home life; meanwhile his or her employees take secret delight in breaking all of the safety rules at work.

People with both mindsets are determined to overthrow the rule of God. The two young men who slaughtered their own classmates at Littleton's Columbine High School, Eric Harris and Dylan Klebold, either saw themselves as God or wanted to be God.

> Harris seemed to feel superior to everyone—he once wrote, "I feel like God and I wish I was, having everyone being OFFICIALLY

> lower than me"—while Klebold was suicidally depressed and getting angrier all the time. "Me is a god, a god of sadness," he wrote in September 1997, around his 16th birthday.[56]

A world full of sinners is a world full of extremes. One man will not or cannot control his urges and so he carries out a bizarre crime. Reactionary legislators respond by creating whole new laws that restrict everyone's freedom when the old laws would have punished the perpetrator well enough. Those with power don't know how to refrain from exercising it, nor do they seem to know how to leave well enough alone.

It is quite possible for these two forces to coexist for a long time in a dying culture, just as fever and chills can live in the same sick body. When a nation permits parents to kill their own offspring with impunity, anarchy is at work. When the same culture criminalizes selling two-gallon flush toilets,[57] buying 100-watt light bulbs, eating Happy Meal toys,[58] or throwing Frisbees on a beach, tyranny is at work.

When anarchy sees an opening caused by some national disaster, it will attempt a coup. Men desire to have no rulers but themselves, thus in many countries anarchy will eventually have its season. Yet, looting and rioting cannot last for an extended period of time and leave survivors. People need to eat. They need rest. When anarchy has completed its course and worn out its welcome, the tyrant will seize power.

Anarchy and tyranny appear to be polar opposites. The proponent of one hates all laws and authority, while the advocate of the other seems enamored with both. One wants no government; one wants an infinite government. Tyrants may ensure the trains run on time (especially when the passengers of those boxcars mustn't be late for their appointments at the gas chamber), while anarchists may prefer to just blow up the trains (regardless of who is on board, friend or foe). Anarchists *destroy* foundations and wrecks things; while tyrants claim to *build* a society, even in the name of heaven. But when God's blueprints are ignored (see the story of Babel, Genesis 11:1-9), the road to "utopia" is often paved over mass graves of unwilling beneficiaries.

While they appear to be enemies, and at times do fight with each other, the anarchist and tyrant are actually blood brothers with a common goal.

---

[56] USA Today, Greg Toppo, 4/13/09, Columbine Myths, online edition

[57] http://dekalbwatershed.com/PDF/plumbingFixturesReplacement.pdf

[58] www.caffeinated thoughts.com, David Shedlock, November 2010, Happy Meal Ban

Anarchists and tyrants have formed an unspoken alliance against Christ and righteousness. This does not mean they are friends, but that they have found a common enemy in Jesus. In Scripture, we see examples of professed political opponents working together against Jesus:

> And Herod with his men of war set him [Jesus] at nought, and mocked him, and arrayed him in a gorgeous robe, and sent him again to Pilate. And the same day Pilate and Herod were made friends together: for before they were at enmity between themselves.
>
> Luke 23:11f

> The Pharisees also with the Sadducees came, and tempting desired him that he would shew them a sign from heaven.... Then Jesus said unto them [His disciples], Take heed and beware of the leaven of the Pharisees and of the Sadducees....[H]e bade them not beware of the leaven of bread, but of the doctrine of the Pharisees and of the Sadducees
>
> Matthew 16:1, 6-8, 11-12

What is the doctrine of the Pharisees and Sadducees? We know from Scripture that the two groups had two different worldviews. They differed on whether the supernatural existed, particularly whether or not there would be a resurrection of the dead (Mt. 22:23). The Pharisees were apparently more "religious" and were legalistic in that they thought law could save them, and they were also unafraid to add their own laws to the law of God.

The shared doctrine of Pharisees and Sadducees was this: they rejected Jesus as Savior and Lord of the World. Common hatred for the Son of God was strong enough it often united those who were otherwise different in both politics and religion. (But God can sovereignly use such division to the good of the church, see Acts 23:6-8.)

The shared doctrine of Anarchists and Tyrants is this: they reject Jesus as Savior and Lord of the World. The anarchist wants the total rule of self, with no accountability to any other person. The tyrant desires to have total rule over all others, without having any rules to guide him from above. Each attempts to dethrone Jesus. Neither one accepts God's sovereignty; therefore, each abandons the Law of God.

Just as blight, ghettoization and demolition projects can occur at the same time as renewal, revitalization and construction projects within the same city, it is quite possible to see the simultaneous rise of anarchy and tyranny in free nations. In the United States, it appears that both agendas are in the ascendancy.

Sometimes would-be dictators use anarchy to force-feed the country its statist agenda, just as Hitler encouraged the riots of the Hitler Youth in order to justify the imposition of his National Socialism (Nazism). This is the practice of creating anarchist problems and offering statist solutions. It is Munchausen Statism by Proxy.[59] This occurred when our own Federal Government required that banks make home loans to citizens who couldn't afford them, then when the inevitable loan defaults began to crush the economy, "rescued" the banks with bailouts and even more government regulations.

Similarly, those whose goal is chaos can use the power of the state to create an atmosphere where they know that anarchy will eventually result. "Green" activists do their best to stop the use of fossil fuels by adding bureaucracy to regulation to legal intimidation in the courts, and then wildly exaggerate the dangers of nuclear energy, for example. When they finally get their wish and the nation begins to subsidize wind farms, they oppose wind farms and prove that what they really want is to make us live like the Flintstones.

The absurdity of the approach is seen in an article entitled "Lawsuit Filed to Stop Construction of WV Wind Farm":[60]

> Environmental and animal rights groups want to stop further construction on a West Virginia wind farm, citing potential harm to the endangered Indiana bat. The Animal Welfare Institute and Mountain Communities for Responsible Energy filed a motion for a preliminary injunction Friday in U.S. District Court in Maryland. The groups last month sought to force developer Beech Ridge Energy LLC of Rockville, Maryland to obtain a federal permit to comply with the Endangered Species Act. Attorney Bill Eubanks, who is representing the groups, says that after the lawsuit was filed,

---

[59] "Munchausen by proxy syndrome (MBPS) is a relatively uncommon condition that involves the exaggeration or fabrication of illnesses or symptoms by a primary caretaker. One of the most harmful forms of child abuse, MBPS was named after Baron von Munchausen, an 18th-century German dignitary known for telling outlandish stories."
http://kidshealth.org/parent/system/ill/munchausen.html

[60] http://www.whsv.com/home/headlines/50492287.html

> Beech Ridge quickly moved ahead with construction. Eubanks says that left the plaintiffs no choice but to file the latest motion.

One is tempted to ask how the Indiana Bat ended up in West Virginia, but it is irrelevant to the animal rights activists, who have carefully designed the Endangered Species Act to protect not only species and subspecies, but also any "any distinct population segment" whose habitat might undergo "modification".

Clash of Worldly Views

Both tyranny and anarchy are religions of the imagination and they must be cast down by the Christian before he casts his vote. Our fathers in Israel watched as the clash of these two philosophies resulted in the breakup of their nation following years of idol worship under Solomon (1Ki. 11:33). A series of events in ancient Israel demonstrates what often happens when governors attempt to control people too much.

It happened after the death of Solomon, as Rehoboam began his reign as new king. Jeroboam had persuaded the Israelite Coalition for Smaller Government into holding a massive demonstration outside the palace demanding that Rehoboam reverse the growing bureaucracy started under the previous Solomon administration. King Rehoboam responded by seeking counsel from two different groups. He first asked the wise and experienced old men what he should do. They suggested that he should serve the people and reply favorably to their requests for less intrusive government, for they knew that "a soft answer turneth away wrath" (Prov. 15:1a). Rehoboam was not satisfied, and instead got advice from the bullies he grew up with, who suggested that he consolidate his power and oppress the people even further (1Ki. 12:6-8). His heart inclined him to go with those whippersnappers and so he told the people,

> My little finger shall be thicker than my father's loins. And now whereas my father did lade you with a heavy yoke, I will add to your yoke: my father hath chastised you with whips, but I will chastise you with scorpions.
>
> I Kings 12:10f

How did the smaller-government conservatives and Jeroboam respond? First, they stomped off in anger and decided to live in passive rebellion (v. 16), perhaps pouring bottles of milk and honey into the river in protest. When the king sent a member of the IRS (Israelite Revenue Service) to collect the taxes due, they murdered him (v. 18). Eventually they decided to secede from the union and start their own country, nearly bringing God's people to civil war (which surely would have been known in the secessionist region as The War between the Tribes or The War of Southern Aggression!). But when Rehoboam was ready to respond with a huge military attack, God intervened through a prophet:

> Thus saith the LORD, Ye shall not go up, nor fight against your brethren the children of Israel: return every man to his house; for this thing is from me. They hearkened therefore to the word of the LORD, and returned to depart, according to the word of the LORD.
>
> I Kings 12:24

What perhaps started out as a harmless *Milk and Honey Party* movement, after three days had turned into out-of-control *Occupy Shechem-Street* protests. Perhaps Jeroboam and his band of rebels had threatened to overturn chariots and set tents on fire; we don't know. We do know they considered revolution, for they said they would serve Rehoboam *if* he met their demands (see 1Ki. 12:1-5).

When it was all over, God's sovereign will had been accomplished in spite of sin on every side. God had avenged the idolatry that Israel had engaged in during Solomon's reign. The over-reaching government of Rehoboam had lost control of over 80% of his kingdom, leaving only Judah and the small tribe of Benjamin loyal to the throne.

Nevertheless, the hopes of a better life for Jeroboam's subjects soon disappeared, too. He led them into idolatry and rebellion against God, setting up the worship of not one but two golden calves, even creating a false religion with a false priesthood, man-made holidays and false worship (1Ki. 12:28-33). The ten northern tribes of Israel would never have a single godly king to rule over them and they would eventually be dispersed over the whole world.

We must be aware that every revolution carries within itself the seeds of the revolutions that follow. Growing discontent against governmental oppression (whether real or imagined) so easily leads to rebellion. The era of the French Revolution demonstrates that war does not satiate the bloodlust stirred up by rebellion. Hardly had the dust settled after the American colonists rose up against King George when our nation—less than fifty years later—would break into a civil war that would kill over 600,000 Americans.

In light of Romans 13, we ought to at least reexamine whether or not many of our ills stem from a national attitude of rebellion spawned by the American Revolution. John MacArthur goes further:

> The United States was actually born out of a violation of New Testament principles, and any blessings that God has bestowed on America have come in spite of that disobedience of the Founding Fathers.[61]

Even if MacArthur is right, we cannot go back and undo what has been done. But we can ask that God put a guard at the door of our rebellious hearts. There is only one way to guarantee that your country, your future home, is a place of peace. Abraham knew that God himself was the source of that place of tranquility:

> By *faith* he sojourned in the land of promise, as in a *strange country*, dwelling in tabernacles with Isaac and Jacob, the heirs with him of the same promise: For he looked for a *city* which hath foundations, whose builder and maker is God. ... These all died in faith, not having received the promises, *but having seen them afar off*, and were persuaded of them, and embraced them, and confessed that they were *strangers and pilgrims on the earth*. For they that say such things declare plainly that *they seek a country*. And truly, if they had been mindful of that country from whence they came out, they might have had opportunity to have returned. But now *they desire a better country, that is, an heavenly*: wherefore God is not ashamed to be called their God: for *he hath prepared for them a city*. (emphasis mine)
>
> Hebrews 11:9, 10, 13-16

If God's people have survived, even thrived, under the persecution of dictators or in the chaos of anarchy, just as Abraham did, it is because our primary citizenship is in another place.

At times, the best a Christian can hope for is found in Paul's command to Timothy concerning prayer:

---

[61] MacArthur, op. cit.

> I exhort therefore, that, first of all, supplications, prayers, intercessions, and giving of thanks, be made for all men; For kings, and for all that are in authority; *that we may lead a quiet and peaceable life in all godliness and honesty.*
>
> I Timothy 2:1, 2

Application in the Voting Booth

First, we should examine the policies and proposals of all candidates. Do they contribute to anarchy or to tyranny? We should be respectful, but skeptical of all politicians, as they suffer the same temptations to power or lawlessness as the rest of us.

Second, it is entirely proper for Christians to petition their civil government for relief of the burdens placed on them by over-regulation and over-taxation. Likewise, we should not directly seek to place in office those who would burden us so. Here is where comparing a candidate's promises with his or her actual record comes in handy.

Third, we have chosen a bowl of pottage over blessing if our desire for more stuff (better jobs, more pay, lower taxes) leads us to abandon the priorities of the Kingdom of God. Shrinking the bureaucracy and the national debt is a good thing unless it is done by trading away the lives of our neighbors yet to be born.

Fourth, neither tyranny nor anarchy tends to the peaceable lives God has called us to. Barry Goldwater conceived the balance as a picture of liberty:

> Freedom under a government limited by laws of nature and of nature's God. Freedom balanced so that liberty lacking order will not become the slavery of the prison cell; balanced so that liberty lacking order will not become the license of the mob and of the jungle.[62]

Tyranny may be preferable over anarchy because anarchy always leads to tyranny, eventually. However, it would be better not to vote, if you have to choose between tyrants and libertines. God will do as he pleases,

[62] Barry Goldwater's 1964 Acceptance Speech for the GOP Nomination for President

but woe unto us if we deliberately choose to stray from the straight path of righteousness found in Scripture.[63]

[63] I do not have in mind here the political distinction between right and left, but the errors of tyranny and anarchy. Politicians on both the left and right can be inclined to tyranny or anarchy. I would hope that members of all parties would mend their ways and seek the face of God in Christ.

Chapter Five

We All Wear Strait Jackets

My sister Shirley and her retired husband Ralph live in the shadows of a great learning institution, The Ohio State University. Their Dutch Colonial-style home is a single-family dwelling and sits perched above—and adjacent to—a small walking park on the edge of the campus where there are many fraternity and sorority houses, apartment buildings and other kinds of "off-campus" housing for students.

Obnoxious parties have always been a part of the landscape, but in recent years things have gone downhill in almost every conceivable way. The blaring music has begun to stretch into the wee hours of the morning. Party nights are no longer just Friday and Saturday; Thursday is the new Friday. Mischief and mayhem are on the uptick, along with their companions, vandalism and graffiti. More students are staggering in the street or losing consciousness in Shirley and her neighbor's yards than ever before. Sadly, the City of Columbus and its police officers don't seem to take it too seriously.

When my sister confronts unruly students (who also happen to be adults) she usually gets blank stares or a "what did I do?" attitude. Even the two inebriated young women who dangerously dangled their legs out into the busy street outside Shirley's house didn't appreciate that it was to their own benefit to get out of harm's way. When asked about the neighbors and their children who are kept up half the night with their antics, some of the belligerents reply with words akin to "who is my neighbor[64]?"

[64] Luke 10:25-37

Are these anti-social acts being committed by socially deprived and unemployed inner city youth who have nothing but time on their hands? No, the perpetrators are mostly privileged students who ought to be in their dorms studying instead of staying up partying and causing their neighbors to lose sleep.[65]

Why do these students behave like this, then? (Shouldn't I say misbehave?) My scientifically researched and academically sound answer is this: They do it because they *want* to. If you want to know why they want to act this way, go back and read Chapter 2 again.

If we are truly inclined to do evil continually, why don't we sin at every waking moment, then? In other words, if the picture I painted of our sinful hearts in the last few chapters is accurate, why don't we all go on maniacal rampages, destroying everything and everyone in our paths? If I am correctly presenting what the Bible teaches, how does society even function, let alone prosper at times?

The answer to these questions is simple, too. Just as the reason I misbehave can be traced to the words "I want to", the reason I don't do evil things all the time is just as simple: "I can't." God won't let me. He has put a whole bevy of restraints on my behavior, so that I cannot do what I would do if I could.

First, each man and woman is made in the image of God and, though fallen, still retains a conscience (Rom. 2:15) And although it is badly distorted so that it is often an unreliable guide, it is like a nagging buzzer that won't let us forget that the evil we contemplate is just plain wrong.

Second, we fear the punishment we might receive whenever we do wrong, whether it comes from a parent wielding the rod of correction for our good or from the sword of the magistrate who was raised up by God to keep our evil in check. Even our fellow human beings might show their anger against us should we wrong them. After Cain killed his brother Abel, he recognized the peril that would come on him and said unto the Lord:

> My punishment is greater than I can bear. Behold, thou hast driven me out this day from the face of the earth; and from thy face shall I be hid; and I shall be a fugitive and a vagabond in the earth; and it shall come to pass, that every one that findeth me shall slay me.
> Genesis 4:13

[65] I must be getting old. When I hear the word "party", I still think of cake and ice cream.

Third, many of us have been trained since our childhood to put others first and to use self-control. Every time our parents denied us the satisfaction of having every goody our hearts desire, they were training us, even restraining us. Christian churches, and even the rituals or teachings of non-Christian religions, can have the effect of restraining outward wicked acts, at least for a season. Cultural traditions and mores have an impact as well.

Fourth, we are physically or providentially incapable of doing all the evil that we would wish. Even if you wanted to destroy all of mankind in one fell swoop, you would fail. There is no doomsday device. On 9/11, terrorists wanted to kill all of the tens of thousands of Americans who worked at the World Trade Center. While what they did was spectacularly evil, they did not kill everyone, even within their targets. The heroes of Flight 93 kept Osama Bin Laden from carrying out all the diabolism he wanted to accomplish with that airplane. Grandiose plans for evil often fail because God has other plans.

The Plan of God vs. the Plans of Men

The Bible tells us of a man named Joseph who was favored by his father Jacob. His envious brothers kidnapped him and eventually sold him as a slave to the Midianites, who in turn resold him to the Egyptians (Gen. 37:28, 36). After experiencing many ups and downs, Joseph was raised up by God to be second-in-command under Pharaoh. Then a great famine arose and Joseph had opportunity to bless the brothers who were unaware of God's shining Providence in Joseph's life. God had given him a plan to rescue the nation of Egypt, which was really for the benefit of the people of God. When his brothers came to Egypt to get food, they eventually learned of the power of the brother they had earlier abused, scorned and criminally mistreated. How did Joseph view the earlier sin against him?

> And God sent me before you to preserve you a posterity in the earth, and to save your lives by a great deliverance. *So now it was not you that sent me hither, but God*: and he hath made me a father to Pharaoh, and lord of all his house, and a ruler throughout all the land of Egypt.... But as for you, *ye thought evil against me; but God meant it unto good*, to bring to pass, as it is this day, to save much people alive. (emphasis mine)
>
> Genesis 45:7-8; 50:20

Not even Satan himself can do all the evil that he would. Job was sorely afflicted, but God would only let the Devil go so far and no further. The whole book of Job shows that even acts once perpetrated by the Devil and permitted by God can simultaneously serve two different purposes. And it is God's purposes for His people that always win out in the end.

As I demonstrated in the last chapter, men want to dethrone God; they are mutineers of the worst sort. But He who sits in the heavens laughs at the plots of wicked men (Ps. 2). Even the most singularly wicked act in all of the world's history failed in its goal: to destroy the Son of God, Jesus our Savior.

> But we speak the wisdom of God in a mystery, even the hidden wisdom, which God ordained before the world unto our glory: Which none of the princes of this world knew: for had they known it, they would not have crucified the Lord of glory.
>
> I Corinthians 2:7f

As the various restraints are removed from people, they begin to brutalize each other. When parents cease to discipline their children or train them in right and wrong, they are preparing them to have outbreaks of socially destructive sin. The trouble brewing on virtually every college and university campus across the country, sometimes breaks forth in full-blown riots or wilding. The latter term refers to groups of marauders who randomly pick and then begin to beat the daylights out of innocent passers-by, sometimes killing them. This is also known as the "game" of "Knockout King."[66]

When people get drunk, one of the earliest casualties is inhibition, an internal mechanism designed as a restraint. Drunkards are displaying another face of humanity unmasked. That drunkard is you and me, dear reader, if left unrestrained. When someone misbehaves under the influence of drugs or alcohol, he or she should not get away with blaming the beer. This is the "real person" coming out.

The relation between restraint and government is almost predictable. In Israel, a pattern can be seen in the book of Judges, typified by the following passage:

> And the children of Israel *did evil* in the sight of the LORD, and forgat the LORD their God, and served Baalim and the groves.

[66] http://www.dailymail.co.uk/news/article-2078484/Knockout-King.html

> Therefore the *anger of the LORD was hot* against Israel, and he sold them into the hand of Chushanrishathaim king of Mesopotamia: and the children of Israel served Chushanrishathaim eight years. And when the children of *Israel cried unto the LORD, the LORD raised up a deliverer* to the children of Israel, *who delivered them*, even Othniel the son of Kenaz, Caleb's younger brother.
>
> And the Spirit of the LORD came upon him, and he judged Israel, and went out to war: and the LORD delivered Chushanrishathaim king of Mesopotamia into his hand; and his hand prevailed against Chushanrishathaim. *And the land had rest* forty years. And *Othniel the son of Kenaz died. And the children of Israel did evil again* in the sight of the LORD: and the LORD strengthened Eglon the king of Moab against Israel, because they had done evil in the sight of the LORD. (emphasis mine)
>
> Judges 3:7-12

The pattern seems to be that Israel sins, God sends judgment in the form of bondage, the people cry out, God sends a leader (called a judge) who brings deliverance and peace to the land, the judge dies, and the people fall into great sin—again (see also Ps. 106:34-45).

There are two lessons to be found in this pattern. First, governors are needed to restrain people from outbreaks of lawlessness stemming from unfettered passions and lusts. Second, such governments do not change the basic nature of the human heart. Restraint is like a strait jacket that surrounds a madman. It keeps him from harming others and himself, but it does not change who the man really is inside. As soon as the restraint is released, man begins to do all that his heart inclines him to do. Like the wild man of Gadara, who could not be bound, even with chains and fetters, a man cannot be truly changed without sitting at the feet of Christ, the Savior (Lk. 8:26-35).

The Los Angeles riots in 1992 demonstrated this principal. Rodney King, a young black man, had been beaten by police and the incident was recorded on video tape for the whole world to see. The nation was divided, some believing the use of force was justified because of the resistance King gave to the police, others believing that the beating was racially motivated. When a jury found the police officers not guilty of assault, the city of L.A. began to experience a series of riots that would eventually spread elsewhere. The civil disorder was aggravated by the apparent fact that in some key places police were nowhere to be found and in others they did not squelch the melee in a timely manner. Over the next several days the unrestrained hoard of unbridled humanity assaulted, robbed and shot others for "no reason" other than "they could." Thousands of fires were set and 53 people died.

Man needs restraint, and government must be big enough to keep us from destroying ourselves.

Chapter Six

How Should We Then Govern?

Government for Sinners

Because we are sinners, we need government. Because we are governed by sinners, those governors need blueprints for righteous government. Thankfully, God has not left us to guess what works or make it up ourselves. What is civil government supposed to do? And how big should it be?

President George W. Bush during his State of the Union address in 2001 said "Some say my tax plan is too big. Others say it's too small. I respectfully disagree. This plan is just right." When I speak of the size of government in this chapter, however, I am not referring to the fiscal size of the government nor to its tax rates but the boundaries of its jurisdiction.

If we were not sinners, we would hardly need civil government at all, for the primary purpose of God-ordained government is to punish evildoers. Civil magistrates can punish certain outward or scandalous sins when they reach the social level of criminality but God has not given human courts the responsibility of punishing sins of the heart and mind.

Though determining the frame of mind of an accused person can help determine whether he or she had the motive to commit a crime or not, it is doubtful whether there is any just reason to prosecute for hate crimes on this basis. All crimes have an element of hate, and hatred no doubt exists that doesn't result in a crime.

I have highlighted two main responsibilities of governors in the passages below:

> Submit yourselves to every ordinance of man for the Lord's sake: whether it be to the king, as supreme; or unto governors, as unto them that are sent by him *for the punishment of evildoers*, and *for the praise of them that do well.*
>
> I Peter 2:13-14

> Rulers are not a terror to good works, but to the evil. Wilt thou then not be afraid of the power? Do that which is good, and thou shalt have praise of the same.
>
> Romans 13:3

Civil laws and rulers, then, were instituted by God to punish wickedness. Many of our nation's founders recognized that government was needed to restrain men. You can hear the echoes of the Apostle Paul in the words of even the unbelieving Thomas Paine: "For were the impulses of conscience clear, uniform, and irresistibly obeyed, man would need no other lawgiver."[67]

> Knowing this, that the law is not made for a righteous man, but for the lawless and disobedient, for the ungodly and for sinners, for unholy and profane, for murderers of fathers and murderers of mothers, for manslayers, for whoremongers, for them that defile themselves with mankind, for menstealers, for liars, for perjured persons, and if there be any other thing that is contrary to sound doctrine.
>
> I Timothy 1:9, 10

At least three observations can be made from this text. First, note the six words used to define who the law is for: the lawless and disobedient; the godless and sinners; and the unholy and the profane. Laws are needed because of who we are (sinners) and what we are like (sinful), and lastly, for what we do (sinful acts). Second, note that the United States has criminalized all of the particular behaviors (sins) listed in the text above at one time or another. The list is not exhaustive. Third, observe that these things are contrary to sound doctrine, yet the Apostle Paul is not talking about modes of baptism here, or the Five Points of Calvinism, or the Divinity of Christ. It is behaviors he addresses. That is the realm of the civil government.

---

[67] Thomas Paine, *Common Sense*

I grant that Paul is likely referring to the moral law in its function as a schoolmaster to lead us to Christ and as a means to bring conviction to sinners who are in rebellion against a Holy God. It does not save. Only Jesus saves. But it is evident that the civil law is to generally reflect the moral law.

Although Thomas Jefferson wasn't a Christian,[68] he also recognized man's natural tendency to seek his own selfish ways. Government must be constructed with that in mind.

> "A small knowledge of human nature will convince us that with far the greatest part of mankind *interest is the governing principle*, and that almost *every man is more or less under its influence*.... It is in vain to exclaim against *the depravity of human nature* on this account; *the fact is so*, and we must in a great measure change the constitution of man before we can make it otherwise. *No institution not built on the presumptive truth of these maxims can succeed*."[69]

Two prominent philosophies typify the anarchist/statist war against righteous governance, and while their end games appear to be vastly different, each has atheism at its source and attempts to place man on the throne instead of God. The first is the Objectivist Libertarianism of Ayn[70] Rand; the second is the Communism of Karl Marx. Both proponents railed against the existence of God and the "bad" effects Christianity had on the culture at large (and on government in particular).

---

[68] There is no evidence that Jefferson ever publicly embraced Christ as the resurrected Savior and much that suggests otherwise. He is oft quoted as saying "To the corruptions of Christianity, I am indeed opposed; but not to the genuine precepts of Jesus himself." It seems clear, however, that belief in the divinity of Christ, his physical resurrection, and virgin birth were among the things he considered distortions of Christianity. He specifically expressed the view that the Apostle Paul corrupted Christianity. Neither was Thomas Paine a Christian. His Age of Reason was an attack upon the deity of Christ.

[69] John P. Foley, *The Jeffersonian Cyclopedia: a comprehensive collection of the views of Thomas Jefferson*, New York: Funk.

[70] Pronounced "ine" as in diner. She rejected the term libertarian for herself but was in essential agreement with virtually all of its tenets.

Chapter Seven

Government Two Sizes Too Small

Ayn Rand Libertarians

Some people do not see the government as the God-ordained means for protecting society from those who would destroy it. On this basis, Ayn Rand libertarianism refuses to protect us against attacks on life and marriage; thus it is godless government, or government-too-small.

Libertarian philosophy[71] has grown in America in recent years, though it has had little impact on national politics until recently. Spurred on by successful talk show hosts such as Neal Boortz, Judge Andrew Napolitano, John Stossel and Larry Elder, the movement has made inroads into the free-market wing of the Republican Party (which is more of an appendage than a wing I am afraid to say.) Politicians who are sometimes considered libertarian include U.S. Representatives, Ron Paul of Texas and Paul Ryan of Wisconsin, and former congressman Bob Barr of Georgia.

Ron Paul's son Rand, also a libertarian, handily won a U.S. Senate seat in Kentucky. Glen Beck and Rush Limbaugh have spoken favorably of Ayn Rand's economic views and her book, *Atlas Shrugged*.

To the true libertarian, all laws of compulsion requiring or forbidding behavior would be disallowed, unless the behaviors involved violence. Those who hold to the philosophy claim it requires no position on the morality of particular immoral behaviors, only that government has no right to create laws concerning them. Pure libertarians then believe in minimalist government and virtually no restrictions on economics

[71] One can belong to the Libertarian Party, and not be a true libertarian.

(no minimum wage, no government mandates to carry car insurance, no requirement that companies pay for unemployment insurance and no income tax, to name just a few). Neither should there be any laws against immoral behavior (commonly called vices, such as drug use, prostitution, pornography.) Many libertarians oppose laws against abortion, while Ron Paul believes that government should have no role in defining marriage.[72]

Modern American libertarianism has two branches: social libertines and fiscal (or economic) Constitutionalists, with self-proclaimed libertarians usually holding to both. To put it most simply, as our nation has grown older, it has generally become less libertarian in its economics and more libertarian in its social mores. If this premise is true, then it is also true that in our nation's early years, we were economically free and socially conservative. Those today who suggest that you cannot have economic freedom unless you have libertarian views on social questions must ignore history. According to Proverbs 28:2, "For the transgression of a land, many are the princes thereof." In other words, the more libertine we become in our moral behavior, the more government be needed.

Ayn Rand's view of government was based upon her Atheism. This brand of libertarianism is anti-Christian at its very core. Are we so desperate for conservative icons and economic freedom that we don't care what poison we have to accept in the mixture?

Onkar Ghate, a spokesman for the Ayn Rand Institute, summarizes Rand's anti-Christian views and asks *Does America Need Ayn Rand or Jesus?*[73]

> Rand's moral teachings are fundamentally different from Jesus' teachings.... In terms of virtues, Rand's is a moral code that upholds rationality not emotionalism or faith; intellectual independence not authority or obedience; earned pride not humility or the belief in man's inherent sinfulness.
>
> In Rand's argument, morality is not about subordination or service to others or to some "higher power"; it is not about self-sacrifice. Hers is a morality that upholds egoism and individualism: it seeks to teach you the difficult task of pursuing the values that achieve your own individual self-interest and happiness.

[72] See Chapter 16 for my response to Paul's arguments.

[73] http://www.foxnews.com/opinion/2011/06/29/does-america-need-ayn-rand-or-jesus

> Only an explicit or implicit individualist and egoist, Rand held, will understand and demand the rights listed in the Declaration of Independence: his inalienable rights to his own life, his own liberty, and the pursuit of his own happiness. He will demand his political freedom and reject all government controls designed to restrict his liberty and make him sacrifice for the "public interest." He will oppose the welfare state.

Given her positive teachings, Rand must reject what is usually taken to be the core of Jesus' moral teachings, the Sermon on the Mount.

The Christian rejects the premise of Ghate's argument that Rand's philosophy is rational. It is not rational to live contrary to the law of Christ. Furthermore, his conclusion is flawed, for it does not follow that the individualist who believes his *own* freedom should not be restricted will care one whit about the other man's freedom. Notice that Ghate five times deliberately emphasized that an egoist would demand his *own* rights.

Ayn Rand said repeatedly that she cared for nobody but herself. She considered the command of Jesus to love others immoral, and believed we should love only those who deserve it.

It becomes clear what this kind of love creates in a culture. Rand had no concerns for others (except as they bounced back to her benefit) and no concept of friendship or self-sacrifice. As many do today, she believed that this life was all that exists. Once a selfish woman's own freedom is assured or secured, why should she care about the freedom of others? Rand proves this to be true in her own life when she rails against the protection of unborn children.

Rand, in 1976, said:

> I urge you, as emphatically as I can, not to support the candidacy of Ronald Reagan. I urge you not to work for or advocate his nomination, and not to vote for him....Most of them [Republican politicians] preserve some respect for the rights of the individual. Mr. Reagan does not: he opposes the right to abortion.

After Reagan became president she said:

> The appalling disgrace of his administration is his connection with the so-called "Moral Majority" and sundry other TV religionists, who are struggling—apparently with his approval—to take us back to the Middle Ages, via the unconstitutional union of

> religion and politics....Observe Reagan's futile attempts to arouse the country by some sort of inspirational appeal. He is right in thinking that the country needs an inspirational element. But he will not find it in the God-Family-Tradition swamp.[74]

The Enigmatic Ron Paul

Ron Paul is a professing Christian who wants to be President. The Texas Congressman is an unabashed libertarian when it comes to economics, which is not inconsistent with the views of most of our founders and the U.S. Constitution.

However, a huge segment of his followers are Randian libertines who clamor for a complete separation of religion and state. Paul himself admits Rand's influence on his viewpoints. His biggest dispute with her was not her hatred of Christianity nor her love of abortion, but her greater willingness to use military force than he would allow. Meanwhile, he endorsed her distinctly anti-Christian book "Atlas Shrugged" as telling the truth.[75]

Why have so many libertines supported Paul's candidacy even though he says he is pro-life? It is because his view of state's rights and libertarianism means they would have next to nothing to fear that abortion (or homosexual "rights"[76]) would be curtailed in a Paul presidential administration.

Scour the dozens of Ron Paul websites and you will find most of his strongest supporters make the same arguments that Ayn Rand makes about abortion, such as these:

> "Perhaps you rail against abortion—yet don't care about the innocent children we kill in our unnecessary wars abroad"[77]

"It's good to see that somebody gets it. I don't think he [Ron Paul] believes it should be legal, but he clearly maintains that the federal government has no business passing any laws regarding abortion, that these matters are for states to work out. I agree with you that his personal belief is pro-life but in no way does he want to use his role in the presidency

---

[74] Caffeinated Thoughts, June 2011, Rand v. Reagan—Jesus

[75] http://www.youtube.com/watch?v=MjwuGHPilwI

[76] Paul is not even convinced that homosexuality is a sin. See http://www.wnd.com/?pageId=88600

[77] http://dailycaller.com/2011/07/29/only-libertarianism-can-save-the-gop-now

and government to force this belief onto others as a matter of fundamental principle."[78]

The influence of Rand on Paul's Christian followers can be seen in this blogger's essay on Religion and Politics, posted on Ron Paul forums by "Iella":

> It really bothers me that Christians insist and expect that the world should live according to God's holy standards....trying to institute holiness using human law indicates a failure to understand that only God can judge sin. It is not our responsibility to demand righteousness from and dole out punishment to those who are unsaved...
>
> Why then does "compassionate conservatism" demand that our human laws punish those who break the laws of God? The point is, demanding holiness, punishing unrighteousness, and offering forgiveness are the business of God, not of us and not of government.[79]

It has been said for over a hundred years[80] that you can't legislate morality, but it depends upon what is meant by morality. It is true that laws cannot make someone righteous or moral. A thief in heart may somehow restrain the impulses he has to lay his hands on another man's goods because he fears civil punishment, but it does not clean up the pollution of his soul. The Christian position has always been that man cannot save himself by the law.

But this is not usually what people mean when they say "you can't legislate morality". What they mean is that you can't or shouldn't regulate behavior that is called immoral or amoral by some religious standard.

There are two errors in Iella's thinking. First, no Christian politicians that I know of are trying to "institute holiness using human law" or "dole out punishment to those who are unsaved." Second, Iella contradicts the very passages that deal with the purpose of government in I Peter, Romans and I Timothy quoted in the previous chapter. Ayn Rand libertarianism refuses to protect life and marriage; thus it is essentially anarchist.

---

[78] http://www.ronpaul.com/on-the-issues/abortion

[79] http://www.ronpaulforums.com/showthread.php?78853-Mixing-Religion-and-Politics

[80] http://www.barrypopik.com "You Can't Legislate Morality"

Libertines like Rand believe in the goodness of man and therefore reject the need for any kind of restraint of man's sinful proclivities. Greed is good. Selfishness is good. Self-sacrifice is bad. Authority is bad. Taken to its natural end, anarchy is its offspring.

We have a basis to be concerned about the inroads of libertarianism among Christians in recent years, but acceptance of a growing collectivist state is also cause for great concern.

Chapter Eight

Government Two Sizes Too Big

You'd need a thousand Sagans[81] to measure the enormity of the federal budget, which is now measured in trillions and trillions of dollars. Might I ask a ridiculous question at this point? What do they do with all that money? I have suggested elsewhere[82] that the problem is not so much the amount of money they take from us, but how they use it. I'd rather they throw almost all of it in the Potomac River than create government agencies called things like the Alternative Agricultural Research and Commercialization Corporation, the Federal Interagency Committee for the Management of Noxious and Exotic Weeds or the Office of Small and Disadvantaged Business Utilization.

We partly rebelled against King George because he had "erected a multitude of New Offices, and sent hither swarms of Officers to harass our People, and eat out their substance," but we are mistaken if we do not understand that *every* government ruled by men will tend towards a tyranny, if God does not restrain it.

The Bible certainly teaches that debt is a curse on a nation:

> For the LORD thy God blesseth thee, as he promised thee: and thou shalt lend unto many nations, but thou shalt not borrow; and thou shalt reign over many nations, but they shall not reign over thee. If there be among you a poor man of one of thy brethren

[81] Scientist/Commentator Carl Sagan became famous for talking about billions upon billions of stars.

[82] http://caffeinatedthoughts.com/2010/06/id-rather-they-throw-my-money-away

> within any of thy gates in thy land which the LORD thy God giveth thee, thou shalt not harden thine heart, nor shut thine hand from thy poor brother: *But thou shalt open thine hand wide unto him, and shalt surely lend him sufficient for his need, in that which he wanteth.*
>
> Deuteronomy 15:6-8

> The LORD shall open unto thee his good treasure, the heaven to give the rain unto thy land in his season, and to bless all the work of thine hand: and thou shalt lend unto many nations, and thou shalt not borrow.
>
> Deuteronomy 28:12

The emphasis on Scripture is not that indebtedness *causes* the judgment of God on a nation, but is a result of judgment. This passage also shows that lending to someone with a genuine need is not wrong. So when my pro-life friends point to a sin of national debt and say that it is as bad as the killing of unborn children, they have mistaken cause for effect.

Government-too-big tends to dehumanize us, making us more like numbers to be counted than people to be served. Almost any business run like the government will fail.

Those old enough to remember the early years of McDonald's restaurants will remember the strange looks you got from the other side of the counter if you ordered a Big Mac with anything contrary to the advertising catchphrase "Two all-beef patties, special sauce, lettuce, cheese, pickles, onions on a sesame seed bun." Because they were the only fast food place in town, they figured it wouldn't matter to us if our fast food for-the-differently-minded meant going to the back of the line and waiting and waiting and waiting.

This is what bureaucracies do. They try to become well-oiled machines. By treating everybody the same way, nobody has to think. The customer becomes subservient to the product. It should have been no surprise to me recently, when I had to "take a number" in a Social Security office branch that could hold no more than six people in the lobby (which also happened to be empty!). It is in the rule book, I am quite sure.

Such "efficiencies" cannot usually withstand competition. By the early 1970s, McDonalds' inflexibility had become legendary and so Burger King took advantage. First, they created a slogan which is still in use today: *Have It Your Way*. Then they created their own jingle: "Hold the pickles, hold the lettuce. Special orders don't upset us. All we ask is that you let us serve it your way!"

McDonalds finally cried "uncle" and gave into the demand by customers that they "have it their way". The problem with Uncle Sam, however, is that its bureaucracies often exist in areas where there is no competition allowed that can make them cry "uncle".

When Governor Sarah Palin objected to President Obama's health care proposal (Obamacare), she expressed what should be obvious to all: demands for efficiency and cost-effectiveness lead to widespread rationing of medical care. In all the debates about whether it is right to require people to carry insurance or require that insurance companies cover pre-existing conditions, no one looked very closely at Mitt Romney's health care bill (Romneycare). It required the creation of a *Health Care Quality and Cost Council (HCQCC)*, whose recommendations included:

> "The strategies proposed here are intended to reduce care that is unnecessary, duplicative, and of no or marginal benefit"[83]

The question we often face is not "What is the best decision in this matter?" but "Whose decision is this to make?[84]" Who decides whether surgery is necessary or that it is of no benefit? A bureaucrat in Boston or Washington (?!), or a doctor and her patient in Provincetown, Massachusetts?

> Spending on end-of-life care in hospitals can be very expensive with little benefit; patients are often more satisfied with less costly hospice care. Medicaid and private insurers would encourage the use of hospice over hospitals...[85]

Hospice is a place where you go to die, not a place to get better; and I can tell you from experience that when money is the motivator and a third-party is the payer, patients will not be making decisions which satisfy their own needs and desires but rather those of the "health care system." The elderly and infirm will be bullied into stopping all efforts to cure or extend life and go someplace where they can die quietly.

---

[83] http://www.mass.gov/hqcc/docs/roadmap-to-cost-containment-nov-2009.pdf

[84] Thomas Sowell (1996) *Knowledge and Decisions*, New York: Basic Books

[85] http://www.rand.org/pubs/research_briefs/RB9464-1/index1.html

President Obama twice admitted during a townhall[86] meeting that health care would be rationed in Obamacare, once when asked about whether he would seek the best care for his own family, if it wasn't covered in the plan.

Dr. Orrin Devinsky asked:

> If a national health plan was approved and your family participated -- and President Obama, if your wife or your daughter became seriously ill and things were not going well, and the plan physicians told you they were doing everything that reasonably could be done, and you sought out opinions from some medical leaders in major centers and they said there's another option that you should pursue, but it was not covered in the plan, would you potentially sacrifice the health of your family for the greater good of insuring millions, or would you do everything you possibly could as a father and husband to get the best health care and outcome for your family?

His answer should have been shocking:

> You're absolutely right that if it's my family member, if it's my wife, if it's my children, if it's my grandmother, I always want them to get the very best care.
>
> *But* here's the problem that we have in our current health care system, is that there is a whole bunch of care that's being provided that every study, every bit of evidence that we have, indicates may not be making us healthier.

When Jane Sturm asked about whether a pacemaker that had been given to her mother at age 100 would be allowed under his plan (her mother, Hazel Homer, was then 105), the president illustrated the risks of socialized medicine when he tried to play a doctor on TV:

> I don't think that we can make judgments based on people's spirit. That would be a pretty subjective decision to be making. I think

[86] http://www.whitehouse.gov Remarks by the President in ABC Prescription for America

we have to have *rules* that say that we are going to provide good, quality care for all people—

(Mrs. Sturm) But the money might never have been there for her pacemaker or for your grandmother's hip replacement.

(The president continued): —Well, and that's absolutely true. And end-of-life care is one of the most difficult, sensitive decisions *we're* going to have to make. I don't want bureaucracies making those decisions.... But understand that those decisions are already being made in one way or another...what we can do is make sure that at least some of the waste that exists in the system that's not making anybody's mom better, that is loading up on additional tests or additional drugs that the evidence shows is not necessarily going to improve care, that at least *we can let doctors know*, and your mom know, that you know what, maybe this isn't going to help, maybe you're better off not having the surgery, but taking the *painkiller*. (emphasis mine)

Carey's Horror Story[87]

Carey Goldberg used to be a reporter for the New York Times. Now she writes about medicine in Massachusetts and elsewhere for NPR. She's an expert. She knows all about end of life care, because she's ended one herself. She doesn't say it that way, of course. She really describes it as something akin to throwing out an old rotten tomato that had sit on the counter too long. In an article she wrote about offing her own mother, she justifies it by telling us that her mother was just "a vegetable." Her biggest nightmare was that she couldn't just poison her mother or something. She had to let her mother come home and take nine whole days to die – NINE DAYS! *Can you believe the audacity* of that old woman (she was 58!) to stay alive that long! She might lived a lot longer if poor old Carey hadn't stopped giving her mother anything to eat or drink and finally ordered the nurse to please give her mom enough morphine to kill her and put her out of her misery (the last "her" being Carey's, not her mother's).

What does this have to do with big government and Romneycare? Goldberg had confessed to the killing in an article she wrote encouraging

---

[87] http://commonhealth.wbur.org/2010/11/end-of-life-menu

her fellow citizens to sign *Medical Orders for Life Sustaining Treatment*[88] forms, part of the recommendations by a panel created by Governor Romney called the *Massachusetts Expert Panel on End-Of-Life Care*, a subcommittee of Romney's *HCQCC*. Sarah Palin would rightly call this a death panel.

He Tinkers with Clunkers

Though the Obama White House claims to stand up for the poor, one of its earliest big programs, Cash for Clunkers, helped car dealership owners and new car buyers, while making life tougher for the poor. The idea was simple. If you went to any new car dealer and picked out a new car to buy, the government would reduce the cost of the car by up to $4500 if you traded in your old gas-guzzling used car. This money was paid to the dealers by the taxpayer.[89]

There were at least two other problems with this plan. Number one, it only helped those who could afford to buy expensive new cars. The deal couldn't be used on used cars, leaving out many buyers. Number two, the program required that the old cars be in drivable condition when they were brought in so that the car dealer could destroy them. Read that last sentence again. Yes, you read it right. The result was that we threw away over half a million perfectly reliable used cars, *on purpose*.

Now try to buy an inexpensive used car. It can barely be done. You'll often find, like I recently did, that your choices are tiny little not-so-Smart-like cars, no bigger than a Cozy Coupe, or very expensive mid-sized cars. Not a luxury car, mini-van or SUV to be found. No bargains. The price of used cars went up sharply immediately.[90] So, who buys used cars? Mostly, it is *not the rich*.

---

[88] http://www.molst-ma.org/sites/molst-ma.org/files/MOLST-Form-SAMPLE.pdf

[89] http://www.cashforclunkersfacts.com/bill-faq/

[90] http://www.autotrader.com/research/article/car-news/117835/used-car-prices.jsp

Government by Sinners

Because we are sinners, we need government. But what kind of government is needed to restrain wicked men? Perhaps your first answer would be a strong central government: one able to respond quickly and forcibly to put down the threats of anarchy, rebellion or chaos caused by a nation of sinners. As a wise mother wouldn't allow her children to run with scissors, a wise governor knows that people are not to be trusted with too much freedom. Since sinful behavior has at its root a sinful mind, you say, a good government should be able to control the very mindset of its citizens through education in order to have a civilizing effect.

The ideas above might combine into a workable philosophy of government were it not for one nagging question: If those who govern sinners are likewise sinners, who will govern the sinners doing the governing?

Scriptures include several warnings about abusive, intrusive government, the most famous being the one when Samuel warned Israel about the perils of demanding to have a king like the nations around them:

> And he said, this will be the manner of the king that shall reign over you: He will take your sons, and appoint them for himself, for his chariots, and to be his horsemen; and some shall run before his chariots. And he will appoint him captains over thousands, and captains over fifties; and will set them to ear his ground, and to reap his harvest, and to make his instruments of war, and instruments of his chariots. And he will take your daughters to be confectionaries, and to be cooks, and to be bakers. And he will take your fields, and your vineyards, and your olive-yards, even the best of them, and give them to his servants. And he will take the tenth of your seed, and of your vineyards, and give to his officers, and to his servants. And he will take your menservants, and your maidservants, and your goodliest young men, and your asses, and put them to his work. He will take the tenth of your sheep: and ye shall be his servants. And ye shall cry out in that day because of your king which ye shall have chosen you; and the LORD will not hear you in that day.
>
> I Samuel 8:11-18:

While determining the ideal size of government—measured in tax rates or government spending as percentage of the Gross National Product (GNP)—is beyond the scope of this book, a couple of observations are in order. First, the king that the Israelites had asked for would soon become the king that would bring them great tears. Second, this king would take the best of their stuff, and the best of their people and he would make them slaves.

I used to think Samuel's warning meant that God was opposed to Israel having a human king, but my pastor has corrected my thinking on this. He reminded me that Jesus was and is a human king. Therefore it is not the humanity, but the impiety of kings that presents a problem. The greater sin was that the Israelites did not want God to rule over them and wanted to be ruled like the pagan nations around them. They thought that the earthly king could take the place of God, fighting their battles for them (1Sa. 8:20). But they soon found that such reliance on a king would be ill-placed. He would not be able to protect them if God was against them, and the king himself would often turn against the best interests of the people.

The lesson for the Christian is plain. Do not put your trust in governors to protect you or provide for you. Any politician who makes such grandiose claims is misleading you, not leading you.

Checks and Balances

The idea that all men are depraved was woven into the very fabric of our Constitution. And while some argue that the document established our government, its primary purpose was to restrain it. Two means of limiting the reach and power of government were utilized: Checks and Balances, and the 10th Amendment.

Checks and balances were not implemented so that just in case one branch of the government happened to get too much power, the others could keep it in line. The idea of an encroaching government was no mere hypothetical. The Constitution was written under the assumption each branch would actively seek more power for itself and must be checked. Children are often taught in the public schools the concept of checks and balances. What is often missing is the reason such a thing is needed: We are sinners, who by nature desire to rule over others.

Government by Prescription

Dangerous medicines that present the risk of misuse are prescribed by licensed physicians and distributed by licensed pharmacists. The prescription tells the patient how many pills to take, when to take them, when to stop taking them, and whether they must be accompanied with the intake of food. The patient is not to "make it up" as they go.

Think of government as God's necessary medicine to keep a nation of poor sinners from killing each other or robbing each other blind, and the U.S. Constitution as one prescription of how that medicine might be dispensed. Government is a treatment for what ails us, but it is not a cure. Just as the moral law cannot save the sinner, neither can the civil law save a nation. Our founders understood the great risk of overdose this medicine of government presented. The U.S. Constitution included the directions necessary—if followed!—to prevent such an overdose. Most importantly, it stated the limits of how much government was allowed. The medicine was not intended to provide nutrition, comfort or entertainment for the patient.

Because government is run by sinners, there is always the risk government authorities will misuse their power, therefore another means of limiting the power of federal government was included in the Bill of Rights: the 10th Amendment. "The powers not delegated to the United States by the Constitution, nor prohibited by it to the States, are reserved to the States respectively, or to the people."

While the concept of checks and balances sought to distribute and balance the power between the three branches of government, the 10th Amendment, the last of the so-called bill of rights, was designed to limit the scope and jurisdiction of the federal government.

Sadly, it seems that both Democratic and Republican presidents feel compelled to create new programs every year and announce them during the State of the Union address, creating an ever bigger and bigger government. Other budget items are debated by Congress and the people, but rarely does anybody ask whether or not the program is even within the jurisdiction of the lawmakers as granted by the Constitution. Therefore we slowly slide down the path to a welfare state or socialism.

We're From the Government; We Are Here to Help You

God has given us many means to help the poor, the widow, the invalid and the orphan, both in our congregations and in our communities: the family, our neighbor and His church. Christians, however, like the rest of the world, are tempted to make civil governors our caretakers and look for a governmental solution to many of our problems. This leads to more dependence on government. We have given ourselves a nanny-state government that has begun to intrude itself into the smallest details of our lives, both at the federal and state level.

The trade-off can be illustrated with President Bush's Faith-Based Initiative. The federal government takes money from private citizens and a Washington bureaucrat then either sends it back to the states (wasting tons of money with all the paper-shifting) or sends it directly to "Faith-based" organizations or charities. Prior to the Bush presidency, some Christians complained that while fellow social aid groups were getting federal dollars, they were being cut out. Bush proposed that religious groups and churches could receive federal dollars as long as they partitioned off how the money was spent, separating the religious from the secular.[91] Christians should never bow to government demands to separate their generosity from the gospel. This was the error of the heretical social gospel movement of the early 20th century.[92]

The Christian is called to sacrifice in helping the poor and to be generous with our wealth; however, it is easy to be generous with *other people's money*. The song says we are supposed to be known by "our love" [93] (based on John 13:35), not by "how well we administer government funds."

Whether it is Social Security, Medicare or Medicaid, we are growing more and more dependent on the government to provide for us. The Obama administration has gotten into the business of loaning us money for schools, as well as bribing car dealers into trashing 650,000 perfectly good used cars.[94] "Obamacare", based upon the supposed right to health care, is the latest—but probably not the last—big government intrusion into our personal lives made for our own good. C. S. Lewis warned:

> Of all tyrannies, a tyranny exercised for the good of its victims may be the most oppressive. It may be better to live under robber

---

[91] The whole idea of groups receiving money and only using it for purposes acceptable to the government is dubious to begin with. The grant simply frees up more of the group's other funds for the supposed unacceptable use. This is the way that Planned Parenthood gets millions of taxpayer's dollars that supposedly do not promote abortion and also how PP receives grants from organizations like Susan G. Komen for the Cure.

[92] Walter Rauschenbusch (1917) *A Theology for the Social Gospel*, McMillian Company

[93] "They Will Know We Are Christians by Our Love", lyrics by Carolyn Arends

[94] http://blogs.cars.com/kickingtires/cash-for-clunkers

> barons than under omnipotent moral busybodies. The robber baron's cruelty may sometimes sleep, his cupidity may at some point be satiated; but those who torment us for our own good will torment us without end, for they do so with the approval of their own conscience.[95]

The Scriptures themselves warn us of those who say they are from the government and are just here to help us:

> And He said unto them, the kings of the Gentiles exercise lordship over them; and they that exercise authority upon them are called benefactors. But ye shall not be so.
>
> Luke 22:25f

The Lingering Effect of Communism

The Communism of Karl Marx was presumed to be dead after the fall of the Berlin Wall, but it thrives at many American universities and law schools, as well as many sectors of the mass media. While Marxism's progeny goes by various names (progressivism, socialism and liberalism), its destructive influences have permeated the whole American culture, including the worldviews of many traditional conservatives and evangelicals.

A brief reading of the short Communist Manifesto would remind us of the destructive force of the atheist ideology of nations such as China, North Korea and the former Soviet Union, but also of its counterparts today in big governments everywhere.

The communists did not hide their agenda as many political Marxists do today. They wrote plainly that they intended to do away with private property, national boundaries, the family and any acknowledgement of God:

> Communism abolishes eternal truths, it abolishes all religion, and all morality, instead of constituting them on a new basis; it therefore acts in contradiction to all past historical experience.[96]

[95] C.S. Lewis, *God in the Dock,* p. 292

[96] Karl Marx and Friedrich Engels, *The Communist Manifesto*

Because Marxism denies the existence of God, it cannot help but attempt to replace God as provider. Marx and Engels told us ten ways to move towards communism. How many of these can be found or promoted in our nation today to one degree or another?

- Abolition of property in land and application of all rents of land to public purposes.
- A heavy progressive or graduated income tax.
- Abolition of all right of inheritance.
- Confiscation of the property of all emigrants and rebels.
- Centralisation of credit in the hands of the State, by means of a national bank with State capital and an exclusive monopoly.
- Centralisation of the means of communication and transport in the hands of the State.
- Extension of factories and instruments of production owned by the State; the bringing into cultivation of waste-lands, and the improvement of the soil generally in accordance with a common plan.
- Equal liability of all to labour. Establishment of industrial armies, especially for agriculture.
- Combination of agriculture with manufacturing industries; gradual abolition of the distinction between town and country, by a more equable distribution of the population over the country.
- Free education for all children in public schools. Abolition of children's factory labour in its present form.

I am a thoroughly convinced believer in the justice of a free market economy.[97] I believe that economic laws, such as the law of supply and demand, are just as genuine as the law of gravity.

I also believe America is at a crucial stage in its history. Unless we have a revival in which a significant portion of the population turns to Christ as Lord, both tyranny and anarchy will probably continue to gain ground, regardless of which party takes control of the government.

The two philosophies we have examined (Libertarianism and Socialism) certainly provide different views of government from each other, but each rejects the sinfulness of man as the basis for government.

On one hand, we have given ourselves a government that has begun to intrude itself into the smallest details of our lives through a "green" move-

[97] For an example of how free market principles apply to health insurance questions, see Appendix 2.

ment that would try to gain jurisdiction over area of business and public life, and a healthcare system that could impose control over virtually every area of our private and family lives right down to the foods we want to eat. On the other hand, the social standards that act as glue for the Republic are fast melting away.

Application in the Voting Booth

We are tempted to call upon the government to help us when *we* are in trouble, but God says that we are to call upon Him, and he will answer (2Ch. 15:4, Ps. 9:9). Our first line of human defense in a time of financial worries is to seek help from our families and then from our churches (1Ti. 5:3-8). We cannot complain about higher taxes and then turn to government to help us every time we are in need.

When politicians promise they will do more and more for us, remember that in order to do so, they must take more and more from us.

Put simply, perhaps even simplistically, we have described two voices that have beckoned us to follow their imaginations:

One voice offers us the "security" of a growing government that will take care of us, while holding out the promise of happiness as a result of being unshackled from the law of God (Ps. 2:3). This is the fast track to a short period of anarchy, followed by an even more controlling government. This must be opposed.

The siren call of libertarianism promises to free us from the shackles of both a giant secularist government and a smothering religious fanaticism. The deceit here is that we can maintain an orderly and free economic system while accepting godless mayhem in our families and our social lives. This too must be rejected. Only when governors please God can the way be found to navigate "the vessel of the State...between the Scylla and Charybdis of anarchy and despotism".[98]

---

[98] Percy Bysshe Shelley, *A Defence of Poetry*, http://www.bartleby.com/27/23.html

Chapter Nine

Government Too Important

Being in the limelight was not something Jane was used to, nor is it something she sought. In fact by all accounts, Providence would seem sure to appoint one of her cousins, either Mary or Elizabeth, to a high and lofty place of worldly renown rather than this young lady, not yet 16 years old. And this all suited Jane just fine. Christ was first, and pleasing Him mattered to her more than anything in this world. And while that sounds like a platitude, for Jane it would become a real test of faith, for she was about to be offered nearly the whole world, in exchange for a little compromise.[99]

Though Lady Jane Grey had many artistic and musical talents and spoke many foreign languages, it was her humility, great integrity and extraordinary love of God which now stand out in contrast to the ambitions of her father and father-in-law[100] who were willing to use all kinds of chicanery in their plot to replace the ailing King of England with a member of their family, namely Lady Jane. These two men used forged documents to lure Mary—the natural heir to the throne—away from her brother, King Edward VI, then used manipulation to persuade the dying king to order that Jane be his successor.

After the king died, the only thing that remained was to gain Lady Jane's consent. When the throne was presented to her, her reaction was one of great resistance. She believed that

> ... it were to mock God and deride justice, to scruple at the stealing of a shilling, and not at the usurpation of a crown. "Besides," said she, "I am not so young, nor so little read in the guiles of fortune, to suffer myself to be taken by them....My liberty is better than the chain you proffer me, with what precious stones soever it be adorned, or of what gold soever framed. I will not exchange my peace for honourable and precious jealousies, for magnificent and glorious fetters. And, if you love me sincerely and in good earnest, you will rather wish me a secure and quiet fortune, though mean, than an exalted condition, exposed to the wind, and followed by some dismal fall.[101]

Nevertheless, against her own better judgment and due to the pressures of all her immediate family members, Lady Jane Grey agreed to her enthronement on July 10th, 1553. When the tables were turned and Mary was proclaimed to be queen in Jane's stead only nine days later, her con-

[99] What could possibly be wrong with that? If you are a Christian, aren't you a king's kid? Shouldn't we be using our talents to rule in this world? It's a good thing to seek out places of influence, isn't it? No, compromise for the purpose of influence-peddling is a deal with the devil. Whatever unethical deed a politician will do to get elected, he will do to stay elected.

[100] The Duke of Suffolk and the Duke of Northumberland, respectively

[101] Chalmer's Biography (1812), Lady Jane Grey (?–1551) [vol. 16, p. 316]

science was given some relief. Upon hearing the news from her father, she told him:

> I better brook this message than my former advancement to royalty out of obedience to you and my mother, *I have grievously sinned*, and offered violence to myself. Now I do willingly, and as obeying the motions of my soul, relinquish the crown, and endeavour to salve those faults committed by others (if at least so great a fault can be salved) by a willing relinquishment and ingenuous acknowledgement of them." (emphasis mine)[102]

By November of 1553, all of the conspirators were rounded up and put in prison, including Jane, her father, and her husband, Lord Guilford. Shortly afterwards, they would all be found guilty of treason and sentenced to death. On February 9th of the following year, Queen Mary would send an envoy, Dr. Feckenham, abbot of Westminster, in an attempt to have Jane renounce her faith in Christ alone and embrace Catholicism. Though he was very kind to Jane, his efforts failed.[103] On February 12th, about an hour after her husband was beheaded, she herself went to the block with this testimony on her dying lips:

> Good people, I am come hither to die; and by law I am condemned thereto. The fact against the Queen's highness was unlawful, as was the consenting thereunto by me; but, touching any procurement and desire thereof by me, or on my behalf, I do wash my hands thereof, declaring my innocence before God and the face of you good Christian people this day....[104] I pray you all to bear me witness, that I die a true Christian woman, and that I look to be saved by no other means but only by the mercy of God in the blood of His only Son, Jesus Christ; and I do confess, that when I did know the Word of God I neglected it, and loved myself and the world; therefore this plague and punishment is happily and

---

[102] Ibid.

[103] In her last meeting with Feckenham she wryly said "God will abundantly requite you, good Sir, for your humanity to me, though your discourses gave me more uneasiness than all the terrors of my approaching death."

[104] http://www.historylearningsite.co.uk/lady_jane_grey.htm

> deservedly happened unto me for my sins; and yet I thank God that He hath given me a time and respite to repent.[105]

Lady Jane Grey learned the hard way that attempting to gain political power or religious influence by abandoning principle was a losing proposition. It was only when she repented of submitting to the manipulations of others and regained her footing that she was able to have the greatest impact possible: as a witness to the Lordship and saving power of Jesus Christ. Robert Godfrey, president of Westminster Seminary in California, adds:

> When you look at the history of the church, it's the people who refused to compromise, who in fact were the greatest influence in the long run.... Because I think as often as not, it's really the person who has made the compromise that has been influenced, rather than becoming a positive influence on others.[106]

Why is the USA Going to Sheol in a Shopping Cart?

Besides the errors of government too big and government too small, there is one other growing temptation for the Christian that may have become more common than either of those other ills and is even more deadly: government too important. We have convinced ourselves that gaining the seats of power is the key to spreading the gospel and changing our world. But we have one who already rules everything for our good, the Lord Jesus Christ, seated at the right hand of His and our Father.

It has become a mantra that the primary cause of our nation's troubles is the Christian's failure to be politically active enough and fulfill the "cultural mandate."[107] Therefore, the cure for our ills is more involvement:

---

[105] http://www.kamglobal.org/Martyrs/martyrs79.html

[106] Interview with Office Hours, http://wscal.edu/resource-center/resource/the-myth-of-influence1

[107] "Replenish the earth, and subdue it: and have dominion over the fish of the sea, and over the fowl of the air, and over every living thing that moveth upon the earth." (Gen. 1:28). It escapes me as to how this passage could be referring to politics, however. It seems to be referring to man's dominion over animals, not other men.

> A great deal of the blame for the state of the nation must fall upon us. It must be placed at the doorstep of the church. We have failed to obey the Great Commission in this country. We have failed to obey our cultural mandate to be involved in every sphere of social activity. We have retreated from politics, from social involvement, from the media, and from higher education. (emphasis in original)[108]

> The church's singular failure in recent decades has been the failure to see Christianity as a life system, or worldview that governs every area of existence... [and it] has crippled our efforts to have a redemptive effect on the surrounding culture.[109]

> Denial of a Christian worldview is unbiblical and is the reason we have lost so much of our influence in the world. Salvation does not consist simply of freedom from sin; salvation also means being restored to the task we were given in the beginning: the job of creating culture.[110]

> For many years Christians have abstained from politics, and now they are shocked that the culture around them has deteriorated.[111]

Many "get-out-the-vote" books have already been written, assigning the blame for many of our cultural woes on Christians. David Limbaugh suggests that

> By refusing to "get their hands dirty" in the material world of politics, or discouraging other Christians from doing so, they might, unwittingly be aiding and abetting the transformation of our culture and society away from Christian values, irrespective of whether they are otherwise doing their part at evangelizing and serving as exemplary witnesses for Christ.[112]

---

[108] D. J. Kennedy and J. Newcombe, op. cit., p. 8

[109] Charles Colson and Nancy Pearcey (1999) *How Now Shall We Live?*, Tyndale House, pp. xi, xii

[110] Ibid, p 283

[111] Kennedy and Newcombe, op. cit., p. 10

[112] David Limbaugh, from the Foreword, Kennedy and Newcombe, op. cit., p. vii

How is that politics has claimed such a huge position in our lives that we accept the denigration or minimization of the importance of winning the lost and living a holy life, pleasing unto God? I fear that it is because we are tied to this world. We've become so earthly minded, we are no heavenly good.

The late D. James Kennedy of Coral Ridge Ministries seemed itching to get Christians more involved in society in general and politics in particular. In his book, *How Would Jesus Vote*, he lamented that "many Christians and pastors are out of touch with the current culture"[113] but cited a study[114] which actually said that 91% of Protestant pastors and 76% of Christians surveyed consider themselves very or somewhat informed about politics.

Wayne Grudem, Professor of Bible and Theology at Phoenix Seminary, has written a huge book about political issues, and it is clear what he thinks the goal is and how it is to be accomplished:

> I believe the Bible's teachings about politics will bring *hope* and *beneficial change* to people in every nation where they are put into practice. When these teachings are put into practice in a nation, it will be good news for those who are oppressed, good news to those who long for justice, good news to those who long for peace, good news for young and old, weak and powerful, rich and poor—good news for everyone who will follow the wonderful paths of freedom and sound government that are taught in the pages of the Bible. The prophet Isaiah extolled the beautiful sound of the feet of a messenger who came running with good news from God himself:
>
> "How beautiful upon the mountains are the feet of him who brings good news, who publishes peace, who brings good news of happiness, who publishes salvation, who says to Zion, Your God reigns"
> Isaiah 52:7
>
> Therefore I hope that as people and nations follow these principles for government, they will begin to see a reversal of the continual decline in peace, civility, liberty, and civic goodness that we have

---

113 Kennedy and Newcombe, op. cit. In fairness to Kennedy, *How Would Jesus Vote* was completed after he passed away; so it is possible that he would not have agreed with every conclusion in that book.

114 http://www.bpnews.net/bpnews.asp?id=24385

> seen in recent decades in our societies, and instead we will begin to see regular progress toward increasingly good, pleasant, productive, low-crime, free, and happy civil societies in which we can live.[115] (emphasis mine)

Grudem has replaced the true gospel with salvation by good government. Of course, it is not wrong for the Christian to want to live in a land where the gospel is freely preached, or where he "may lead a quiet and peaceable life in all godliness and honesty" (1Ti. 2:2). However, Grudem posits a near utopia[116] for unbelievers that God doesn't promise and bases it upon conditions that no nation full of unbelievers can attain. The errors are numerous.

First, in the real world there does not seem to be a strong correlation between law and obedience. Men are obstinate. Even when shown "what is best for them", they resist. Unconverted sinners don't want Biblical morality, let alone Biblical law.[117]

> The kings of the earth set themselves, and the rulers take counsel together, against the LORD, and against his anointed, saying, Let us break their bands asunder, and cast away their cords from us.
>
> Psalm 2:2f

The people of ancient Israel opposed the commandments of God. In spite of being given perfect civil law, the nation became filled with bloodshed and idolatry. Righteous law cannot save individuals nor can it save nations. Any view of the future that expects a universal age of peace and prosperity apart from the converting power of the gospel of Jesus Christ apparently does not account for the incorrigibility of man. When Stephen

---

115 Wayne Grudem (2010) *Politics—According to the Bible: A Comprehensive Resource for Understanding Modern Political Issues in Light of Scripture* , Zondervan, pp. 15-16

116 Sadly, some of my fellow Huckabee supporters succumbed to the temptation of thinking that the election of one man would result in a country where there will be "low crime" "stable families" and a place "no one litters." Perhaps the last idea was tongue-in-cheek, but the sentiment among some was that he would "save our country and the world from spiritual famine." This is not just a vain hope, I fear it borders on idolatry.

117 By the moral law, I am referring to the Ten Commandments; by Biblical Law I mean the civil ordinances typified in Exodus through Deuteronomy.

reminded the Sanhedrin that the prophet's message was met with this resistance, they stoned him:

> Ye stiffnecked and uncircumcised in heart and ears, ye do always resist the Holy Ghost: as your fathers did, so do ye. Which of the prophets have not your fathers persecuted? and they have slain them which shewed before of the coming of the Just One; of whom ye have been now the betrayers and murderers: Who have received the law by the disposition of angels, and have not kept it.
> Acts 7:51-53

Second, the nations of the world are not promised the kind of prosperity Grudem suggests. The only nations promised any kind of blessing are the nations which make up the church.[118]

Third, and most dangerously, Grudem has taken a passage which plainly refers to the good news (or gospel) of Jesus Christ and confounded it with the Bible's teachings about law, government and politics. Law cannot save; because we are sinners, it can only condemn. Only Jesus saves. Also, the passage he quotes is a promise to Zion, which regardless of your theology, refers to the people of God, and certainly not to nations like the United States, Afghanistan, Russia or Brazil. Finally, the passage itself ties the preaching of the gospel to recognition of the Lordship of Jesus Christ and God's sovereignty, not the rule of mere men.

Exceptional Christians

Many godly Christians only think about politics and government when an election day approaches or when the latter imposes some obtrusive regulation upon their lives. I don't see a problem with that. Those folks don't eat, drink and sleep politics, nor spend the day trying to figure out how to wheedle their way into the corridors of political power nor impose narrow and bigoted notions on the backs of an unsuspecting public as they are often accused of doing by the left. For some Christians, the stereotype simply doesn't apply.

The standard day for these Christians is spent doing the things other Americans do: working hard, playing with the grandkids, taking out the trash and praying for a way to pay the bills. Some of us worship together at home with prayer, the singing of Psalms and the reading of Scripture.

---

[118] See Chapter 10 on the relationship between the nations and the Church.

Nevertheless, we put our pants on one leg at a time, just like everybody else. Government is not in all our thoughts (cf. Ps. 10:4). If dominion means being the best grocer or school teacher one can be, many of us are already doing that. If it means to witness and do what is right in the field of medicine or law or business, we are doing that, too.

It is not that we deny Christ's Lordship in every area of our lives, nor do we deny that God should rule in the workplace, family or church, as well as our personal lives. God rules in the civil realm as well, so even governing magistrates should behave like Christians. What we do deny is that politics and culture, which shall soon pass away, should be central to our lives. We are only pilgrims living under the world's systems, which too shall pass. Even present suffering due to persecution is bearable only in light of eternity (Rom. 8:18-20).

It is central to the theme of this book, likewise, that more political involvement is not the key to pleasing God, but it is that our involvement should be righteous, both in our motivations and our actions.

It is our worldview that deceives us. Francis Schaeffer pegged it when he said:

> There is only one perspective we can have of the post-Christian world of our generation: an understanding that our culture and our country deserves to be under the wrath of God. It will not do to say the United States is God's country in some special way. It will not do to cover up the difference between the consensus today and the Christian consensus that prevailed sixty years ago.[119]

[119] Francis A. Schaeffer (1984) *The Great Evangelical Disaster*, Crossway Books, p. 29

Chapter Ten
A Separation of Faith and State

Lord, bless and pity us,
  shine on us with thy face:
That th' earth thy way, and nations all
  may know thy saving grace.

Let people praise thee, Lord;
  let people all thee praise.
O let the nations be glad,
  in songs their voices raise:

Thou'lt justly people judge,
  on earth rule nations all.
Let people praise thee, Lord; let them
  praise thee, both great and small.

The earth her fruit shall yield,
  our God shall blessing send.
God shall us bless; men shall him fear
  unto earth's utmost end.

Psalm 67, Scottish Metrical Psalter of 1650

The Governor and the Devil at the Airport

It happened at an airport. Satan slithered in to tempt a man. Quiet—yet insistent—he whispered, "You want to be President, don't you? The most powerful man in the world? Think of all the good you can do: a gospel minister in the White House. God will be glorified, the name of Jesus lifted high!"

The Devil paused, wondered if the man was listening to him. The Governor seemed to be fumbling for the right words to say to another man, who was pouring out his heart. *Good*, Satan thought.

"Just tell him what he wants to hear," Satan said. "This will come up again and again. People already think you're narrow-minded. Now is your chance to show the whole world how compassionate you are—how compassionate *God* is."

Was it working? Satan couldn't tell. He tried another tack. "This man who is pouring his heart out to you, he has power, too. Millions of people listen to him. You can win him over, right now; he will be on your side. He will tell everyone how kind and considerate you are. He's already deceived. Just give this poor sap what he wants—what difference does it really make? You don't know his heart. It's such a little thing, after all. See the tears, how sincere he is? Why are you so judgmental, anyway? This is your chance to show them you're not like that at all."

The Devil could see that the Governor's mind was racing.

Should I apply more pressure? Maybe I should just wait 'til the crying man quits talking. The Governor has always been a sucker for such things.

Then came the moment Satan was waiting for: *Now. Time for the coup de grâce.*

"Just tell Glenn Beck that Mormons are Christians, too, Mike. After all, there are many ways to heaven, and just one god. Do this and you *will* be the next President of the United States."

In December 2007, Glenn Beck sought out Governor Mike Huckabee in an airport. Other than Beck's radio account of the encounter,[120] the event went virtually unnoticed—except in the heavenlies. God often tests and proves a man by such as this.

In Whose Kingdom Will You Serve?

> Therefore take no thought, saying, What shall we eat? or, What shall we drink? or, Wherewithal shall we be clothed? (For after all these things do the Gentiles seek:) for your heavenly Father knoweth that ye have need of all these things. But seek ye first the kingdom of God, and his righteousness; and all these things shall be added unto you. Take therefore no thought for the morrow: for

[120] http://archive.glennbeck.com/news/12142007a.shtml

> the morrow shall take thought for the things of itself. Sufficient unto the day is the evil thereof.
>
> Matthew 6:31-34

At every moment the Devil goes about seeking to devour the people of God. And while the enticement to commit sins against the second table of the law (murder, adultery, theft, perjury and envy) will be more or less constant for all of us in this life, those of us in a democratic republic constantly face the temptation to put our country or our party ahead of the Kingdom of God, violating both the First and Second Commandments. If we find ourselves more worried about defending our standard of living, being on the gold standard, or supporting or opposing CAFÉ standards than following the standards of God's word for kindness and personal generosity, for example, we are serving the wrong king.

Because it describes the attitude of those who know not God, Matthew 6 also shows the unlikelihood of getting cooperation from unbelievers in an effort to make the nation conform to the Bible's teachings. They seek the temporal because that is all they have. They love to say "eat, drink and be merry" because they think this is the whole meaning of life. But we are not to be like the world.

Christian politicians are tempted to violate Christ's command to seek first the Kingdom of God, and seek a kingdom of this world instead. This can be illustrated by a pair of questions I once posed: *Should I Pray When I Smoke?* and *Should I Smoke When I Pray*?[121] At first glance, it might appear the two questions are basically the same. But upon closer examination, the questions illustrate a crucial distinction. In the first case, praying is incidental to smoking, which is the main focus of the smoker. So, of course you can certainly pray while you are smoking. In the second case, praying is central. At those times specifically devoted to prayer, smoking is inappropriate because it takes the focus away from the main purpose, which is prayer. An analogy exists between those questions and two others pertinent to this chapter:

May I commend a man who is right on politics even though we greatly differ in religion? (Of course!)

May I commend a man's false religion because he is right on politics? (Of course not!)

Failure to make the distinction between these two questions is much more serious than smoking while praying and probably comes up more

---

[121] http://caffeinatedtheology.com/should-i-pray-when-i-smoke

much often in the lives of politically active Christians. While I deal with the question of identity politics and religious questions pertaining to a candidate in a later section, here I take a stand to defend the good news of Jesus Christ. Many pundits worry about the encroachment of religion into politics. Much worse is the harmful influence partisan politics can have upon the Christian and the church.

Two Mormons have begun to play a more prominent role in American culture and politics over the last four years: Mitt Romney and Glenn Beck. Make no mistake, these men have a Constitutional and historical right to practice their religion and participate in politics as they see fit, as all men do in the USA. They can mix these two aspects of their lives in any way they wish. My quibble is with neither of them on the issue at hand. They both are patriotic men who want the best for our country, and I agree with many of their political positions. I am dealing here with purely religious questions, and my concern is that many Christians are following misguided leaders who are setting aside sound Biblical doctrine in the name of political expediency.

I will speak plainly. While it is quite possible to work together with unbelievers to stop abortion, work on economic issues, further political goals or protect marriage, it is not okay to do so at the price of denying Christ or the gospel and losing one's own soul. Well-known Christian public figures, such as Texas Governor Rick Perry, Pat Robertson, David Barton, James Robison and Joel Osteen have already said that Mormons are Christians. However, patriotism and love of country must not take priority over our service to the True and Living God, and his only Son, Jesus. To do so is to make patriotism an idol.

I have come to the conclusion I'd rather sit under a thousand Mormon presidents than hear one more minister deny the gospel by affirming that Mormonism is a Christian religion. Mormonism is not Christianity; in fact it resembles the original false religion promoted by Satan in the Garden of Eden when he promised Adam and Eve that they would be as God,[122] knowing good and evil. Mormonism teaches that Christians *will* become gods and that the eternal God was once a man. They believe that God has a father and mother.

It is not necessary here to extensively defend the belief that Mormonism is a false religion, a view which has been held by virtually the entire church since Mormonism began formally under the leadership of

---

122 http://www.mormondoctrine.net/don't_know_that_we_teach_it.htm

Joseph Smith in the early 1800s. For those who believe the Bible to be the only inspired Word of God, it is fairly straightforward.

So what in the world does this have to do with politics? Am I worried about the influence of Mormonism on politics? Not at all. Mormons are often outstanding citizens, who agree with other conservatives on many political issues. My concern is not even that Mormons want to have an impact on the culture with their religion. Errors from outside the church are not my concern here; it is the wave of error overtaking the church from within. As the quality of preaching and teaching from American pulpits has deteriorated in recent decades, even as the church has gotten more involved in politics, the crumbling of her walls has nearly reached the foundation (which of course cannot be touched, for it is the Word of God, delivered once and for all to the saints by the prophets and apostles).

It is not the Mormon influence on politics that is the problem; the problem is the compromise of the pure gospel of Christ which alone is able to save souls from hell. Politics and patriotism have become the great tempters of the American Christian. The Scriptures repeatedly warn us that the cross is offensive to the unbeliever. The belief in justification by faith alone through the unique Son of God is foolishness to the wise of this world.

> As it is written, Behold, I lay in Sion a stumblingstone and rock of offence: and whosoever believeth on him shall not be ashamed.
>
> Romans 9:33

> If the world hate you, ye know that it hated Me before it hated you
>
> John 15:18

> And I, brethren, if I yet preach circumcision, why do I yet suffer persecution? then is the offence of the cross ceased.
>
> Galatians 5:11

An American Idol

I love my country. I am thankful for the manifold blessings God has given her. Christians can certainly see God's gracious hand in our history. But our freedoms and Christian legacy are a result of the blessing of God, not the cause of it. This may seem to be trivial, but it is really the difference between honoring the Creator and deifying the creature, between salvation by grace and damnation by good works, between godly worship and godless idolatry.

It is evident that a legitimate patriotism has grown into patriolatry, with all of the trappings of any other false religion. Just as counterfeiters work hard at making their currency look as much as possible like the real McCoy—by using the same typeface, paper, ink and symbols as genuine money—so too, the American civil religion has replaced the sweet doctrines of Christianity with super-sweet, cancer-causing substitutes. Patriolatry has set up a false religion right in the middle of the church.

False Apostles

It is true that some of our founding fathers were orthodox Christians, including Patrick Henry, John Quincy Adams and Samuel Adams. But it is futile to deny the huge influence Deism, Unitarianism, Freemasonry and other vain philosophies had upon our founders. Many of these men did indeed believe in providence but it was not a Divine Providence based upon the promise of God that everything in history is geared toward the blessing of the church. God still rules over all *for his people*:

> That in the dispensation of the fulness of times He might gather together in one all things in Christ, both which are in heaven, and which are on earth; even in Him.
>
> Ephesians 1:10

> The eyes of your understanding being enlightened; that ye may know what is the hope of His calling, and what the riches of the glory of His inheritance *in the saints*, And what is the exceeding greatness of His power *to us-ward who believe*, according to the working of His mighty power, Which he wrought in Christ, when He raised Him from the dead, and set Him at His own right hand in the heavenly places, Far above all principality, and power, and might, and dominion, and every name that is named, not only in this world, but also in that which is to come: And hath put all things under His feet, and gave Him to be the head over all things *to the church*. (emphasis mine)
>
> Ephesians 1:18-22

These men believed in a god, but many—like Jefferson and John Adams—rejected the deity of Jesus Christ and His virgin birth, resurrection and second coming. This shows that they knew not God. You cannot know God unless you know Jesus, because Jesus is God in the flesh and has displayed Him. When you have seen Jesus, you have seen the Father:

> All things are delivered unto me of my Father: and no man knoweth the Son, but the Father; *neither knoweth any man the Father, save the Son, and he to whomsoever the Son will reveal him*. (emphasis mine)
>
> Matthew 11:27

> Whosoever denieth the Son, the same hath not the Father: but he that acknowledgeth the Son hath the Father also.
>
> I John 2:23

> For had ye believed Moses, ye would have believed me: for he wrote of me.
>
> John 5:46

Whenever parachurch leaders, pastors, political leaders or Christian historians tell us that to save the country we must return to our founders, they are treating them as if they were apostles. But the Apostles of Christ wrote the only book that can teach us how to be saved. The Constitution is not equivalent to the Bible. Hope lies in Jesus, not Jefferson.

False Religious Ceremonies and Artifacts

A true revival, reformation or great awakening, if it is to occur, will be demonstrated by widespread repentance and faith in Christ as our only Savior, and will come as a result of the preaching of the gospel. Once we grasp this, all attempts to manipulate our emotions or convince us that we need to do this or that patriotic act in order to save our country will leave us cold and unaffected.

Promotion for Kirk Cameron's new film, *Monumental: In Search of America's National Treasure*, illustrates two problems that have plagued the church in recent years.

First, we have begun to think that one event or experience will be the catalyst that saves the country. For example, virtually every leader in the evangelical church got behind Mel Gibson's 2004 barbaric film "The Passion of Christ" which implied that the suffering of Jesus was almost exclusively physical and primarily at *the wrath of men*, while ignoring the

Atonement, which is Christ suffering *the wrath of God* for sinners. Many blasphemously implied that that film's impact would be greater than the preaching of the gospel itself.[123]

Second, we believe that going back to the founders is the key, not going back to Biblical religion. Here, Cameron is clear:

> We need groups of families, churches, schools, political clubs to come out together to experience it as one community—and then share the message with others.[124]
>
> What's wrong with America, and how can we make it right? This is the question Kirk Cameron asks as he retraces the footsteps of our forefathers in the hope of rediscovering America's true "national treasure." What made us one of the most exceptional nations the world has ever seen? How did we stray from such a great beginning? Journey with Kirk throughout America and Europe as he explores the foundational doctrines and governing principles on which America was founded.[125]

We cannot redeem the culture by making pilgrimages to Massachusetts, literally or figuratively. Moreover, the Puritan forefathers would likely have rejected honoring men with statues of remembrance such as the *Monument to the Forefathers,* which the Cameron film venerates. We can indeed honor the Lord by remembering what He did in the lives of His people in our country, but we must guard ourselves against grandiose claims about the benefits of human endeavors or the necessity of going back to 1620 or 1776.

False Salvation

I am afraid that the neo-patriotic fervor we are being called to experience is offering a false salvation. We are being told that if we somehow "restore liberty" in our country, we will then see some great awakening of religious blessing. But liberty is a result of blessing, not the cause of it.

---

[123] See http://www.seekgod.ca/gibsoncomments.htm

[124] http://www.monumentalmovie.com/

[125] Ironically, Cameron appeared on the Glenn Beck show and suggested that what Beck and other Americans do at their dinner tables can bring about a Third Great Awakening, never once suggesting that Beck turn to the Christ of the Bible.

Right now we can freely preach the gospel, but many worry that it may someday become illegal. What shall we do then, we fretfully ask? The answer is simple. We will freely preach the gospel:

> Remember that Jesus Christ of the seed of David was raised from the dead according to my gospel: Wherein I suffer trouble, as an evil doer, even unto bonds; but *the word of God is not bound* [chained]. (emphasis mine)
>
> II Timothy 2:8f

The effect of the grace of God, the work of Christ, and the preaching of the gospel are not dependent upon Constitutional protections and the backing of the U.S. Supreme Court, as Pastor John MacArthur notes: "The ideal human government can ultimately do nothing to advance God's kingdom, and the worst, most despotic worldly government in the end cannot halt the power of the Holy Spirit or the spread of God's word."[126]

> And when he saw a fig tree in the way, he came to it, and found nothing thereon, but leaves only, and said unto it, Let no fruit grow on thee henceforward forever. And presently the fig tree withered away.
>
> Matthew 21:19

> That fig-tree, full of leaves, but barren of fruit, was a striking emblem of the Jewish church, when our Lord was upon earth. The Jewish church had everything to make an outward show. It had the temple, the priesthood, the daily service, the yearly feasts, the Old Testament Scriptures, the courses of the Levites, the morning and evening sacrifice. But beneath these goodly leaves, the Jewish church was utterly destitute of fruit. It had no grace, no faith, no love, no humility, no spirituality, no real holiness, no willingness to receive its Messiah.[127]

The Christian patriot movement seems to suffer the same malady. We are willing are to talk about the founders and freedom, but not Jesus and the gospel.

---

[126] MacArthur, op. cit.

[127] Ryle's Expository Thoughts on Matthew

Over the last several years, rallies have been promoted under the auspices of religion and have been passed off as calls for spiritual revival to an unwary American church. In many cases politics was supposed to take a back seat to religion, if it was allowed to come along at all. Each rally provided its own pitfalls for the Christian.

Religious Convocation #1

Glenn Beck planned and conducted what he called a *Restore Honor* rally for a crowd of hundreds of thousands on the Washington DC Mall on August 28th, 2010, in front of the Lincoln Memorial. The program was filled with references to the founding fathers and God, but what might have been seen as a traditional patriotic rally in which Christians could have freely participated, became much more in the eyes of Beck:

> This is something that 8-28, we prayed about and prayed about and prayed about and prayed about and I told you some things were going to happen on 8-28 that hadn't been done in over 238 years. I told you that this is the period of awakening, not the period of enlightenment....The founders didn't agree on religion....We all have principles that are the same. God is universal... I have been reaching out to the biggest names in faith for the last year. It has been extraordinarily difficult because of my faith and because of who I am. I have met with the biggest leaders of faith in the country privately and I have asked them *to help me put differences aside and to reach out with one another so we can remind people to get down on their knees...* for our brothers' shield in our danger's hour.
>
> I have been telling you for awhile this will be a historic moment. I promise you that it will be....I have told you, prepare to witness mighty and powerful miracles. I have already seen them. What you will witness...the beginning of a restoration you and your children will never forget...nationally known religious figures from all faiths will join me on stage....[128]

It seems many evangelists and pastors have taken the position of Jerry Falwell, Jr. when he said concerning Beck's religious rally: "There

---

[128] http://www.glennbeck.com/content/articles/article/198/44048

are bigger issues now, we can argue about theology later after we save the country."[129] This could not be more wrong. No country will be saved without revival, and no revival will arise without the true preaching of the gospel of Christ. We have traded away the gospel for patriotism. Love of country has replaced love of God.

To Falwell, "save the country" does not mean save souls or bring about moral reformation, for Falwell immediately discussed banking regulations and problems with the Federal Reserve. That this was a religious rally begs two questions. First, what are Christians doing joining hands with unbelievers in an effort to bring about spiritual revival? Would the average evangelical join hands in going door-to-door with members of the Jehovah Witnesses? Apparently a common political goal justifies joining together with unbelievers. The Bible teaches otherwise:

> Be ye not unequally yoked together with unbelievers: for what fellowship hath righteousness with unrighteousness? and what communion hath light with darkness? And what concord hath Christ with Belial? or what part hath he that believeth with an infidel? And what agreement hath the temple of God with idols? for ye are the temple of the living God; as God hath said, I will dwell in them, and walk in them and I will be their God, and they shall be my people. Wherefore come out from among them, and be ye separate saith the Lord
>
> II Corinthians 6:14-17

Second, can we have the kind of political reform Falwell and Beck desire without spiritual revival? It is unlikely to happen, and I'll go so far to say that it ought not to happen if it is at the cost of denying the gospel of Jesus, and the law of God. Though Beck is thought of as a "social conservative", he supports the claim that homosexuals can get married, as shown in an interview with Bill O'Reilly:

O'Reilly: Do you believe that gay marriage is a threat to the country...?

> Beck: "Are the gays going to come and get us? I believe that Thomas Jefferson said 'if it neither breaks my leg, nor picks my pocket, what difference is it to me?[130]

---

[129] http://www.glennbeck.com/content/articles/article/198/42325

[130] http://hotair.com/headlines/archives/2010/08/12/glenn-beck-whats-the-problem-with-gay-marriage

Looking at the Restore Honor rally in hindsight, one Scripture comes to mind:

> Ye shall know them by their fruits. Do men gather grapes of thorns, or figs of thistles? Even so every good tree bringeth forth good fruit; but a corrupt tree bringeth forth evil fruit.
>
> Matthew 7:16f

One evangelical thinks that Christians should thank Beck for giving Protestant Christians a platform to call a return to the God of the Bible,[131] though Jesus *is* the God of the Bible, a fact Beck flatly denies.

Southern Baptist leader Richard Land also joined in praise of Beck's event:

> Land told National Public Radio that the rally was neither political nor sectarian. "We had rabbis praying. We had Catholic priests praying. We had Muslim imams praying and participating. We had Protestant Christians," said Land. "And [Beck] kept saying over and over again: This is not a political event, and politics is not the answer. The answer is spiritual renewal and rebuilding a civil society one person, one family, one church, mosque, synagogue, temple and one community at a time." [132]

When Land said the rally was not political, and that politics was not the answer, he means you can't rebuild a decaying society by voting, lobbying and legislating. This is certainly true.

When he said the rally was not sectarian, he means it was religious but not Christian: it included Jews, Mormons and Muslims. In other words, Beck believes that getting people to pray to their own gods will bring about revival and cultural transformation. This is certainly not true.

We cannot have spiritual renewal without the Spirit of God. The Bible says of Jesus: "Now the Lord is that Spirit: and where the Spirit of the Lord is, there is liberty (2Co. 3:17). The passage in context tells us there is a veil over the hearts of those who know not Jesus, so that they cannot understand God or His commandments. Those still bound to false religions such as Judaism, Mormonism and Islam then cannot contribute to

[131] http://www.renewamerica.com/columns/fischer/100903

[132] http://www.christianitytoday.com/ct/article_print.html?id=89354

spiritual[133] renewal unless and until they turn to Christ, who is the God of the Bible.

Religious Convocation #2

A prayer meeting called "The Response" attracted 30,000 plus to Reliant Stadium in Houston on August 6th, 2011. The rally, initiated by Governor Rick Perry of Texas, was billed as non-political, though other similar rallies were planned in Iowa, Florida and Arizona, all coinciding with early Republican primaries in those states. Exactly one week to the day after the Houston rally, Governor Perry announced his intent to pursue the presidency of the United States. Perry also attended The Response rally in South Carolina, just days before that state's crucial primary.[134] After a poor South Carolina showing, Perry dropped out of the race and did not attend the Response Rally in Florida held the week before that state's primary.

Former Baptist pastor, Mike Huckabee, received criticism for mentioning that he was a Christian leader in a commercial in 2008 and broadcasting another Christmas commercial with a subliminal cross supposedly in the background. Ron Paul even implied that Huckabee was a fascist[135] and criticized him for "wrapping himself in the flag"[136], yet hardly a word was said by any Republicans about Perry's use of these rallies as a platform to promote his campaign or the commercials and mailing ads which were also chockfull of references to his faith and Christianity.

Perry even spoke at a rally in South Carolina, just before a debate in Myrtle Beach, suggesting his campaign might help bring about a spiritual revival:

> Don't let the voices of secularism in government silence your voices. Together we can build more than just a winning campaign. We can bring about the next great awakening in this world, and we can make America more than just the freest and the most pros-

[133] That does not mean they cannot be good earthly citizens, but that only in Christ is one spiritually renewed.

[134] http://blogs.star-telegram.com/politex/2012/01/perry-to-attend-another-response-prayer-rally-in-south-carolina.html

[135] http://www.nationalreview.com/campaign-spot/11006/ron-paul-charges-huck-implies-hes-only-christian

[136] http://caffeinatedthoughts.com/2011/10/is-ron-paul-a-fascist

perous nation on the earth, but as Ronald Reagan said, we can again make it that shining city on the hill.[137]

Taking Back the Country

A favorite chant of whichever political party is out of power is that "come next election—watch out!—we are going to take our country back" from the evil forces who have "taken over the country." Some form of the phrase has been used by Howard Dean, Sarah Palin, Glenn Beck, Hillary Clinton, Tim Pawlenty, Rick Santorum, Michele Bachmann and President Barack Obama, to name just a few.

Most of the time, this kind of rhetoric is used to shore up the candidate's base of support. Think of it as "hitting the panic button." It is a lot easier to rake in the political dough and get out the vote if you have convinced your followers that they are about to lose their country. Therefore, any candidate who uses this line should be asked what he or she means by the phrase. Who owns the country? Are you implying that your opponents weren't democratically elected? If you suddenly claimed to take ownership of the country, wouldn't you expect your political opponent to be up in arms about it?

An "us vs. them" mentality has developed among politically active Christians. Everything bad that has happened to us is the fault of "them", usually meaning Democrats or liberals. Sad to say, it has resulted in dividing our families and nation up into political factions. This is not a Christian attitude. Indeed, the Bible is clear that while there are enemies of the church, these are motivated by doctrinal and religious differences, not primarily political ones.

For the Christian, this raises even more important questions: "Doesn't God own the country?" "When did Christians ever own the country?" and "How do Christians go about taking back their country from unbelievers?" "Is this a Christian Nation, and what are the implications if it is not?"

In the introduction of his book, *Why Government Can't Save You,* Pastor John MacArthur expresses his concern that Christians are going about this whole cultural transformationalism thing the wrong way. He writes:

---

[137] http://abcnews.go.com/blogs/politics/2012/01/perry-tells-evangelicals-together-they-can-create-next-great-awakening

> Imagine what the world must think of our God. Do we think Him so weak and incapable of caring for us that we prefer using protests and political pressure rather than the spiritual resources He offers? And do we believe He has lost control and we have to get it back for Him?[138]

One way popular historian David Barton attempts to makes the case that we are a Christian nation is by using the lives of the founders; but arguing this way is of no help if in his very arguments he denies the true gospel. It might be easy to side with Barton against the skeptics who would deny our Christian heritage, except that Barton tends to minimize the obvious influence of Deism and Unitarianism on the founders and the Republic they established. To make matters worse, he refuses to distinguish between Christianity and Mormonism, lending considerably less credibility to his claims about the founders being Christians:

> It has always been interesting to me throughout my political and religious life that many Christians seem more intent on whacking allies than enemies... I have watched the Christian debate surrounding Glenn Beck's religious beliefs devolve not to a consideration of him individually but rather to label him with a group identity. That is, folks repeatedly say, "Since Mormons believe XYZ, then Beck therefore also believes XYZ." That's as ill-informed as to say that since redheads are universally known to have a temper, then if you are an individual redhead, you have a personal problem with anger. Absurd! Such a statement rejects the principle of individual identity and replaces it with group identity, which is not Biblical.[139]

Barton seems to ignore the frequent opportunities Beck takes to either promote Mormon doctrines[140] or affirm[141] that he agrees with those doctrines. No one is putting words in his mouth. Glenn Beck chose Mor-

---

[138] John MacArthur, op. cit.

[139] http://www.facebook.com/note.php?note_id=150770881618696

[140] http://caffeinatedthoughts.com/2010/08/827-828-glenn-beck-takes-another-bite

[141] http://caffeinatedthoughts.com/2010/08/827-828-glenn-beck%e2%80%99s-divine-destiny-evangelicals-without-the-evangel

monism, it did not choose him. The bigger problem with the Barton defense of Beck's professed Christianity is that it denies the scores of passages that warn the Christian of false gods, false religions and false prophets. Here is just a small sampling:

> Then the LORD said unto me, The prophets prophesy lies in my name: I sent them not, neither have I commanded them, neither spake unto them: they prophesy unto you a false vision and divination, and a thing of nought, and the deceit of their heart.
>
> Jeremiah 14:14

> Beware of false prophets, which come to you in sheep's clothing, but inwardly they are ravening wolves.
>
> Matthew 7:15

> For such are false apostles, deceitful workers, transforming themselves into the apostles of Christ.
>
> II Corinthians 11:13

> But there were false prophets also among the people, even as there shall be false teachers among you, who privily shall bring in damnable heresies, even denying the Lord that bought them, and bring upon themselves swift destruction.
>
> II Peter 2:1

The Crux of the Matter

What is crucial[142] here is not whether Glenn Beck is personally a Christian. Ultimately, that question is left to God. We cannot see the heart. Sadly, however, that has not stopped many leading evangelicals from telling us that Beck *is* a Christian. Joining David Barton have been many prominent evangelicals, and it is no coincidence that all are highly involved in politics. Jim Garlow, pastor of the huge Skyline Wesleyan Church in San Diego, CA, was instrumental (along with the Mormon church), in getting Proposition 8 passed in California. This bill defined marriage as between a man and a woman. Garlow, along with Baptist leader Richard

---

[142] Both "crux" and "crucial" come from the Latin word for cross or torture. What precious providence that God would preserve in English a reminder of the centrality of the Cross of Christ.

Land and evangelist-turned political activist James Robison, seems mesmerized with Glenn Beck, hanging on his every word in order to affirm the legitimacy of Beck's faith:

> On one of his TV shows about a month ago, he laid out the gospel, using his well-known blackboard, in the clearest explanation of the crucifixion and the resurrection that I have ever heard on national TV. I called James Robison, and asked, "Did you hear that?" James said, "Richard Land (Southern Baptist) just called me and said he never expected to hear the Gospel so clear on secular television." It was quite remarkable. A few days ago, Glenn laid out America's problems and then concluded, "We need God!" [143]

These leaders and many others appear unable to resist Beck's fame, political accomplishments and the lure of his radio and television platform. He often brings them onto his show to promote their books and other projects, which are then often lavished with praise by Beck. The Scriptures warn us that "A man that flattereth his neighbour spreadeth a net for his feet" (Proverbs 29:5). Garlow implies that meeting the talk show host was unrelated to the following public praise he had made about Beck:

> Candidly, I made a statement publicly about three months ago, before I ever knew I would even meet Glenn Beck. The statement was (as nearly as I can reconstruct it from memory): "If this nation collapses in the 2010-2012 time frame, historians will have to report, if they are honest, that American (sic) fell because of silent pastors and inactive pews. If, on the other hand, this nation is saved from self-destruction in the 2010-2012 timeframe, those same historians will have to report that one of the major reasons for the turnaround was Glenn Beck." That was before I had ever been with him. I had no idea that two days later, I would receive a call to come meet with him. I still believe that. Glenn Beck is being used by God – mightily.[144]

Garlow proceeded to minimize Beck's Mormonism, implying that he was less committed to that religion than his wife, and that apparent public statements affirming Mormonism should be accepted with a grain of salt.

---

[143] http://www.torenewamerica.com/evangelicals-mormons-and-glenn-beck

[144] Ibid.

Garlow is deceived on this point, but I think it shows that even among the compromisers there is some hope that their eyes will eventually be opened.

Chapter Eleven

Is America a Christian Nation?

"Nation" in the Old Testament

Is there any basis in Scripture for the Christian to take back a nation for Jesus? Nations are first mentioned in Genesis 10:5. The scattering of those nations across the globe is described in the next chapter and came as God opposed man's first efforts at building a Utopia. The leaders of this early one-party system wanted to construct a tower that would reach heaven and make a name for themselves.

> And the LORD said, Behold, the people is one, and they have all one language; and this they begin to do: and now nothing will be restrained from them, which they have imagined to do. Go to, let us go down, and there confound their language, that they may not understand one another's speech. So the LORD scattered them abroad from thence upon the face of all the earth: and they left off to build the city. Therefore is the name of it called Babel; because the LORD did there confound the language of all the earth: and from thence did the LORD scatter them abroad upon the face of all the earth.
>
> Genesis 11:6-9

The idea that "if it weren't for God's holding them back, they could and would do whatever they imagined" is not a compliment, because it is really speaking of the conjured up thoughts from the hearts of men which are only a cesspool of continuous evil (cf. Gen. 6:5). Unimaginable blood-letting occurs when men cooperate without restraint. From the French Revolution to the Third Reich, citizen cooperation in nations demonstrates a putrefying picture of man as a savage beast. It is important to remember that the perpetrators of these unspeakable crimes were just ordinary people. We must not think of them as different from ourselves in their basic make-up.

Democratic principles and freedom to vote are no guarantee that the people won't elect a blood-thirsty tyrant, especially when nationalism flourishes or when the people have an opportunity to eliminate the weak and powerless who might stand in the way of their continued prosperity. Adolph Hitler remained popular right up to the end among the German people.

When the people of Israel were in rebellion against God, it could not look ahead and fathom the atrocities they would commit under God's judgment, but the Bible doesn't mince words. Fathers and mothers would soon be eating their own newborn children, while hiding this "food" from their spouse and older children who were themselves starving to death. It would get worse:

> And there was a great famine in Samaria: and, behold, they besieged it, until an ass's head was sold for fourscore pieces of silver, and the fourth part of a cab of dove's dung for five pieces of silver. And as the king of Israel was passing by upon the wall, there cried a woman unto him, saying, Help, my lord, O king. And he said, If the LORD do not help thee, whence shall I help thee? out of the barn floor, or out of the winepress? And the king said unto her, What aileth thee? And she answered, This woman said unto me, Give thy son, that we may eat him to day, and we will eat my son tomorrow. So we boiled my son, and did eat him: and I said unto her on the next day, Give thy son, that we may eat him: and she hath hid her son.
>
> II Kings 6:25-29

No law can make people live righteously; it may at best keep them from killing and cannibalizing each other. In the midst of this nightmare, there is hope. The tragedy of Genesis 11 is contrasted with the promise of God to Abram in Genesis 12 that he would have a great name, be made into a great nation,[145] and receive a great blessing.

---

[145] In Genesis 17, God expands the promise to include many nations and kings.

Because God deals with nations throughout the Bible, it is certainly relevant to ask what the word "nation" means in the context of Scripture. It does not seem to have the same meaning as the English word country (which usually denotes a place of fixed borders), but rather the idea of a people or nationality. This is clear from the following passages:

> And the LORD said unto her, Two *nations* are in thy womb, and two *manner of people* shall be separated from thy bowels; and the one people shall be stronger than the other people; and the elder shall serve the younger.[146] (emphasis mine)
>
> Genesis 25:23

> Now therefore, I pray thee, if I have found grace in thy sight, shew me now thy way, that I may know thee, that I may find grace in thy sight: and consider that *this nation is thy people*.
>
> Exodus 33:13

> And ye shall not walk in the manners of the *nation*, which I cast out before you: for *they* committed all these things, and therefore I abhorred *them*.... I am the LORD your God, which have separated you from *other people*. And ye shall be holy unto me: for I the LORD am holy, and have severed you from *other people*, that ye should be mine.
>
> Leviticus 20:23-26

> Keep therefore and do them; for this is your wisdom and your understanding in the sight of the *nations*, which shall hear all these statutes, and say, surely this great nation is a wise and understanding *people*.
>
> Deuteronomy 4:6

[146] I unequivocally reject Kinism (the philosophy that the most important connection people have is race). When God promised Abraham that many nations would come from him, and emphasized one seed, the Bible is talking about all of those of the faith of Abraham who would come to Christ from every ethnicity and nationality (see Rom. 4:12-25, 9:6-13, Gal. 3:16-20). Though the word "nation" can include the concept of race in some contexts, the Bible does not for a moment consider the kingdom of God to be made up of one race, physically. It is quite the opposite. God has invited all, without distinction (see Rom. 10:11, for example). Revelation 5, verses 9 and 10, describe the fulfillment of the promise to Abraham.

> And there was given him dominion, and glory, and a kingdom that all the *peoples, nations*, and men of every language might serve Him.
>
> Daniel 7:14

"Nation" in the New Testament

The word "nation" has two primary connotations in the New Testament. In both cases, the focus is on people, not governments or borders of a country. In the first example (Mt. 21:43), after Jesus told the parable of the vineyard, He warns that the kingdom of God was about to be taken from those who outwardly rejected Him and given to those who received Him. Since we know that Jesus is not referring to Egypt or Syria or any other physical nation with borders, we can only conclude He means the church (people of all languages, tribes, tongues, nations)

The following passages also seem to me unintelligible unless the word "nations" refers to a people group.

> When the Son of man shall come in his glory, and all the holy angels with him, then shall he sit upon the throne of his glory: And before him shall be gathered all nations: and he shall separate them one from another, as a shepherd divideth his sheep from the goats: And he shall set the sheep on his right hand, but the goats on the left. Then shall the King say unto them on his right hand, Come, ye blessed of my Father, inherit the kingdom prepared for you from the foundation of the world.... Then shall he say also unto them on the left hand, Depart from me, ye cursed, into everlasting fire, prepared for the devil and his angels.
>
> Matthew 25:31-34, 41

This is obviously the last day, the judgment day. He is addressing people, who will be judged as individuals. God is not bringing Australia or Zimbabwe, Botswana or Yugoslavia before himself. He is bringing every man to account out of every nation, and those that are saved will enter the kingdom, planned from the foundation of the world.

> Go ye therefore, and teach all *nations*, *baptizing them* in the name of the Father, and of the Son, and of the Holy Ghost: *Teaching them* to observe all things whatsoever I have commanded you:

> and, lo, I am with you alway, even unto the end of the world. Amen.
>
> Matthew 28:19

Governments and borders cannot be baptized or taught; He is referring to people, here.

> And they sung a new song, saying, Thou art worthy to take the book, and to open the seals thereof: for thou wast slain, and *hast redeemed us to God by thy blood out of every kindred, and tongue, and people, and nation*; And hast made us unto our God kings and priests: and we shall reign on the earth.
>
> Revelation 5:9f

God promises in Revelation not to save the nations, but save His people *out of the nations*, and make them kings.

The second meaning of the word "nation" appears to be a synonym for the word "Gentiles", as shown in this passage:

> Therefore take no thought, saying, What shall we eat? or, What shall we drink? or, Wherewithal shall we be clothed? (For after all these things do the Gentiles seek:) for your heavenly Father knoweth that ye have need of all these things. But seek ye first the kingdom of God, and his righteousness; and all these things shall be added unto you.
>
> Matthew 6:31-33

The words "nations" and "Gentiles" are sometimes used interchangeably in English translations. In those cases "the nations" refers to all nations *except for Israel*. What you have then in the New Testament, is "the nations" (the Gentiles) and THE nation, the people of God. This was true of the church in the Old Testament as well as in the New.

> Thou shalt not lie with mankind, as with womankind: it is abomination. Neither shalt thou lie with any beast to defile thyself therewith: neither shall any woman stand before a beast to lie down thereto: it is confusion. Defile not ye yourselves in any of these things*: for in all these the nations are defiled which I cast out before you.*
>
> Leviticus 18:24

> But ye are a chosen generation, a royal priesthood, *an holy nation*, *a peculiar people*; that ye should shew forth the praises of him who hath called you out of darkness into his marvelous light: Which *in time past were not a people*, but are now *the people of God*: which had not obtained mercy, but now have obtained mercy.
>
> I Peter 2:9f

Why is it said of Christians that they were not a people? It is because they were not a distinct nation. Those particular Christians that Peter addressed were previously only citizens of their earthly nations. Only in Christ had they become truly a people, under one king, the Lord Jesus Christ. It is fitting then, that the people of God would be physically scattered among the Gentiles and yet spiritually gathered out of them to become a distinct people, a holy nation.

When a child is adopted, his birth certificate is changed to reflect that as a matter of law, he receives the same right to the inheritance as any natural born child. The parents listed on the certificate are now the adopting parents, not the biological parents. The boy is to be treated exactly *as if* he had been theirs from the very first day, no matter how old he actually was when adopted. In the Scriptures the same concept is applied to citizenship:

> Glorious things are spoken of thee, O city of God. Selah. I will make mention of Rahab and Babylon to them that know me: behold Philistia, and Tyre, with Ethiopia; this man was born there. And of Zion it shall be said, This and that man was born in her: and the highest himself shall establish her. *The LORD shall count, when he writeth up the people, that this man was born there.* Selah. (emphasis mine)
>
> Psalm 87:3-6

It does not matter what country you were born in (or what your nationality); if you are born again, it is counted as if you were born in God's heavenly city Zion, giving you citizenship in heaven. This does not just mean that in the future you get to "go to heaven"; it means you have the rights *and responsibilities* of citizenship *now*. We are to seek after God's things, not our own, for He has promised to take care of us.

What Kind of Nation?

Having defined a nation, according to Scripture, I will address the question as to whether or not the United States is a *Christian* Nation. Gary North recognizes the flaws in some approaches to this question:

There have been many detailed intellectual defenses of the United States as a Christian nation. These studies invariably rest on a conceptual error: equating *state* (civil government) with *nation* (society). That the United States has been a Christian society during its post-1788 period is obvious. This is not the same thing as the United States civil order when considered in terms of its defining judicial document, on which the United States rests its civil covenant.

> In contrast, humanistic historians turn to the U.S. Constitution and point out that it is a secular document, and uniquely secular for the eighteenth century. They, too, confuse state with nation. They conclude that the United States is a non-Christian nation[147]

To put it more succinctly, the question can only be answered effectively if you make a distinction between the official/legal status of Christianity and the informal impact of Christianity on the society as a whole. The latter is sometimes called the civil or civic religion,[148] and carries no binding authority in the courtroom or chambers of legislatures, though it may include "official" recognition of God in the civil realm, such as in the phrase "In God We Trust" on our money or the mention of God in our pledge of allegiance.

Just because we were greatly influenced by Christianity in many ways does not mean we are *now* a Christian nation in any legal sense. Certainly the Mayflower Compact's statement that the Pilgrim's efforts were "for the Glory of God and the advancement of the Christian gospel" could be used to demonstrate the reasons the Pilgrims came to the USA, for example. In addition, all but one of the thirteen states had established churches or oaths of office requiring a witness to Christianity, prior to the ratification of the United States Constitution.[149] Here are just a couple of examples:

---

[147] Gary North, *Conspiracy in Philadelphia: Origins of the United States Constitution* (2004) Online Version, p. XVI

[148] http://www.robertbellah.com/articles_5.htm

[149] http://undergod.procon.org/view.resource.php?resourceID=69

> I _______do declare, that I believe the Christian religion, and have a firm persuasion of its truth" [150]
>
> Massachusetts Oath of Office

> I _______, do profess faith in God the Father, and in Jesus Christ His only Son, and in the Holy Ghost, One God, blessed for evermore; and I do acknowledge the holy scriptures of the Old Testament and New Testament to be given by Divine Inspiration. [151]
>
> Delaware Oath of Office

Something, however, changed from the time the Declaration of Independence (1776) was penned and the Constitution (1788) was created, in that the latter refused to make official recognition of our prior Christian heritage. This is why the latter document makes no mention of God, according to North:

> This new covenant meant a new god. The ratification of the United States Constitution in 1787-88 was not an act of covenant renewal. It was an act of covenant-breaking: the substitution of a new covenant in the name of a new god.... a "grand experiment" in which the God of the Bible was first formally and publicly abandoned by any Western nation.[152]

John Lofton seems to agree:

> Patrick Henry was one of the key anti-federalists and they were the ones who were, relatively speaking, really the Christian faction, and they opposed the Constitution in part because it gave short shrift to the Christian religion. [153]

North argues that the Constitution was thrust upon the thirteen states illegally, as it was ratified in a manner contrary to the Articles of Confederation. Here was Article 13:

---

150 http://www.malegislature.gov/Laws/Constitution#cart011.htm

151 http://undergod.procon.org, op. cit.

152 North, op. cit.

153 Gregg Jackson and Steve Deace, op. cit.

> The Articles of this confederation shall be inviolably observed by every State, and the union shall be perpetual; nor shall any alteration at any time hereafter be made in any of them; unless such alteration be agreed to in a congress of the united States, and be afterwards confirmed by the legislatures of every State.

Instead of being ratified by the Articles Congress and state legislatures, the document was given to state constitutional conventions to ratify. Because the states had differing state churches, it is understandable that the framers could not set up a single established church for the whole country. This conundrum alone, however, does not explain the decision to deliberately omit recognition of our Trinitarian God in the document, nor does it explain Article Six, making the oath of office secular. The Articles of Confederation had made mention of "The Great Governor of the World", so it was not unprecedented to have legal documents carry the recognition of our sovereign God.

Three Possible Marks of a Christian Nation

Before we settle on whether or not we are a Christian Nation, I must define Theonomy, the Establishment Principle, and the Judeo-Christian Ethic.

Theonomy is a system of thought that all nations are required by God to institute the Old Testament civil laws[154] lest they be punished for breaking covenant with Him. Proponents have included R. J. Rushdoony, Gary North, Greg Bahnsen, George Grant and David Chilton. There have been varied approaches among theonomists as to how Old Testament civil laws might be instituted in a democratic republic, none of them undemocratic, as far as I can tell, though some on the left believe that having a religious basis for any law is verboten.

The Establishment Principle was debated among the founders of our country and was rejected in the 1st Amendment with the "Establishment Clause." A range of views exist of this concept, including some who hold that the nation should be considered officially a Christian nation with a particular denomination being the representative of that Christianity. Others see establishment as simply the requirement that Christian magistrates carry their Christianity into the workplace with them.

---

[154] http://reformed-theology.org/ice/newslet/bet/bet98.02.htm

By either of these two definitions, we are not officially "Christian." Jesus has not been declared Lord, as has been the case in the United Kingdom, for example. Nor can it be argued that we have submitted ourselves to the Old Testament civil laws.[155] So, using the standards of theonomy or the establishment principle we cannot conclude that the United States is a Christian nation.

One other concept, the Judeo-Christian Ethic, is sometimes used to make the argument that we are a Christian nation, but use of the prefix "Judeo" is problematic on several counts. First, it seems self-refuting. If the idea is that there exists some blending of two religions (Judaism and Christianity) then, of course, we are not a Christian Nation, but a Jewish-Christian Nation. But Judaism and Christianity are religions in conflict, because the one accepts Jesus, the Savior of the world, and the other explicitly rejects him.

Finally, a case can be made that the Christian consensus has largely disappeared, and pluralism has gained the upper hand, leaving just remnants of a Christian heritage found on early documents and courthouse walls. The widespread acceptance of psychological viewpoints about human behavior, the emphasis on material wealth over spiritual health, the focus on self in worship, the abandonment of a Biblical sabbath view, the rejection of children as a gift of God and the ascendancy of cultic or heretical views about Christ, the Bible, God's Foreknowledge and the existence of hell have all contributed to the decline of any Christian worldview we once may have had.

Surprisingly, in some ways, the answer to the question of whether or not America is a Christian nation is irrelevant. As I will demonstrate in the next chapter, the focus in Scripture is godly governors and godly subjects, not establishing a Christian government. The only truly Christian nation is the Church. Just as France is made up of Frenchmen, a Christian nation is made up of only Christians, a nation without borders, and with Christ as her head.

Notwithstanding all that is said above, I am in essential agreement with the idea that an indelible mark has been clearly made by the Bible and Christianity on the American society and its legal system. There is no need to review that history here. We can be thankful for the freedom to worship and evangelize as Christians in this country. These facts cannot

[155] I would argue that much of the American political/legal system has its roots in these laws, such as the right to subpoena, the distinction between murder and manslaughter, the importance of making restitution, and a host of other comparable laws, too numerous to mention here.

be denied by the atheist unevangelist. Turning on more lights won't help the blind to see.

To sum up: we are a Christian nation only in an informal sense and that only in so far as we retain the consensus of Biblical values. That consensus is quickly disappearing among people.

Having now disposed of the two previous questions (*What is a nation*? and *Is America a Christian nation*?), I now return to challenging the idea that a Christian can "get the country back" for God through gaining political power.

In the face of a growing tyranny/anarchy state, it is tempting for the Christian to become a cultural wallflower: a Christian who just wants to blend in with his surroundings. To the other extreme, however, some Christians have sought not to influence culture, but transform it. God, on the other hand says to us, "be not conformed to this world: but be ye transformed by the renewing of your mind, that ye may prove what is that good, and acceptable, and perfect, will of God," (Rom. 12:2) and requires that we be "conformed to the image of his Son" (Rom. 8:29). Paul longed to "know him, and the power of his resurrection, and the fellowship of his sufferings, being made conformable unto his death" (Phi. 3:10). Notice the emphasis on *us being transformed*, not *us transforming the culture*. We are to keep ourselves from being corrupted by the world as we take care of orphans and widows (Jam. 1:27b).

Mike Horton says:

> We're never called to transform the world (or even our neighborhood). We're never called even to bring millions to Jesus Christ. We're called to be faithful in our vocations at work, at home, in our neighborhoods and in our witness to those individuals whom God brings across our path in ordinary ways every day.[156]

Cups of Cold Water

> And whosoever shall give to drink unto one of these little ones a cup of cold water only in the name of a disciple, verily I say unto you, he shall in no wise lose his reward.
>
> Matthew 10:42

[156] http://www.whitehorseinn.org/blog/2009/10/05/two-kingdoms-questions-part-3

God brought Dutch Sichina into my life, about the time my father died, when I was in the 8th grade. Dutch became like a father to me, frequently giving me tidbits of wisdom and opening up his own home to me, all hours of the day and night. But my classmate and Dutch's son, Ty, is the one who set the example of a Christian for me in so many ways. For one, he had to share his dad with me, which he did without complaint.

Sports have always been a big part of Ty's life. But his only big break in athletics was the fractured arm he got when he quarterbacked our high school football team. A little over three years ago, Ty did have a dream come true. After about 25 years of plugging away as an assistant football coach, an opportunity for him to become a head football coach came at last.

I'd like to tell you how he took a small-town gridiron program to a state championship within those three years. I'd like to, but I can't. Instead, Ty endured the agony of defeat much more frequently than he did the thrill of victory.

Ty's fruit, nevertheless, will remain long after the thrill of winning a trophy that gathers dust in a display case has worn off. Ty's players and some of his students (he teaches elementary school) come to him if they need someone to pray for them or a family member. They feel comfortable in visiting his home, too. A few have visited his church. No, Ty hasn't jammed the Bible down the throats of those under him in hopes of adding them to the church rolls. But he has not been ashamed of his faith, nor of sharing a Scripture that might encourage them to seek God. Most of all, he has lived as an example. Not perfect, but one who walks in the grace of God.

His wife, Joellen, told me:

> While sitting at home over Christmas break trying to figure out if he should resign as head football coach he gets a call from a very homesick exchange student from Brazil who plays football for him. He just wanted to tell "Coach" Merry Christmas. My husband only won one game that year but he realized all his work and time spent with these young men was actually making a difference because they learned about prayer, faith, courage, character, compassion and teamwork. My husband's coaching was not all about X's & O's. It was more about life's lessons that could help them throughout their lives.

When Ty's father, Dutch, died a couple of years ago, the whole football team showed up at the funeral home to honor Ty. If many of these young men turn to Christ, as they might, it is possible they may turn into "conservative" voters. But I can tell you, that is the furthest thing from Ty's mind. He has learned what is important in this life, and that is the life to come.

Paul Thorn was an eighth grader, one year older than me at Pleasant City Junior High. One day Paul asked to borrow a pencil from me. When I complied, he thanked me and I thought that would be the end of it. Not so. The next day he thanked me again and *returned the pencil.* Who does that? I knew Paul and his family were Christians, and that little piece of integrity impressed me.

Two days later an announcement was made to the whole school. Paul Thorn had accidentally drowned the previous day. I didn't know Paul well; we weren't close friends. At most we had shared a few pleasantries. Nevertheless, that young disciple made a difference by giving me refreshment in the name of Jesus.

Paul never grew up and never had a chance to vote, and I have little idea what Ty thinks about politics. But they both changed the world—my world.

My first youth pastor, Greg Black, taught the kids in our youth group to do what he did naturally, witness to others about Jesus. He never came across as pushy, but had a keen ability to know when people were open to hearing about the Lord. He still witnesses to neighbors and strangers to this day.

One time, Pastor Black took me door-to-door witnessing. After being turned down a few times, someone finally let us in to talk with him about Jesus. It was actually just a kid, named George McElroy. George refused our appeals for him to trust Christ, and I don't think I ever spoke to him again about Jesus, though we would later go to the same junior and senior high schools. George and I had little in common. He became a bodybuilder and weightlifter, while I have been a weakling all my life. George went to cussing school, and though Ty says that in the sixth grade I was so foulmouthed I could cuss the paint off the wall, by the time I got to high school God had washed my mouth out with holy soap. George continued to swear at everyone but his mother.

The Watering Can

A number of years ago, George became very sick and contracted cancer which weakened his once powerful body. His best friend, Ty Sichina, was there for him every day, if need be. Ty ran errands for George and took him places when he was too weak to drive. Even when he was demanding, as very sick people can be at times, Ty was faithful. Although he continued in his other duties of teaching, coaching and preparing Sunday school lessons, he didn't let his busyness keep him from taking care of George. Though Ty tried to witness about Jesus from the Word, he was often rebuffed. Yet, he continued to show Jesus to George in his actions.

Before George died, the love of God broke thru to him and changed him completely. He changed George's vocabulary by changing his heart. He that had become weak was now forever strong in the Lord. Greg Black planted the seed; Ty Sichina watered; but it was God who gave the increase.

What Are We to Do?

First of all, there is the risk that politics will lead us further down the path of a false gospel which bishop Richard B. Wilke lamented had occurred in his own United Methodist Church. Preaching had almost exclusively become a recitation of the duties of the Christian to change the world:

> However, the sermon, in all likelihood, would not tell me what God was doing to me, in me, through me, for me. The preacher would not tell me how God changes the sinful heart into a heart of faith and love. Is God at work in the world? Is God at work in the church? Is God at work in me? Tell me what God is doing right here and now...!
>
> ...Historians remind us that Susanna and Samuel, John's [John Wesley's] mother and father once quarreled over politics and did not sleep together for a considerable time. Their reconciliation of love (not of politics) caused John to be conceived.[157]

Second, I fear that many of us have taken our cues from sources other than the Bible in making politics the be-all and end-all of our relations to

---

[157] Richard B. Wilke (1986) *And Are We Yet Alive? The Future of the United Methodist Church*, Abingdon Press, pp. 35f

others in society. Francis Schaeffer, in his important work *Evangelical Disaster,* warned the church of failing to heed the Apostle's advice in I Corinthians to recognize "the wisdom of this world" which is at odds with "the wisdom of God":

> Paul is speaking...of a worldly wisdom which claims to be self-sufficient in itself, quite apart from God and his revelation. It is a kind of worldly wisdom which leaves God and his revelation out of the picture and thereby ends up with a completely distorted conception of reality.[158]

Too many Christians have become so consumed with politics and government it has caused them to stray off God's paths, either in rejecting Christian ethics in much of what they do, or subscribing to the worldly notion that all is fair in love and war (and politics is war, *doncha know*?). Or we have become so fearful of electing the wrong president that we have put all our eggs in that basket. We have not trusted the One who has promised His people that he will never leave us nor forsake us.

While we are enamored with making the whole world better, we have ignored the little worlds that God has placed in our hands. And we have become too busy: too busy to honor our parents, too busy to worship God as a family, too busy to raise our own children, too busy to bless our grandchildren, too busy to reach out to our neighbors.

Choosing the Better Part

Carol Douglas rescued unborn children in Iowa by joining others in blocking the doors of the sites where babies were scheduled to be killed. For several months after retirement, she devoted herself to fulltime picketing and used sidewalk counseling to try and talk mothers out of killing their children. But sometime later she began to realize her own grandchildren were needing her attention, and that devoting oneself to activism can tempt one to all kinds of sins: pride, neglect of one's familial duties, loss of integrity, anger, and other things that demonstrate it is possible to gain the whole world and lose one's own soul (Mt. 16:26). That Biblical warning doesn't just refer to material things, but also to worldly pride in our accomplishments. I don't mean to say that Carol had any of these

[158] Francis A. Schaeffer (1984) *The Great Evangelical Disaster*, Crossway Books, p. 27

sinful qualities coming out in her; on the contrary, she lived her life in great integrity at that time. But I think she saw these things in others and by God's grace did not want to shipwreck all that was rightly important to her. So she left the rescue movement to spend time with her family.

This new found freedom in the grace of God also kept Carol from getting overly involved in church busyness as well. We can so easily become obsessed with serving God in some public way that we forget the importance of spending our lives for him in our own homes and neighborhoods. Jesus condemned the practice of devoting things to God but neglecting our family duties:

> For Moses said, Honour thy father and thy mother; and, Whoso curseth father or mother, let him die the death: But ye say, If a man shall say to his father or mother, It is Corban, that is to say, a gift, by whatsoever thou mightest be profited by me; he shall be free. And ye suffer him no more to do ought for his father or his mother; Making the word of God of none effect through your tradition, which ye have delivered: and many such like things do ye.
> Mark 7:10-13

While I am not advocating either pietism or isolation from this world, the current emphasis on public service at the expense of the worship of God and personal devotion is leading many men to neglect their families and other obligations closer to home. A Christian man who fails to provide for his family has denied the faith and is worse than an infidel (1Ti. 5:8).

My wife Judy looks forward to the gift of each Lord's Day, hearing the Word of God, singing Psalms of praise, fellowshipping with the saints and offering prayers. Our own time worshipping as a family together blesses her beyond measure. This rest is necessary because she spends herself so selflessly the other six days of the week. Every day she takes time to attend to her elderly mother's needs, gives her time to help in her widowed sister's cleaning business, cares for many of our 16 grandchildren while the parents are working, and supplements our family income by spending long hours typing at the computer in our home business. Once a week she also hosts a three-hour "grandma day" for at least seven little ones, usually doing all the work herself. The reasons Judy does all of this are beyond the ordinary.

For one, Judy has put into practice her understanding of the Fifth Commandment. God commands that children honor their parents. This command is binding upon us even as we become adults, though the honor is carried out in different ways. Our parents continue to concern themselves for our lives even as we enter middle age, and they are in the graying years. On the other hand, children often neglect their parents once they have gotten all the benefits out of the relationship. We need the commandment because we are not inclined to honor our parents.

Judy isn't doing this to change the world, but in obedience with a heart of thanksgiving for God's grace.

I disagree with Kennedy and Newcombe when they tie too closely evangelism with cultural transformation:

> Do you realize that just buy inviting people to church, you could change this country? They *might* hear the gospel[!], and their hearts could be changed... Our duty is to share His message and influence people in the public sector, not only through political involvement, but also through the ultimate "political espionage", namely, evangelism.[159] (emphasis and exclamation mine)

So it has come to this. Can't you imagine one of Newcombe's neighbors reading his book and saying to himself: "You want me to come to church so you can change the country? No thanks, I'm not interested in being anybody's political football."

Averting One Other Extreme

One small group of Christians focuses on the imminent return of Christ and believes that we shouldn't bother to "polish brass on a sinking ship." These folks don't just believe that Jesus may come at any time (a viewpoint which has been widely held by the church since its inception), but that he is *certainly* coming *very soon*. Why worry about policies implemented by a government in 2012 (or 2016, 2020, etc.) when we probably won't be around that long? I have several reasons for not addressing this viewpoint in full:

First, because much of the church has become materialistic and worldly, only a small and shrinking segment of the American church focuses on the second coming. We have become fat and sassy and have largely abandoned the blessed hope, the return of the Lord of glory, and

[159] Kennedy and Newcombe, op. cit., p. 35

our everlasting home where righteousness dwells.[160] Believing Jesus *will* definitely come today presents some problems, if he doesn't come today. The errors of Harold Camping come to mind. But caring not if Jesus comes at all (or supposing it is thousands of years away) is far worse, in my opinion. It means we have lost our first love.

Second, trying to deal with dispensationalism and other date-setting errors would require a book-length response and until that theology is challenged, its proponents are not likely to concern themselves too much with voting booths at all, or they separate themselves from their world-view every four years and vote anyway, so I would think they would still receive benefit from the advice contained in this book.

Third, scores of "get-out-the-vote" books have already been written, and most of those authors go after these non-polishers with a vengeance, assigning them the blame for everything from high taxes to every part of our cultural decline.

[160] See Dave Hunt (1988) *Whatever Happened to Heaven*, Harvest House Publishing

SECTION THREE

RIGHTEOUS GOVERNANCE

Chapter Twelve

God Is King

The Bible is full of analogies, metaphors and other figures drawn from the physical world *and* used to explain spiritual truths. For example, the Bible compares human beings to sheep who tend to wander off, and likens false prophets to wolves with a design on gobbling up the sheep. These comparisons—and a thousand like them—did not originate in the imaginative minds of creative authors grasping for something in the "real world" to compare their spiritual notions. Instead, the likenesses began in the very creation of those things by God *prior to* the associations given to them by Prophets and Apostles. We often ignore the implications of this, even though we believe God created everything.

Sheep and snowflakes were made white by God on purpose, so that we sinners might better understand that our sin-stained lives could be as wool, and made as white as snow, through the blood of Christ (Isa. 1:18). Sheep were also made harmless to show the passive way in which Christ was made the Lamb of God, just as lions were made ferocious to demonstrate the idea of wrath. God created water, dirt, stars, bees, trees, honey, milk, little dependent babies, eyes, ears, noses and throats, even creepy spiders and snakes. These were all made by God for particular use in His Revelation. They were no accident of evolution and then twisted in their significance by well-meaning writers of Scripture. Instead, they were specifically created and ordained by God to help us understand the Word.

All of this should cause us to reflect on the subject at hand: God and Government. Did the writers of Scripture just grasp at whatever kind of leaders they had at hand, in order to describe God or were the very kind of leaders in existence when the Bible was written appointed by the providence of God for a specific purpose?

Even as early as Genesis, when cities or nations must have been relatively small, kings were in existence. So what about kings? Is God *like* kings? No, not exactly. It is more precise to say that earthly kings are patterned after the King of Kings, the Lord Jesus Himself. Of course, they are fallen and wicked and He is righteous. They are limited and He is all-powerful. Therefore, earthly kings are mostly *contrasted* with the Original King in Heaven:

> For who in the heaven can be compared unto the LORD? who among the sons of the mighty can be likened unto the LORD? God is greatly to be feared in the assembly of the saints, and to be had in reverence of all them that are about him. O LORD God of hosts, who is a strong LORD like unto thee? or to thy faithfulness round about thee? Thou rulest the raging of the sea: when the waves thereof arise, thou stillest them.
>
> Psalm 89:6-9

In Chapter 1 we learned that God both puts up and sets down earthly kings, but the Scriptures teach of another king, which was described in a dream that great conqueror of kings, King Nebuchadnezzar had:

> Thou, O king, sawest, and behold a great image. This great image, whose brightness was excellent, stood before thee; and the form thereof was terrible. This image's head [was] of fine gold, his breast and his arms of silver, his belly and his thighs of brass, His legs of iron, his feet part of iron and part of clay. Thou sawest till that *a stone was cut out without hands*, which smote the image upon his feet that were of iron and clay, and brake them to pieces. Then was the iron, the clay, the brass, the silver, and the gold, broken to pieces together, and became like the chaff of the summer threshingfloors; and the wind carried them away, that no place was found for them: and the stone that smote the image became a great mountain, and filled the whole earth....in the days of these kings shall the God of heaven set up a kingdom, which shall never be destroyed: and the kingdom shall not be left to other people, but it shall break in pieces and consume all these kingdoms, and it shall stand for ever (emphasis mine).
>
> Daniel 2:31-35, 44

The Babylonian king was shown that his kingdom would be followed by other kings who would eventually fall before the true King of Kings. Though many people today seem worried about a one-world government, Nebuchadnezzar saw that God would decimate the power of all other kingdoms in one moment.

Jesus rules now. We wait neither for Him to return, nor for the church to get more politically active. The kingdom is made without human hands, just as salvation was shown to be all of God when the temple altar was to be made with a stone untouched by any human tools (Ex. 20:25).

All of us, including the political class, are commanded to do obeisance to Jesus:

> The kings of the earth set themselves, and the rulers take counsel together, against the LORD, and against his anointed, saying, Let us break their bands asunder, and cast away their cords from us. He that sitteth in the heavens shall laugh: the Lord shall have them in derision. Then shall he speak unto them in his wrath, and vex them in his sore displeasure. Yet have I set my king upon my holy hill of Zion. I will declare the decree: the LORD hath said unto me, Thou art my Son; this day have I begotten thee. Ask of me, and I shall give thee the heathen for thine inheritance, and the uttermost parts of the earth for thy possession.
>
> Psalm 2:2-8

Sennacherib, the King of Assyria, sent a taunting letter to King Hezekiah of Judah, threatening the people of God and demanding surrender. In the message, Sennacherib bragged about his victories over other nations and their gods, saying that they could not count on the LORD to deliver them. Here is how Hezekiah responded:

> And Hezekiah received the letter of the hand of the messengers, and read it: and Hezekiah went up into the house of the LORD, and spread it before the LORD. And Hezekiah prayed before the LORD, and said, O LORD God of Israel, which dwellest between the cherubims, thou art the God, even thou alone, of all the kingdoms of the earth: thou hast made heaven and earth. LORD, bow down thine ear, and hear: open, LORD, thine eyes, and see: and hear the words of Sennacherib, which hath sent him to reproach the living God. Of a truth, LORD, the kings of Assyria have destroyed the nations and their lands, And have cast their gods

> into the fire: for they were no gods, but the work of men's hands, wood and stone: therefore they have destroyed them. Now therefore, O LORD our God, I beseech thee, save thou us out of his hand, that all the kingdoms of the earth may know that thou art the LORD God, even thou only.
>
> II Kings 19:14-19

The Christian has plenty of promises from God that such obedience will be rewarded by God, not necessarily in material wealth or prosperity but in eternal blessings. Here is one:

> And we know that all things work together for good to them that love God, to them who are the called according to his purpose.
>
> Romans 8:28

Though debates rage concerning the relation between church and state, the Christian must remember that only the church has been given the following promises by God:

> I will never leave thee, nor forsake thee. So that we may boldly say, The Lord is my helper, and I will not fear what man shall do unto me.
>
> Hebrews 13:5b, 6

> When I cry unto thee, then shall mine enemies turn back: this I know; for God is for me.
>
> Psalm 56:9

> And hath put all things under his feet, and gave him to be the head over all things to the church.
>
> Ephesians 1:22

> Though I walk in the midst of trouble, thou wilt revive me: thou shalt stretch forth thine hand against the wrath of mine enemies, and thy right hand shall save me.
>
> Psalm 138:7

The Idea of the Kingdom of God

Your view of the Kingdom of God likely lines up with your eschatology (or view of the end of the world), though this is a subject well beyond my purposes here. I do suggest that there is a kingdom concept that ought to be universally acknowledged no matter how you see the "end things." That is this: We must not confuse the kingdoms of this world with the Kingdom of Christ.

Though God overrules the actions of kings for the benefit of His people, they are called the kingdoms of this world because they are part of a worldly system, ruled by the god of this world. To expect that unbelieving kings will willingly submit to the claims and rule of Christ this side of glory is a pipe dream. It is true that "The kingdoms of this world are become the kingdoms of our Lord, and of his Christ; and he shall reign for ever and ever" (Rev. 11:15), but this is at the commencement of God's wrath against unbelievers and the rewarding of the saints in the final judgment (v. 18).

One theologian wrote:

> The Kingdom of God is primarily an eschatological concept. The fundamental idea of the Kingdom in Scripture is not that of a restored theocratic kingdom of God in Christ—which is essentially a kingdom of Israel—as the Premillenarians claim; neither is it a new social condition, pervaded by the Spirit of Christ, and realized by man through such external means as good laws, civilization, education, social reforms, and so on, as the Modernists would have us believe. The primary idea of the Kingdom of God in Scripture is that of the rule of God established and acknowledged in the hearts of sinners by the powerful regenerating influence of the Holy Spirit insuring them of the inestimable blessing of salvation,——a rule that is realized in principle on earth, but will not reach its culmination until the visible and glorious return of Jesus Christ. The present realization of it is spiritual and invisible.[161]

[161] Louis Berkhof (1932) *Systematic Theology*

Defense Against Our Enemies

> It is well that war is so terrible, lest we grow fond of it.
>
> General Robert E. Lee

No sane man ever loves war. Like divorce, there is no such thing as a no-fault war. Somebody is to blame, usually a lot of somebodies on every side. It may come as a result of an ego or power trip by a political leader, but it is almost always either a result or cause of the judgment of God.

As a country, the U.S. has enemies. It is naïve to think that we can fend off forever the threats of dictators and terrorists with talk alone. While our foreign policy is often confused and inconsistent—propping up dictators in one place, while sticking our noses in where it doesn't belong in another—we are not the "bad guys." I honestly think one of our problems is a result of changing our leaders (and foreign policy) every four to eight years. Another is the fact that every conflict we have entered since World War II has been without a formal declaration of war. Thankfully, with the exceptions of the December 7th, 1941, Japanese attack on Pearl Harbor in Hawaii and the Al Qaeda attacks of September 11th, 2001, our own borders have been exceptionally safe for 200 years.

We must remind ourselves, however, that promises for military conquest such as found in Deuteronomy 20:1-4 were made specifically to the people of God. These promises concerning "enemies" are not promises to the United States that it is destined for victory in future wars; it is a promise to Christ and His church. We mustn't think that the promise can be transferred to the U.S. simply because we have many citizens who are Christians, because our country's enemies may also include Christians, too.

While I will not go into just war theory here, I will simply make one observation from the Scripture, in keeping with the focus on trusting God:

> There is no king saved by the multitude of an host: a mighty man is not delivered by much strength. An horse is a vain thing for safety: neither shall he deliver any by his great strength. Behold, the eye of the LORD is upon them that fear him, upon them that hope in his mercy; to deliver their soul from death, and to keep them alive in famine.
>
> Psalm 33:16

If we trust in the world's finest military to save us, we will have become idolaters. This is true whether we make our fighting forces bigger and stronger, or pull them all back home in an isolationist scheme. This passage applies to kings or leaders of every nation.

After presenting many of the failing schemes of man to govern himself without God (or in God's name, but misunderstanding His blueprints), I now present a model for governance I believe is pleasing to God, will eternally benefit his people, and may brim over to temporal blessings to our country. It is simply this. Both the ruler and the ruled are to recognize the Kingdom of God and the Lordship of Christ.

What follows in the remainder of this chapter is a discussion of the Christian duty of submission and a very brief discourse on when civil disobedience is permitted. Chapter 13 then deals with the separation of church and state, followed by a chapter on identity politics. Finally, this section ends with two chapters devoted to social issues coming from an unusual perspective I like to call "principle."

Citizens Must Submit, Even When They Cannot Obey

> Men are not corrupted by the exercise of power or debased by the habit of obedience."
>
> Alexis de Tocqueville, *Democracy in America*, 1835

> Power tends to corrupt, and absolute power corrupts absolutely. Great men are almost always bad men.
>
> Lord Acton, letter to Bishop Mandell Creighton, 1887

I believe Acton was wrong and Tocqueville was right. Just as Jesus taught us that it is not what goes into a man (what he eats, for example) that corrupts him, but what comes out of his wicked heart; so too, it isn't government or politics that corrupts a man, but man who corrupts the process. God holds all power and he is not corrupted. He has even condescended to give man power, which he expects to be yielded in righteousness, for God is even ruling now, in Christ:

> All the ends of the world shall remember and turn unto the LORD: and all the kindreds of the nations shall worship before thee, for the kingdom is the LORD's: and he is the governor among the nations.
>
> Psalm 22:27f

It is the second part of the Tocqueville quote (the habit of obedience) that is potentially the most offensive notion in this book to the ears of some Americans because it affirms that we are "subjects". The idea may be repugnant to a people who are accustomed to hearing rousing speeches from politicians about liberty (or freedom) and rights. The former term is often understood to mean that we can do whatever we want, even to the point of telling all of our rulers how they must rule. But is this the Biblical approach to citizenship? I am not suggesting that hard-fisted rulers are to be commended. God certainly comes to the defense of those oppressed and afflicted by heavy-handed governors. Nevertheless, the stance towards those God has placed over us is to be as those under subjection:

> Submit yourselves to every ordinance of man for the Lord's sake: whether it be to the king, as supreme; Or unto governors, as unto them that are sent by him for the punishment of evildoers, and for the praise of them that do well. For so is the will of God, that with well doing ye may put to silence the ignorance of foolish men: As free, and not using your liberty for a cloke of maliciousness, but as the servants of God. Honour all men. Love the brotherhood. Fear God. Honour the king.
>
> I Peter 2:13-17

Many on the right have been guilty of dishonoring Barack Obama by personally attacking him, passing on lewd or racist jokes or doctored pictures garnered from the internet, or poking fun at his appearance. This is to disobey God and is unbecoming for the Christian, and is without excuse.

While ambition can cause leaders to seek office simply to run the lives of others, Joe Q. Citizen must also fight off developing a bad attitude against those God has placed over them. It is easy to become rebellious against officials and bureaucrats when government policies are clearly in violation of God's law or appear to be designed to do more harm than good. It is easy, but it is not right. God calls for submission. This is an attitude that recognizes the lawful authority that GOD has placed over you (even if the power was usurped against both the laws of God and man). This attitude of Honoring the King is due, even when the King is wicked and knows not God.

The default position of the Christian is submission. This does not mean that governors have the right to destroy their own people or order them to do evil. Ruling this way is proof that the leader is no Christian.

What is a Law?

Legal Positivism is the view that laws gain their authority and validity only because they have been implemented by a recognized authority, not because they are based upon some moral law.[162] On the other hand God says,

> Shall the throne of iniquity have fellowship with thee, which frameth mischief by a law? They gather themselves together against the soul of the righteous, and condemn the innocent blood.
>
> Psalm 94:20

The two views of law above are at complete odds with one another. According to the positivist, all laws ought to be obeyed simply because they are laws, period. He does not ask whether they are moral or immoral, or whether they are legitimate in what they require or forbid of those under their jurisdiction. Finally, he does not ask whether the laws are right, they simply are. That is all that matters.

But according to the Word, no human law is presumed to be inherently moral, for kings are able to create mischief by decree (as the New American Standard Version puts it in the above passage). They could order (or permit) the killing of Jews, blacks, Ukrainians, the handicapped or unborn babies, but those are laws are no laws at all.

Civil Disobedience, but Not Revolution

The fact that some governments step outside their lawful boundaries is insufficient reason to take a rebellious stance. If some foolish politician outlaws green socks, the Christian complies.

Fearing God and honoring the King are not contrary to one another, but when an earthly governor requires disobedience to God or forbids obedience, then that ruler must be disobeyed, even while submitting. This was done by the apostles (who said they ought to obey God rather than men, Acts 5:29), Rahab the prostitute (who "treasonously" hid the spies of God, Joshua 2:3f), and the Hebrew midwives (who feared God more than the King, Exodus 1:17) among many others.

It must not be assumed that such disobedience should only occur when the government requires you to do something evil. All three of the cases

[162] http://www.businessdictionary.com/definition/legal-positivism.html

above, in fact were positive acts of righteousness that had been forbidden. Though we have the example in the book of Daniel of the three Hebrew youths refusing to bow down, the same book tells us that Daniel simply prayed in violation of the law.

Suppose an unrighteous government imprisoned your pastor and his wife because he preached the gospel, and was slowly starving them both to death. Would it not be right to sneak food to them if given an opportunity? Are we bound to put the laws of men above doing what is right? Surely if Rahab can please God by treasonously hiding Spies for God in her home, we can give food to a member of Christ's body.

What if the law forbad the use of the rod on your children? Would you obey God or men? Again, while discretion in this case would forbid you from flaunting the law of men, it is clear that you should pray for strength and then obey God, trusting that He will vindicate His righteous ones.

None of this justifies doing what the passage above clearly forbids, which is "using our liberty as a cloke of maliciousness". When the Devil cannot tempt us with fear of men he will tempt us to belligerence, instead. We ought to be considered model citizens, not seen as rabble-rousers, as much as some of us might be tempted to glory in the "limelight" of being arrested. Even in the lawful rescue of unborn children, I must confess that I frequently sinned in failing to honor God by showing due respect to God's authorities.

Years later, I recall watching a newscast that featured a young couple who had gotten off scot-free after being arrested in Ohio for transporting their baby in their car without using a baby car seat or seatbelt. In fact, the mother had held the newborn baby in her lap while driving. They escaped the charges on a technicality having to do with jurisdiction. What was awful was the display of hatred toward the government and disregard for the safety of their own child, which they admitted was not their main concern. They were trying to make a point: they were only interested in their rights.

Providentially, I believe my life was changed by the Spirit of God when I saw what looked like me in that story. In fact, it was me, every time I screamed at an officer or simply tried to make life tougher for them. Sadly, I see this same attitude among many so-called patriots. Just as we are not to worship at the feet of governors, nor should we be mischief makers ourselves, challenging everything they do.

Chapter Thirteen

Christians Rule with Their Bibles Open

In the Introduction I suggested that some Christians, who have little involvement in politics, just want to be left alone. I don't criticize them. They don't expect much from their government. But I also don't want to leave the impression that I agree with those who argue for a "separation of church and state".

America has a long history of electing presidents who profess to be Christians. In fact, nearly every U.S. president has made such a profession. Yet this leaves open the question as to how much an American president should be influenced by his faith in Christ. The range of views on that question can be illustrated by looking briefly at Thomas Jefferson's view of the Separation of Church and State, comparing that with the actual practice of a few politicians since then.

Jefferson's Separation of God and State

When the separation of Church and State is debated, I usually cringe as each side makes it case, without really understanding the other.

When my Christian brothers suggest that we are a Christian nation, and that Thomas Jefferson's phrase "separation of church and state" was in a private letter and had nothing to do with the Constitution, they are missing the point. Jefferson was strongly opposed to having an established religion, at the federal *or* state level. An established religion is one in which the state church is associated with a particular religion or denomination.

When Jefferson was governor of Virginia, he argued that other states did just fine without an established religion. He wrote in his autobiography:

> Our sister States of Pennsylvania and New York have long subsisted without any establishment at all.... They flourish infinitely. Religion is well supported ... their harmony is unparalleled, and can be ascribed to nothing but their unbounded tolerance, because there is no other circumstance in which they differ from every nation on earth. They have made the happy discovery that the way to silence religious disputes is to take no notice of them.[163]

Many voices, including some on the Supreme Court, have used Jefferson's viewpoint to suggest that laws cannot have a basis in religion, and that Christian politicians should keep their religion to themselves.

Four Western Leaders Who Invoked Scripture, and Not a Theocrat Among Them

Some detractors have frantically warned us that politicians like Michele Bachmann are theocrats, people who believe that God will or should rule in the civil realm via the church or clergy. These naysayers are hyperventilating. A similar term, "theonomist", refers to those who believe the Mosaic judicial laws should be implemented in our day. Only a small number of Christians hold the latter view, but even they believe that those laws would be implemented through the democratic process, not from a takeover of the government by the church. There is not one shred of evidence that any of the candidates listed above has ever been a theocrat or a theonomist. The accusation is mostly put forth by bloggers who oppose these candidates' views on abortion and homosexual marriage. A few well-known liberal pundits have made the charge as well.[164] Many of them took offense at George W Bush because he dared pray about whether to enter into war with Iraq or not.

---

163 Thomas Jefferson, *Notes on Virginia*, Ford Edition, viii, 402; iii, 265 (1782)

164 See Kevin Phillips, *American Theocracy: The Peril and Politics of Radical Religion, Oil, and Borrowed Money in the 21st Century* (2006) Viking Adult
See also Schaeffer, Frank *(12/1/2009)* http://www.bradblog.com/?p=7551
"Franky" wrote an important pro-life book called *A Time for Anger: The Myth of Neutrality* (1982), Crossway Books: University of Michigan. Schaefer now opposes both the religion and political viewpoints of his father, Francis Schaeffer.

The detractors forget that nearly every president who has ever sent us to war believed that the war was just and therefore, we would be blessed by God. Whether the war was just or not is a separate question; what is undeniable is that leaders who are not theocrats also make claims of God's favor or pray for wisdom.

It is also true that Governor Huckabee was unashamed of his Christian testimony in 2008, his personal belief in The Ten Commandments, and the view that the underpinning of good civil law is the moral law. He believes in a God that actually exists, though he never claimed God[165] (or Ronald Reagan[166]) would endorse him.

It is sad when a candidate feels compelled to present their testimonies in the subjective, rather than if the gospel were objective truth. For example, when a person says "My belief in God sustains me" or "My faith is important to me", that is different than when a candidate says "God sustains me" or "Jesus was raised from the dead."

Before we examine a few of the most controversial aspects of certain politicians and their faith and testimony, it would be good to provide a little historical background. I have already made the case that we are not a Christian nation. Nor do I reject the obvious fact that our nation has a strong Christian heritage and is greatly blessed of God. What I aim to do is take three leaders, who at three critical junctures of Western Culture invoked God's name and His Law to justify certain national or legislative ends. All of them took heat for their decisions at the time, but none were called theocrats in their day. Would they be called theocrats today?

God and the American Civil War

There is considerable dispute over whether Abraham Lincoln ever truly embraced the Christian faith. However, such questions are irrelevant to my pleading here. The text of his Second Inaugural Address contained this description of the two sides at the height of the Civil War: *"Both*

---

[165] If God had wanted Huckabee to become our president in 2008, *he would be president* today (see Chapter 1).

[166] John McCain, Ron Paul and Mitt Romney all gave reasons at the 2008 Simi Valley Reagan Library debate as to why Reagan would endorse them. Huckabee received a huge ovation when he answered "I think it would be incredibly presumptuous and even arrogant for me to try to suggest what Ronald Reagan would do, that he would endorse any of us against the others. Let me just say this: I'm not going to pretend he would endorse me. I wish he would. I would love that. But I endorse him, and I'm going to tell you why."

read the same Bible and pray to the same God, and each invokes His aid against the other." At first glance, it resembles the pleas of those who would tell us that religion only divides people and should play no part in politics or public policy. But Lincoln, whatever his personal faith, was not playing with words. He was not afraid to say that the God the North and South had in common was very much involved in the recent unpleasantness, though not as either side might wish:

> The prayers of both could not be answered. That of neither has been answered fully. The Almighty has His own purposes. "Woe unto the world because of offenses; for it must needs be that offenses come, but woe to that man by whom the offense cometh." If we shall suppose that American slavery is one of those offenses which, in the providence of God, must needs come, but which, having continued through His appointed time, He now wills to remove, and that He gives to both North and South this terrible war as the woe due to those by whom the offense came, shall we discern therein any departure from those divine attributes which the believers in a living God always ascribe to Him?.... Yet, if God wills that it continue until ... every drop of blood drawn with the lash shall be paid by another drawn with the sword, as was said three thousand years ago, so still it must be said "The judgments of the Lord are true and righteous altogether."

Though no specific legislation is explicit in this portion of Lincoln's speech, it is clear that he believes that slavery is a moral evil bringing about a judgment of God upon the whole land and he wants to end the war and slavery. How is this different than statements by Christian leaders today warning of judgments on America because we spill innocent blood or abandon the covenant of marriage?

William Wilberforce

The battle over slavery across the pond was fought in the halls of Parliament rather than fields of blood. William Wilberforce introduced bills to outlaw the slave trade as early as 1789 and persisted year after year until shortly before his death in 1833, when he was notified that slavery as an institution was about to be voted out of existence. No one today looks at Wilberforce as someone who stubbornly imposed his religion on others.

No one equates his efforts with the Taliban, though he feverishly opposed slavery based upon his Christian viewpoint. He wrote:

> Policy, Sir, is not my principle, and I am not ashamed to say it. There is a principle above everything that is political. And when I reflect on the command that says, 'Thou shalt do no murder,' believing the authority to be divine, how can I dare set up any reasonings of my own against it? And, Sir, when we think of eternity, and of the future consequences of all human conduct, what is here in this life which should make any man contradict *the principles of his own conscience, the principles of justice, the laws of religion and of God?* (emphasis mine)

Martin Luther King, Jr.

Martin Luther King, Jr. was never a politician, but profoundly impacted politicians and the politics of his day. Many call him Dr. Martin Luther King, Jr. who never call him *Rev.* Martin Luther King, Jr.; but he was a Baptist minister who was not afraid to interject Scripture into his civil rights speeches. In particular, his letter from Birmingham Jail was peppered with Scriptures and the notion that God's law is higher than man's law.

> How does one determine whether a law is just or unjust? A just law is a man-made code that squares with the moral law or the law of God. An unjust law is a code that is out of harmony with the moral law...
>
> Of course, there is nothing new about this kind of civil disobedience. It was evidenced sublimely in the refusal of Shadrach, Meshach and Abednego to obey the laws of Nebuchadnezzar, on the ground that a higher moral law was at stake. It was practiced superbly by the early Christians, who were willing to face hungry lions and the excruciating pain of chopping blocks rather than submit to certain unjust laws of the Roman Empire....
>
> There was a time when the church was very powerful--in the time when the early Christians rejoiced at being deemed worthy to suffer for what they believed. In those days the church was not merely a thermometer that recorded the ideas and principles of

> popular opinion; it was a thermostat that transformed the mores of society.... By their effort and example they brought an end to such ancient evils as infanticide and gladiatorial contests.[167]

Mike Huckabee and Amending the Constitution

Many in the pundit-world became apoplectic when Mike Huckabee, during the 2008 presidential campaign season, dared suggest four facts, none of which would have been denied by Christians or most conservative pundits when taken separately, but are apparently a sign that Huckabee is a Jihadist when put together as he did (see below):

> [Some of my opponents] do not want to change the Constitution, but I believe it's a lot easier to change the constitution than it would be to change the Word of the living God, and that's what we need to do is to amend the Constitution so it's in God's standards rather than try to change God's standards," Huckabee said, referring to the need for a constitutional human life amendment and an amendment defining marriage as between a man and a woman.[168]

The four facts:

1. The Constitution Can Be Amended (Gasp!)
2. The Bible Cannot Be Amended (Another Gasp!)
3. The Bible affirms the pro-life, anti-abortion position and the truth that marriage can only be between a man and a woman.
4. The best way to defend these issues is to amend the Constitution[169]

How Soon They Forget

Apparently, guest chaplains for the U.S. House are given *The Official Instructions for Guest Chaplains in the U.S. House of Representatives*

---

167 http://www.africa.upenn.edu/Articles_Gen/Letter_Birmingham.html

168 http://firstread.msnbc.msn.com/_news/2008/01/15/4431338-huck-the-constitution-and-gods-standards

169 One could perhaps disagree on the best strategic approach to these issues, but it would not change the argument that Huckabee was making about the legitimacy of changing the Constitution.

Concerning the Opening Prayer, which is another voice testifying against godless government:

> The purpose of the opening prayer for the House is to pray on behalf of, and for, the Members of the Congress as they seek to know and do God's will for America and in the work of the House of Representatives. God is Sovereign Lord of our Nation. The prayer should affirm our heritage as a Nation "Under God" and the calling of the Senate to lead our Nation in His righteousness and justice. We accept the separation of church (sectarianism) and state but affirm the historic American Tradition that there is no separation between God and state.

When a culture is in decline, there is always the possibility that those resisting the decline will be seen as culturally backward. Recent history itself will quickly be distorted to the point where events from even 20 or 30 years ago are ignored or treated as if they were a million years ago. This is particularly true in the two most hotly debated issues among Republicans: Abortion and Homosexual Marriage. Just 40 years ago, states were permitted to outlaw abortion, and hardly a soul in the Republic thought that two men could get married. Was the whole country filled with Neanderthals, Theocrats or Jihadists? No. How soon we forget.

Your Bible: Don't Leave Home Without It

Suppose you are defending the proposition that it should be illegal to kill unborn children. Or that the government should not recognize something called "gay marriage". If you are a Christian, you are likely to resort to using Scripture, which may be either offensive to, or considered irrelevant by, your unbelieving opponent, who neither believes in God nor accepts the relevancy of God's Word. To him, the book is nonsense. It seems reasonable at that point, doesn't it, to take a different approach and leave the Bible out of it?

On the abortion question, for example, you could make your appeal to science and say that the offspring of human beings is a human being (of course, you would be making the Scriptural argument from Genesis 1:24 that creatures bear offspring of their own kind). However, understand that those who want to kill babies may acknowledge the humanity of the unborn child, just not his or her "personhood". How do you prove the personhood of persons? Read a debate on abortion and watch the protagonists. Notice that the actual arguments, logically speaking, are quite simple. The debaters go round and round because they cannot agree on foundations or presuppositions.

You could also point to pictures of unborn children either produced by an ultrasound, or display the bloody remains of an unborn child scalded in a saline abortion, cut up alive in the womb, or simply thrown in a dumpster. But these are not so much rational arguments meant to persuade the mind, but an attempt to bypass the fallen reasonings of man and go directly to the conscience. You may have recognized this already. There is nothing wrong with doing this.

But once you begin to appeal to the mind of your opponent, you must not grant his premise that the Bible is irrelevant. He is a creature made in God's image. Granting the premise of your opponent that God is irrelevant to the discussion is to lose the argument. If you do not bring to bear the unchanging Word from an unchanging God on a subject, your nemesis can and will change the rules of argument and debate at his every whim. And what will you say then?

Suppose someone wanted to tempt your teenage son to break your rule that he must be home by 11:00 p.m. What if the tempter said "your father doesn't really exist, so his rules don't really matter"? Such a claim should rightly be considered foolishness by your son. He knows you exist, and any further argument on the issue of what the other guy said is moot. Furthermore, your son could correctly say to himself that the other guy obviously knows that you exist and is simply being obstinate.

In the same way, the Bible teaches that all men know that God exists (Rom. 1:20, Ps. 19:1-3) even if they have suppressed such knowledge into the recesses of their minds. But perhaps God will use your appeal to Scripture to awaken their minds.

Presuppositions

Man is incapable of building something from nothing. What is true in the physical universe is also true in the area of knowledge. No man can or does know everything, therefore he must build upon assumptions that he himself has not tested or proven. He must trust someone or something to begin to build a philosophy of life. That someone may be his own self. Man may trust in his own ability to reason or think, but he cannot gain proof that such a philosophy is rational.

In other words, man must begin with unproven assumptions. The Christian begins with God. He believes that God has revealed Himself not only in nature, but in His Son, Jesus, and in the written Word.

Chapter Fourteen

Can You Identity with Me?

Identity politics entails the notion that voters tend to vote for people like themselves or perhaps even vote against someone not like themselves, i.e., someone they cannot identify with. The practice is usually denigrated as being beneath the dignity of the American voter, and sometimes "identity voters" are called bigots, unless they are themselves from a favored group. Blacks vote for blacks[170], Mormons for Mormons[171], and women for women, or so the theory goes. As it turns out, sometimes this is true, sometimes it is not[172].

Equality under the Law: A Christian Notion

> Christianity, which has declared that all men are equal in the sight of God, will not refuse to acknowledge that all citizens are equal in the eye of the law.[173]
>
> Alexis de Tocqueville

> There is neither Jew nor Greek, there is neither bond nor free, there is neither male nor female: for ye are all one in Christ Jesus.
>
> Galatians 3:28

---

170 http://www.politico.com/news/stories/1108/15297.html

171 http://www.irr.org/mit/voting-mormon-president.html

172 Time Magazine Online (6/5/08) *Why Didn't More Women Vote for Hillary?* by Amy Sullivan

173 Alexis de Tocqueville, *Democracy in America*, Volume 1, p. 7

There are privileges exclusive to citizens of any country, including the United States, such as the privilege to vote. But the "unalienable" rights belong to all, because they came from our Creator. Within our borders, all people have an equal right to life, liberty and the pursuit of happiness. Our government was created to secure and protect those rights. One of the important distinctions between the U.S. and some other countries is the source of rights. As has been noted by many others, citizens of the former Soviet Union had many rights, including the right to practice religion and the right to free speech. But where did those rights come from in the USSR? They came from the State (the government).

Does equality under the law require that citizens treat everybody the same or only that the law treats everybody the same? The answer to this question is not easy, but it is relevant to the Christian as he enters the voting booth.

How Do We Know Who is Qualified to Hold Office?

What may a man rightly use to judge whether another person is fit for office? Can he question the man's religion? Those sold on religious pluralism will answer unequivocally "no." What about race? Those who know the Bible will be clear that race is not relevant to the question. Whether or not a woman should run for office is still a matter of controversy to some, particularly as it pertains to mothers who have young children at home.

While the world has its ideas, God has given us many measuring sticks that we might lawfully use to measure the candidate. The worldview, experience, positions, character and record of the competing candidates are just some of the factors we usually consider when we decide who to vote for. Of course, not all Christians will agree on how to interpret all of those standards. In this section of the book we will consider the legitimacy of considering a person's religion, gender and race in determining who to vote for. Interestingly, all three of these issues came up during the 2008 campaign season: the religious views of Mitt Romney and Mike Huckabee; the race of Barack Obama, and the gender of Hillary Clinton and Sarah Palin.

I begin with the premise that a man may enter the voting booth totally free to vote according to his own conscience, without consideration of the consciences of others. Without this freedom, there are no free elections. It seems a voter may vote for a particular candidate for any reason he or she jolly-well pleases, irrespective of whether that decision is wise or foolish according to the opinions of our friends, family, pastor or party leaders. I offer one ubiquitous caveat. We do answer to *God* and Him alone.

Feminism and Androgyny

The State Department announced in 2011 that passport forms for children will no longer ask for the name of the mother and father, but instead the form now asks for the name of "parent one" and "parent two." It is got to be gender-neutral just to be fair to all those non-gendered parents. Google+ is a social networking site that asks those registering whether they are "male," "female," or "other." Someone should tell Google: There is no "other".

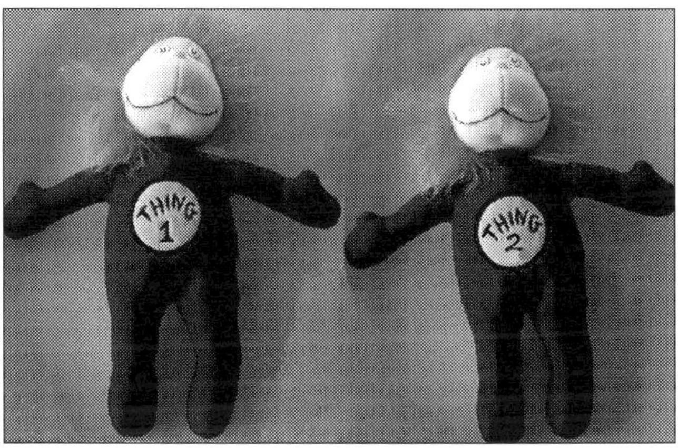

The Dog in the Blog

None of us wore pink or blue,
Our parent's names are One and Two.
Neither were we girls and boys,
We all played with Barbie toys.

No son or daughter, sister, brother,
Grandpa, Grandma, dad nor mother.
No one here can rule the house,
Parent One nor Two, its spouse

Two little siblings here with me,
No one's he and no one's she.
We were never him or her
The differences are all a blur.

Our Parents gave us tots no aunts
For all their siblings wear the pants.
My sibling's kids are all obese,
But none of them is named DeNiece.

The kitty cried, I thought they'd shoot her,
Instead they took her out to neuter.
They took our puppy to be fixed
I guess that means its gender's mixed.

Are you my daddy? I asked my father
He said be quiet and not to bother
Are you my mother? I asked my mama
Hush yourself, go ask Obama.

The lead Dr. Seuss character in *The Cat in the Hat* pulled out of his box two indistinguishable little brats called "Thing One" and "Thing Two". Coincidentally, these two genderless creatures also took on a mission to utterly destroy the family dwelling of two little children, "Sally and me". At least Seuss had the sense to identify the parent wearing a dress, as "mother".

Many different issues have animated conservatives over the last three or four decades: gun control, crime and punishment, terrorism, pornography, the wars in Vietnam, Afghanistan and Iraq; the economy, prayer in schools, and the general encroachment of political correctness and secularism. Two things, however, have occupied the front burner in more recent years and don't appear to be going away very soon: abortion and gay "rights".

Is there a connection between the alleged right to kill one's own offspring and the right of two men or two women to get married to each other? I believe the connection is feminism or its natural end, androgyny. It is rather simple. Children have a way of interfering with a woman's plans for a career outside the home. And that interference is not based upon cultural training alone. It is first of all based upon biology, pure and simple: Women bear the children, and breast-feeding requires the kind of attention only a mother can give. But, for the Christian, motherhood is more than biology. It reflects the different roles God has ordained for men and women by decree. The idea that mothers *ought to* stay at home with the babies is downright offensive to many college-educated women, who might otherwise vote Republican or consider themselves conservative, but can't stomach the idea that men or women are different.[174]

As to biology, every pregnancy is a reminder that men and women are physically different. Not only is the anatomy different, the ways in which each contributes to the reproductive cycle are different. We used to call these things the facts of life. They will not go away, even though we ignore them.

Alaska Governor, Sarah Palin, came into the national limelight when John McCain made her his pick for a spot on the Presidential ticket in 2008. Most conservatives embraced her candidacy and did not consider it their business to weigh the impact of her running on her five children, for they recognized that this was ultimately a choice for Palin and her husband to make. But in the intervening years between 2008 and 2011 Palin made several statements that caused some Christians to take pause:

> I'm a feminist who believes in equal rights and I believe that women certainly today have every opportunity that a man has to succeed, and to try to do it all, anyway. And I'm very, very thankful that I've been brought up in a family where gender hasn't been an issue.
>
> And Geraldine [Ferraro] has also been grossly attacked back in '84, and I remember as a young college student watching what it was that you were going through and knowing that and more power to you for busting that glass ceiling you know and standing on the shoulders of Elizabeth Cady Stanton, and Susan B. Anthony, and others who had come before you, of course, so many years ago. And, then you busting through and then the opportunity that I and other women following you have, have been able to seize. That's

[174] Here I only discuss the different *roles* prescribed for husbands and wives, or fathers and mothers, and not any differences in the *constitution or make up* of men and women, which is of only secondary importance, according to Scripture.

> just been wonderful. It's been great for our nation, it's been so good.
>
> But, yeah, it kind of seems, Geraldine that some things haven't changed.
>
> There are still the Neanderthals out there, who pick on the petty little superficial meaningless things like looks, like whether you can or can't work outside of the home if you have small children. All those type of things where I would so hope that at some point, uh, those Neanderthals, will evolve into something a bit more, um, with it, a bit more modern, and a bit more understanding that, yeah, woman can accomplish much..."

Palin's remarks might be without controversy among many American Christians and be considered an effort on her part to repossess feminism from those she greatly differs with on, say, abortion. Indeed, the Scriptures teach that before God in Christ there is neither male nor female. There is no superiority inherent in males and hardly any Christian thinks that "women can't accomplish much".

The real question raised is not about the fitness of Palin for office as a woman, but whether the Christian is a Neanderthal for believing the Scriptures which teach that a wife or mother is to be a "keeper at home" and "obedient or submissive to her husband" (Titus 2:5, Eph. 5:22-24), ideas which are indeed anathema to most women who identify themselves as feminists.

The great scandal here is not that Palin would run for office. It is that she would use that platform to challenge the Word of God's plain teaching concerning the roles of wives and husbands and the role of mothers in the home. It is not her personal position which is critical. If she and her husband have decided that she should run for president or hold public office, it is her family's decision.

But can a woman "do it all"? Is it really a "petty thing" to decide "whether you can or can't work outside of the home if you have small children?" Whichever side you come down on for your own life, it is not a little thing. This is another example of politics having a bad influence upon the Christian as he or she seeks to maintain a Biblical worldview while seeking political office.

I do not believe anything in Scripture forbids a woman from seeking political office. God providentially raised up Deborah as a Judge to lead ancient Israel for a season (Jdg. 4:4-6). The Bible does not teach that every man is the head over every woman, that her place is inherently subservient. While the Scriptures do teach that a wife should submit to her husband, my wife is not required to submit to other men.

Michele Bachmann ran for president in 2007 and for a short season was leading the Republican pack, winning the Ames, Iowa Straw Poll in August of 2011. I believe she votes on principle and has a good understanding of the role of government. She is 100% pro-life and has never endorsed a pro-abortion candidate, as far as I was able to discover. In spite of the fact she was often mocked for her faith, she was never ashamed of her Savior.

I stood for her in my own caucus site, but Bachmann finished with only 5% of the vote in Iowa and dropped out of the race shortly thereafter.

Pluralism and the Voter

Before I discuss the place religion plays in the political arena, we should first consider what it means that we live in a *pluralistic society*. It is true that we do not live under the legal constraints of a particular religion in the United States, and that there is no state religion. Every person is free to practice his or her religion in this country almost without restriction. However, it does not follow that a Christian is bound to consider all religions equal. If freedom of religion means anything, it surely means that we can freely speak of the warnings the Bible gives concerning false prophets and teachers, as well as false religions.

In 2010, talk show host Glenn Beck, traveled around the country holding "American Revival" meetings. He has often suggested "we need another Whitefield". He was referring to Great Awakening preacher, George Whitefield. Beck regularly lays it on thick with affection for Whitefield, but he grossly misunderstands or greatly misrepresents his preaching by suggesting the thrust of Whitefield's ministry was "freedom" and "individualism". It would be good for Beck's soul to read some of Whitefield's sermons, before he says things like "And we all have principles that are the same. God is universal,"[175]—a notion which Whitefield would have rejected outright.

George Whitefield was a consistently orthodox gospel preacher whom the "Prince of Preachers", Charles Spurgeon, considered his role model. Whitefield preached faith in the one Triune God, Jehovah, who alone is

[175] http://www.glennbeck.com/content/articles/article/198/44048/

eternal. Beck, on the other hand, frequently says things like "I don't care what God it is that you worship or what church you go to" and calls upon Christians to "put all differences aside on everything". Beck is wrong. There is only one God. And we don't get to pick him. He is the chooser, not we.

Whitefield did not preach that morality would lead to freedom. He actually said:

> People have been so long misled, they have been taught that they must do so and so, and though they were under a covenant of works, and then for DOING this, they should be saved. Whereas, on the contrary, people should be taught, That the Lord Jesus was the second Adam, with whom the Father entered into covenant for fallen man; That they can now do nothing of or for themselves, and should therefore come to God, beseeching him to give them faith, by which they shall be enabled to lay hold on the righteousness of Christ; and that faith they will then show forth by their works, out of love and gratitude to the ever blessed Jesus, their most glorious Redeemer, for what he has done for their souls.[176]

Having recognized that according to the Constitution we are free to practice any religion and that according to Scripture, there is only one true religion, how do we reconcile the tension these ideas create while in the voting booth? Do we hear voices from heaven telling us for whom we should vote? I say "no"[177]; but the Bible does tell us how a ruler should *rule*. It seems to follow that if you are picking your leaders, they should be "qualified". The Constitution only requires that our congressmen be 25 years old, our senators 30, and our presidents 35. The president must also have been born in the USA. But the Word of God tells us much more. Compare the two Scriptures immediately below with the quotes that follow.

> He that ruleth over men must be just, ruling in the fear of God.
> II Samuel 23:3

> Be wise now therefore, O ye kings: be instructed, ye judges of the earth. *Serve the LORD with fear,* and rejoice with trembling. *Kiss the Son*, lest he be angry, and ye perish from the way, when his

176 http://www.ccel.org/ccel/whitefield/sermons.txt

177 http://caffeinatedtheology.com/god-spoke

wrath is kindled but a little. Blessed are all they that *put their trust in him*. (emphasis mine)

Psalm 2:10-12

The demand for a statement of a candidate's religious belief can have no meaning except that there may be discrimination for or against him because of that belief.

President Teddy Roosevelt[178]

"No religious test shall ever be required as a qualification to any office or public trust under the United States."

Article 6 of the Constitution

Providence has given to our people the choice of their rulers, and it is the duty, as well as the privilege and interest, of our Christian nation to select and prefer Christians for their rulers. [179]

Justice John Jay

Politics are totally directed by worldview. That's why when people say, "We ought to separate politics from religion," I say to separate the two is absolutely impossible.

Mike Huckabee, from his 1997 book *Character is the Issue.*

"Given our grand tradition of religious tolerance and liberty, some wonder whether there are any questions regarding an aspiring candidate's religion that are appropriate. I believe there are...I did not confuse the particular teachings of my church with the obligations of the office and of the Constitution—and of course, I would not do so as president. I will put no doctrine of any church above the plain duties of the office and the sovereign authority of the law."

Mitt Romney's Faith Speech (December 6, 2007)

I do not think I could myself, be brought to support a man for office, whom I knew to be an open enemy of, and scoffer at, religion. Leaving the higher matter of eternal consequences, between

[178] Americanism in religion: a letter from Theodore Roosevelt, 1858-1919 Chicago: Blakely-Oswald

[179] William Jay, 1789-1858. *The life of John Jay: with selections from his correspondence and miscellaneous papers,* New York: J. & J. Harper

> him and his Maker, I still do not think any man has the right thus to insult the feelings, and injure the morals, of the community in which he may live. If, then, I was guilty of such conduct, I should blame no man who should condemn me for it; but I do blame those, whoever they may be, who falsely put such a charge in circulation against me.
>
> Abraham Lincoln[180]

A political candidate's positions on various issues are a reflection of his religious beliefs, whether he attends church regularly or not. The press intimates that only candidates "on the right" are influenced by their religion. Thus, we have the term "religious right" (you will get almost 7 million Google hits for the term). But there *is* a religious left (though you will only get about 400,000 hits on Google for that one).

The religious left are generally influenced by churches that bear the name Christian, but are liberal. That is, they reject the Biblical doctrines of the bodily resurrection of Christ, the virgin birth, Christ's miracles, a literal heaven and hell, the inspiration and infallibility of the Scriptures, and the Incarnation. Politically, they often interpret the Constitution the same way they do the Bible, without concern for its original intent. These churches (and by extension, many of their adherents) oppose the death penalty and restrictions on the murder of unborn children, while supporting assisted suicide[181] and gun control. They are often pacifists, and are opponents of America's traditional support of the nation of Israel.

Talk show host, Dennis Prager, applies the ideas that basic assumptions effect politics with an illustration from modern life. Suppose a person is sitting at a baseball game. On one side of him is a man smoking like a chimney, on the other is a man cursing like a sailor. The fan that offends the person in the middle most is likely determined by the middle man's worldview. Our culture has virtually banned the man on the right because of fear and concern that he will cause harm to his neighbor's physical well-being. Bans of smoking seem to be reaching a wider and wider sphere. On the

---

[180] Abraham Lincoln, Handbill Replying to Charges of Infidelity. Religious infidelity is in view here.

[181] While fighting against the expansion of euthanasia in Iowa in the early 1990s, I came across a small booklet about "the right to suicide", published by what was then called the Hemlock Society. They had completed a survey of the religion of its members. Almost all of the members were atheists, agnostics, or members of three religious denominations: Unitarian/Universalist, United Church of Christ, or Reformed Jews.

other hand, the man on the left may hardly receive a rebuke at all from the culture at large. Though his profanity may pollute the morals or the mind, our culture by-and-large ignores it. Cable television and modern discourse welcomes that kind of speech and sees no harm in it. This represents an historical change of perspective, based upon a change of worldview, in turn based upon a change of religion. Belief in an afterlife, and that your destiny may be based upon some idea of justice, means you will consider moral corruption more harmful than cigarette smoke. If you believe the material world is all there is, and we should "eat, drink and be merry, for tomorrow we die," you will look at not only the environment at a stadium, but legislation differently.

To deny the relationship between religious views and politics is to deny the obvious. Religion is an expression of what we believe to be most important. We get our morals from our religious views. It is natural that politics flows from our worldview, which comes from our views of God, the Bible, the nature of man, our destiny, the Kingdom of God, the source of morality, our definitions of justice, even the role of God in raising up and tearing down kings.

I would suggest that on any given Sunday you will be much more likely to hear a sermon on politics in a liberal church than a conservative one. Because modernists reject the notion of a literal heaven and often reject the Ten Commandments, all they are left with is this world, which is passing away. If you believe in an afterlife and focus on the spiritual and unseen aspects of faith, politics will end up in the periphery. This is not to deny that some Conservative local congregations have found themselves focusing on abortion and other public issues, but they are probably a small minority within conservative churches. Most fundamentalists and conservative Evangelical churches only mention these issues near elections, and then briefly by comparison.

There is another *practical* reason why attention has been focused on the right, however. The prominence of televangelists from the late 1970s to the early 1990s no doubt focused the press attention on the religious right. An awakening of political clout began on the right that had already existed on the left.

Other reasons for keeping religion out of politics seem reasonable enough. Is the candidate's view on the proper mode of baptism (sprinkling, pouring or immersion) or what kind of bread should be used with the Lord's Supper relevant? No, and for obvious reasons. Those questions bear no direct connection on how the office bearer will rule in the civil realm.

On the other hand, certain religiously-based views of the candidate may indeed bear on the candidate's approach to a host of political issues. If Governor Huckabee has a view of the imminent return of Christ or Israel that bears on his foreign policy, can that be fodder for discussion? Of course, it can. Perhaps his view of creation will impact legislation about science in the classroom. Shouldn't we know how one's views will or will not affect how that candidate will govern? Religious views direct ones political views because they deal with such questions as "what is man like?" and "how do we determine what is right and wrong?"

Race Relations

It is doubtful a legitimate reason exists to vote for or against a candidate based upon race. Unlike religious views, a candidate's race tells you little that is significant about his or her world view.[182] While there are plenty of prominent conservatives who happen to be black, such as Justice Clarence Thomas, Thomas Sowell, Walter E Williams, Alan Keyes and Ken Blackwell, this too is largely irrelevant. Our goal should line up with Martin Luther King, Jr.'s desire that we look past the color of the skin and look to the content of a candidate's character.

To inquire about a politician's *view on* race is surely a reasonable thing to do, whether the discussion is about immigration, the status of Israel or other current events where race or ethnicity comes into play. However, we need to get past both racism and race baiting. Sadly, like so many other sins, the evils of the one sin are used to justify the other.

[182] Catholics and Mormons do not always hold similar political views as their co-religionists, to be sure.

Chapter Fifteen

No Matter How Small

Kelly didn't have the best work ethic. She had a tendency to be lazy and easily bored. But her new employer was willing to hire her, because while finding help was easy, finding good help wasn't. And Kelly was friendly and seemed eager to work.

Her new job was really quite simple. Follow the policy manual. Maintain all machines on the premises. Report any machines making unusual noises or overheating. The hardest part was helping discard any machines that had ceased to function, but the system overall seemed to work quite nicely.

Kelly was not a people-person and this job seemed like the perfect fit. Like many occupations, training was mostly on the job and only required watching some videos and practicing on some dummy machines available at the learning center. There was some technical jargon she needed to eventually learn, but a couple of classes at the community college would soon take care of that.

A typical shift consisted of making sure fluid levels were within range. Fluid leaks occurred on these old contraptions almost every day, but she got the hang of the cleanup procedure pretty quickly. Some machines needed a wipe down daily, others needed taken to the shop for more thorough cleaning once a week or so. Some of the machines were heavy, so gurneys were provided to help move them or another employee could help in some cases if they weren't on break.

Kelly did not need to understand how the pieces of equipment really functioned, because there were always one or two maintenance experts available for advice or for taking care of the hard jobs. For this reason, stress was mostly a minimum, although each machine was equipped with a bothersome alarm system. At times these seemed to go off at inopportune times, for example, during smoke breaks. And more often than not the alarms were nothing, just a simple switch needed to be turned or a filter replaced, hardly worth the trouble of walking across the building to check on them. It's not like these pieces of equipment could "die" on her or something. She laughed at the thought. One day, she got so mad at the continuous alarm going off from Machine 15B, she just gave it a good slapping. It had little effect on the machine, but it made her feel better.

Since these contraptions belonged to various companies and were being maintained in a common facility, Kelly had been warned that if she were caught messing up on maintenance, in rare cases she could be sued.

But she didn't worry about it too much; after all, these machines are just machines. And her superiors rarely asked questions. As long as the basic maintenance list was checked off each shift, nobody cared whether you went the extra mile or even really did your job. In fact, it was discouraged. The pressure to not rock the boat by "caring" was overwhelming, especially to newcomers like Kelly.

After six months on the job, the combination of boredom with the routine and Kelly's laziness finally caught up with her. Three machines had to be discarded in one week, raising the suspicions of the local examiner. Apparently, Kelly had been neglecting to add fluids to two of the machines and had put the wrong fluid in another; moreover, none of the machines had been cleaned for weeks and she had been falsifying documents.

Kelly was quickly fired, but that was not the worst of it. Days later, she was arrested for negligent homicide. But she was not arrested because some prosecutor thinks machines are really human. She was arrested for thinking certain humans are only machines. You see, Kelly was working at Friendly Manor *Nursing Home*.

A Person's a Person, No Matter How Small[183] (or Sick or Old or Disabled)

Kelly's flaw is our own. She had come to consider folks in a nursing home as more like robots than persons. Reread her story, noting all the ways she depersonalized a whole class of people. How we speak of things is often how we truly look at them (Mt 12:34).

Though the Bible declares that "the LORD God formed man of the dust of the ground, and breathed into his nostrils the breath of life; and man became a living soul" (Gen. 2:7), and that "God created man in his own image, in the image of God created he him; male and female created he them" (Gen. 1:27), man has continually used his own reason to challenge the self-evident truth that all men are created equal. Unborn children, Jewish people,[184] the handicapped, Ukrainians, Gypsies and blacks have all suffered from being considered less than human or less than persons.

---

[183] Dr. Seuss, *Horton Hears a Who!* (1954), Random House Books for Young Readers. The full quote is "I'll just have to save him, because, after all, a person's a person, no matter how small." This has been a rallying cry to rescue particular unborn children.

[184] I add the word "people" here because the word "Jews" itself has been used so pejoratively in the past by anti-Semites.

In 2010, Governor Mike Huckabee spoke about equality at the Value Voters Summit[185]:

> It's all based upon the *value* of every single individual. Our founders had it right. When in the Declaration of Independence they said "We hold these truths to be self-evident, that all men are created equal, and are endowed by their Creator with certain unalienable Rights, among these, Life, Liberty and the pursuit of Happiness."
>
> The basic idea is that there is no such thing as a person who is more valuable than another, that all of us have the same intrinsic worth, that no person is worth more because of his last name, or landownership, or occupation, or who his father was or grandfather was, or what city he came from, or what color he is, or what gender he or she may be. Nobody has greater worth because the IQ level in one person is higher than that of another.
>
> I'd like for us to believe and surely this country can accept the fact that a child with Down's Syndrome, a child with a severe disability—whether it's Cerebral Palsy or any other disability—is equally as precious and valuable not only in the eyes of God but in the eyes of the rest of us, as the kid who is Mensa-level in intelligence, and could be the NFL Player of the Year.
>
> There is no difference in the essential basic worth and value of that individual. But if those of us who truly believe that, do not continue to say...
>
> We will not be silent on the issue of the unborn, and we will not be silent on the value of every human life from the moment of conception until the end of life.
>
> Let it be clear I will not vote for, I will not support any candidate who does not value the worth and value of every human life and I urge you, don't do it either.

185 http://www.valuesvotersummit.org/2010archive (browse to the Huckabee speech, beginning at the 37:00 minute mark)

It is easy to say these words. It is harder to mean them. Christians should hold Governor Huckabee to this statement. We cannot let fear of Obama or another candidate force us into compromise. I will take the advice from Governor Huckabee; I will not vote for or support Mitt Romney who still believes in exceptions, should he be the Republican nominee.

Humanity and personhood are synonyms. Dividing humanity into classes (persons and non-persons) requires a new definition of humanity. As I show below, many people claim to be pro-life but their language betrays otherwise. Sometimes it's done deliberately in order to justify killing people. Sometimes, the idea to kill or enslave comes after dehumanization. Christians are not immune from this sin. And the pressure to succeed in politics will tempt us to play to the crowd. When candidates say they are pro-life but believe in exceptions for rape and incest, they deliberately or ignorantly dehumanize the unborn child. Can you imagine that we would consider it acceptable to kill an eight-year old because her mother was raped? The only difference is the age of the child and her place of residence.

Senator Rick Santorum doesn't think it is okay to kill unborn children simply because of the manner in which they were conceived, as he has advocated for outlawing abortions even in the case of rape because "one violence is enough."

"Would you allow no exceptions for cases of rape or incest?" Fox News host, Byron York asked Santorum. "Polls have shown that large majorities of Americans support some exceptions for abortion. Are your views too much, even for many conservatives to support?"

"That child is an innocent victim," Santorum replied. "To be victimized twice would be a horrible thing. It is an innocent human life, genetically human from the moment of conception."

Losing the Language

When I was growing up, a noun was defined as a person, place or thing. I challenge my college students by suggesting the definition is misleading. A noun is *a word that represents* a person, place or thing. The distinction is crucial. We are always tempted to equate the words we use with realities. I follow it up with this riddle. Say you have a dog with four legs, and then you call the tail a leg. How many legs does it now have? Many students answer "five". Of course, the answer is "four", because you can call a tail a leg all day long and that don't make it so.

> Woe unto them that call evil good, and good evil; that put darkness for light, and light for darkness; that put bitter for sweet, and sweet for bitter!
>
> Isaiah 5:20

Although all three comparatives in this passage represent curse-worthy[186] redefinitions, each has a different focus. Men take what is evil and call it good, and vice-versa. They do so against the revelation of God, which clearly defines those terms. It is a sign of maturity to discern the difference between good and evil (Heb. 5:14).

At first glance it might seem ridiculous that anyone could be fooled by someone calling darkness light. For while good and evil are moral decisions, dark and light seem to be plainly and physically differentiated. But that is simply not the case. We are deceived all the time. How is it we call her a *baby* in the womb when the mother intends to keep her, but call her a *fetus* when the mother desires to kill her? If the woman changes her mind, does that change what is in her womb? Or how is that a pregnant 16-year old who wants to keep her child is a *baby having a baby*, but a 13-year old who wants to abort her child is a *woman* exercising her rights? How is that people can watch videos of Terri Schiavo laughing with her mother, or following the motions of a balloon after opening her eyes wide at the command of her doctor, and still call her brain dead? Then we sit back while they take her food and water away from her, and call her death sweet, just because soft music was played and scented flowers were used to cover the bitterness of starvation. We are blind. We cannot tell the difference between darkness and light, good and evil.

Language matters, not because we are trying to mold the world into our image, but because we either speak the truth or we do not. We should strive to have our words match up with reality.

Another example of the acceptance of worldly definitions is when we are willing to call people who are very ill "vegetables". This has long been a method of dehumanization. People are never vegetables. They are not turnips. They are made in the image of God. We unwittingly do the same thing when we call those about to have their vital organs removed "dead". However, they are not really dead. *Yet*.

---

[186] "A curse" is the essential meaning of "woe" in this passage.

How Much Do We Value Human Life?

My wife and I used to own a resale clothing store called Refried Jeans. Occasionally, a customer would come into the business and express real interest in a particular item, but then try to dicker with us over the price. The final outcome of such dickering was as predictable as human nature. If we lowered the price as they wished, such customers often changed their minds and decided not to buy the item. However, if we stood our ground, they usually bought the item. The reason is simple. Our willingness to lower the price was seen as a concession that the item was not that valuable in the first place. Conversely, sticking to our guns raised the value of the item in the customer's eyes.

A similar dynamic has been at work in politics, though it is a little more complicated. For years, principled pro-lifers were painted as unreasonable for opposing all abortions, including those that resulted from rape or incest. This caused some who were unprincipled to admit these exceptions. Meanwhile, the pro-life community attempted to marginalize the other side by focusing on abortions induced for the convenience of the mother, or abortions done for sex selection. This dubious effort failed because it would require crafting laws that outlawed abortions, based on the motive of the mother. It also implied that killing some children was socially unacceptable, but other motives were more reasonable.

The approach taken by the pro-life community changed dramatically when a Life Advocate magazine article in 1995 highlighted a gruesome procedure called partial-birth abortion (PBA). This procedure involved removing the torso of the baby alive and then jamming scissors into the back of the skull of the baby, essentially deflating it, in order to extract the head from the mother's womb. But murders that are less gruesome are no less murder. Nevertheless, for more than a decade, resources in the pro-life movement were almost solely focused on preventing this one method of killing, even though it was a rare procedure. It was surely known that even if it was outlawed, it would be replaced by a different method that would still kill the same baby. In other words, not a single life would likely be saved by legislation banning PBAs.[187]

Nevertheless, this effort immediately captured the pro-life public's imagination. Congressional hearings were held, and many formerly "pro-choice" politicians got on board with an effort to outlaw PBAs. Without question, it accomplished something, something that may have set the pro-

[187] For a fuller discussion of the politics surrounding Partial Birth Abortion, please read Appendix Two, an article by one of the people responsible for first publicizing this "procedure", Paul Du Parrie.

life movement back for decades. Though the Supreme Court actually upheld the law in Gonzales v. Carhart, it should be no surprise that Carhart himself is still killing babies in the womb who are more than 20 weeks old. Outlawing a particular procedure would be like having specific laws against stabbing someone in the back of the head, but no laws against cutting people into little pieces. In fact, that is exactly what we did do. Carhart simply uses a different method to kill babies the same age as the ones he killed before. The Supreme Court itself gave graphic descriptions of how child killers could continue to kill, even as they voted to uphold the law banning the procedure. How twisted is that! So what did the law accomplish?

It was a distraction from making the case that all human life should be protected, and wasted huge amounts of time, energy and money.

It gave cover for pro-abortion politicians to call themselves pro-life or at the very least make themselves appear moderate next to the "radical" pro-lifers. This includes Republican candidate for Governor of California, Meg Whitman[188]; and former Speaker of the House, Democrat Tom Daschle.

Many pro-lifers made a flawed distinction by saying that PBA was not really about abortion, but rather infanticide. This however, is to give away the farm. The principle is that the life inside the womb is worth no less or no more than the one half-way out or the one all the way out. The Bible describes life as a thread. This is the seamless garment of life.

A Preliminary Question

Being pro-life does not begin with concerns about abortion, euthanasia or the inhumane neglect of the elderly. It begins, like all else, with God. It is interesting that the creation/evolution debate and the pro-life/pro-abortion debate begin with almost identical questions: How did life begin? When does life begin?

For the Christian, God has given us the answer to both questions in one verse:

> And the LORD God formed man of the dust of the ground, and breathed into his nostrils the breath of life; and man became a living soul.
>
> Genesis 2:7

---

[188] http://amormundi.blogspot.com/2010/10/meg-whitman-pro-life-pro-choice-it.html

One of the arguments of the evolutionist is to explain how subtle changes in living creatures help them adapt to their environments over time. Given enough time, those changes result in sufficient adaptation to account for different species, they say. The phrase "given enough time" is really being used to counter a typical response by a creationist that "the odds against random change resulting in favorable evolution are astronomical, equivalent to a monkey sitting at a typewriter and randomly typing the complete works of Shakespeare". The problem for the creationist is that he is betting against the monkey because of the long odds in his favor. The debate then becomes a matter of playing the percentages. It is not necessary to go there. The argument is really much simpler: Non-life doesn't adapt. It is passive. Dust of the ground can't make itself alive. Life doesn't come from non-life. Not only can scientists not explain how life began, they can't begin to explain why we are alive now. Or why we die. If they could, they could keep us alive. Or raise us from the dead:

> In the sweat of thy face shalt thou eat bread, till thou return unto the ground; for out of it wast thou taken: for dust thou art, and unto dust shalt thou return.
>
> Genesis 3:19

> All they that go down to the dust shall bow before him: and none can keep alive his own soul.
>
> Psalm 22:29b

The Changing Politics of Abortion

While the definition of life has not changed, the battle to protect the preborn child has. In 1996, National Review took issue with Ralph Reed:

> The Christian Coalition's Ralph Reed finds himself, not for the first time, in the middle of a dustup over abortion. This time, uncharacteristically, the fault was partly his own. He *inadvertently led a New York Times reporter to believe that he would accept a rape-and-incest exception to a Human Life Amendment*. Although Reed immediately denied the report and the Times issued a clarification, some pro-lifers were furious at the perceived sellout. The public-relations damage was not insignificant: attention was diverted from partial birth abortion to abortions involving rape

> and incest—from President Clinton's *extremism* to *squabbling within the pro-life movement.*
>
> (National Review, 1996, emphasis mine)

This story perfectly illustrates my point. The pro-life author wants desperately to paint President Clinton as extreme, yet thinks arguing for the life of every child is squabbling. We obviously need a new ethic, informed by pro-life, Biblical principles.

Another example of a "prolife" Republican was plastic surgeon Dr. Greg Ganske of Iowa who won two terms as a Republican in the U.S. House. He portrayed himself as pro-life even though he supported the right to an abortion through the first trimester and also exceptions for rape and incest. In other words, this Republican supported nearly every abortion. The local Planned Parenthood was so pleased with his position that they rewarded him with a picture and write-up in their quarterly newsletter. But he continued to maintain he was pro-life and Republicans defended him. Pundits like Hugh Hewitt even endorsed Ganske over pro-life stalwart Bill Salier.

Would that God would grant us Christian statesmen like William Wilberforce who in England faithfully spoke the truth and overcame the evil of slavery with godly principle.

Policy, Sir, is not my principle, and I am not ashamed to say it. There is a principle above everything that is political. And when I reflect on the command that says, 'Thou shalt do no murder,' believing the authority to be divine, how can I dare set up any reasonings of my own against it?

Real LIFE Example

> My son, if sinners entice thee, consent thou not. If they say, Come with us, let us lay wait for blood, let us lurk privily for the innocent without cause: Let us swallow them up alive as the grave; and whole, as those that go down into the pit: We shall find all precious substance, we shall fill our houses with spoil: Cast in thy lot among us; let us all have one purse: My son, walk not thou in the way with them; refrain thy foot from their path: For their feet run to evil, and make haste to shed blood.
>
> Proverbs 1:10-12

Suppose you are a Senator sponsoring a bill that would outlaw every single abortion in America. It needs 60 votes to overcome a filibuster, and you've been able to scrape together 59 "yes" votes. You are finally approached by the lone Senator yet sitting on the fence who said he would be your 60th vote, if you added exceptions for rape and incest, and fetal deformity. Would you strike the deal with confidence that you could come back and outlaw the exceptions, later?

The logic to take the deal seems straightforward enough. In fact, one could try to argue that to not take the deal is tantamount to sentencing millions of babies to their deaths, all because your perfect has become the enemy of the good.

This is exactly how Richard Land does argue:

> If you have an opportunity to pass a law that would ban most abortions and you turned it down because you couldn't get the rest, I believe you would be morally culpable for the ones you allowed to be slaughtered. I would rather not have that on my conscience.[189]

The argument sounds good. It is evil. Before I explain, let us try the same scenario with one slight twist.

Now what if the conniving senator says he will only vote for the bill if you allow black mothers under the age of 21 to kill their babies. Then what? Let me suggest that there is not a Senator within 10,000 miles of Washington DC who would be willing to sign on to that piece of legislation (and rightly so). Don't tell me you are pro-life if there are some babies you would let people kill.

Politics has corrupted our sense of right and wrong. If you are truly pro-life, what should you do then? After publicly denouncing the man for his foolishness you should pray, trust God, and then call for a vote. Righteous men do not commit evil acts under the threats of terrorists. That principle is not hard to understand. You cannot stop all the evil in the world. But you can refuse to participate. Perhaps your courageous stand will persuade one of the other Senators to join the side of righteousness. Perhaps not. Either way, the other man is responsible for his vote and the millions of deaths afterwards, not you.

If a terrorist threatened to blow up the city of Pittsburgh unless you killed all your family members, would God hold you responsible if you refused the terrorist's demand and he followed through on his threat? Absolutely not. If on the other hand, you killed your family in order to save the city, would you be guiltless? No. You are to do the right

[189] Gregg Jackson and Steve Deace, op. cit.

thing, and trust that God will bring about justice. Pray that the terrorist is caught or dies of a heart attack. Perhaps it is a hoax. But you cannot do what is wrong, in order to bring about good (A damnable prospect, see Romans 3:1-8)

Suppose you did agree to the compromise with the other Senator, as I proposed above. A few minutes later, one of your own supporters loses courage and decides to vote against you unless you allow exceptions for the health of the mother. Where do you draw the line? I tell you where you end up drawing the line. You pass a bill that saves no lives, wastes millions of dollars, and allows your opponents to claim to be pro-life while painting you as an extremist. *Solomon had it right, we cannot cut the baby in half.*

> Then came there two women, that were harlots, unto the king, and stood before him. And the one woman said, O my lord, I and this woman dwell in one house; and I was delivered of a child with her in the house. And it came to pass the third day after that I was delivered, that this woman was delivered also: and we were together; there was no stranger with us in the house, save we two in the house. And this woman's child died in the night; because she overlaid it. And she arose at midnight, and took my son from beside me, while thine handmaid slept, and laid it in her bosom, and laid her dead child in my bosom. And when I rose in the morning to give my child suck, behold, it was dead: but when I had considered it in the morning, behold, it was not my son, which I did bear.
>
> And the other woman said, Nay; but the living is my son, and the dead is thy son. And this said, No; but the dead is thy son, and the living is my son. Thus they spake before the king. Then said the king, The one saith, This is my son that liveth, and thy son is the dead: and the other saith, Nay; but thy son is the dead, and my son is the living.
>
> And the king said, Bring me a sword. And they brought a sword before the king. And the king said, Divide the living child in two, and give half to the one, and half to the other. Then spake the woman whose the living child was unto the king, for her bowels yearned upon her son, and she said, O my lord, give her the living child, and in no wise slay it. But the other said, Let it be neither mine nor thine, but divide it.

> Then the king answered and said, Give her the living child, and in no wise slay it: she is the mother thereof. And all Israel heard of the judgment which the king had judged; and they feared the king: for they saw that the wisdom of God was in him, to do judgment.
> I Kings 3:16-28

This passage shows that the love of the real mother for her child made her willing to give up that child, rather than see any harm done to it. This parallels the heart of a young unmarried mother and father who gave up their child for adoption and allowed me to be blessed with my wonderful son, Samuel.

The passage also shows the heart of a woman who would rather have the baby cut in half than watch someone else raise her. This happens every time an abortion is committed, especially when there have been offers by others to raise and give love to the baby. In the case above, we shouldn't be surprised that a woman willing to kidnap another mother's baby would be willing to kill the baby. The problem with the evil mother was that she saw children primarily as something to give her pleasure, rather than both a gift and a responsibility. Do any parents seriously believe that their kidnapped child is safe in the hands of someone "who just wants to raise" him or her?

Finally, this passage shows the pitfalls of half-measures, sometimes called the "half a loaf" approach (I'd rather have half a loaf than none at all, or so it goes).

Life of the Mother Exception

What if you couldn't save everybody? This is a hypothetical question found in the "lifeboat game" and often designed in our day to persuade people into accepting the notion that some lives are less valuable than others and therefore expendable. The origins of the game itself in 1974 can be attributed to ecologist Garrett Hardin, whose purposes were not to promote the situation ethics of Joseph Fletcher in individual cases, but rather to illustrate the dangers of a population explosion and promote his notions on how to implement coercive world-wide population control. There is a connection between the two, however, as Planned Parenthood and many advocates of birth control also support Population Control.[190] Hardin wrote:

[190] http://cdn.abbyjohnson.org/wp-content/uploads/2011/11/jaffememo.pdf

> The only way we can preserve and nurture other and more precious freedoms is by relinquishing the freedom to breed, and that very soon. "Freedom is the recognition of necessity"--and it is the role of education to reveal to all the necessity of abandoning the freedom to breed. Only so, can we put an end to this aspect of the tragedy of the commons.[191]

Usually the teacher or professor in the lifeboat "game" sets up a scenario where you must choose to save some and choose to throw one or more other passengers in a lifeboat overboard. The "leader" usually also defines the race, age, gender, occupation, marital and parental status, handicaps and other information about the passengers, lending a supposed rationality to your decision making.

In real life, nobody wants to face a decision on who they must try to save if you can't save everybody. Firemen and EMTs must cringe at the thought it could happen to them. There is a legitimate "triage" used to determine the priorities of treatment at the scene of a catastrophe or on the battlefield, based upon the medical conditions and needs of the patients. But in all of my readings on the subject, no one has ever dared determine treatment based upon the social or personal attributes of the patients or victims as listed above.

The pro-life movement has allowed itself to be conned into playing this game. When we say in advance that there is an abortion exception "for the life of the mother", we have given away the core of the life argument. To be sure, this dilemma rarely—if ever—occurs. Providence has given us an answer that is rather simple in most cases: Doctors and families must try to save both lives. The most frequent circumstances don't require "the choice" often presented in these discussions. In rare emergency cases, for example, the mother may be at risk of dying if the baby is not removed right away. If the baby is too young to live outside the womb, obviously he or she will die if the mother dies. This is not a matter of choosing to save the mother over the baby. The baby needs the mother. Since you can only save the mother, it is acceptable, though tragic to take the baby. An ectopic pregnancy would be in this category. There was no choice to be made. Only one person *could* be saved: the mother.

If a baby could potentially survive outside the womb, you must remove the baby and try to save him or her, as well as the mother. This might be the case later in the pregnancy when the mother has severe complications

---

[191] Garrett Hardin, *The Tragedy of the Commons*

from gestational diabetes or high blood pressure and is at great risk of dying if the pregnancy continues. Again there is no choice to be made. You must try to save both.

Finally, in the case where cancer has been detected in the mother and the treatment will certainly kill the baby and perhaps allow the mother to survive or live longer, what should the family do? With great gravity I would suggest that the mother must forgo that kind of treatment at least until the baby can be safely removed from her womb. The key words in the scenario I gave were "certainly" and "perhaps". The decision, of course, becomes more difficult depending on the diagnosis.

The evil found in the aphorism "the life of the mother exception" is that we are expected to immediately sacrifice the life of the child for the mother, without thought and without condition. If you have a doctor who comes to you with the attitude of "what baby?" in a scenario like this, get a different doctor. For example, if one doctor told you that you must have major surgery tomorrow and that you would only have a 3% chance of getting out of the surgery alive, you would get another opinion before making a decision. Give the baby the same consideration you give the mother, and you have begun to deal justly.

Half-A-Baby Legislation

What if a bill passed the Iowa legislature that reinforced the state's homicide laws, protecting the citizens of the state against murderers. Now suppose that the law specifically excluded from protection any citizens of Asian descent or who claimed the legal status as a Native American. If anybody in these groups happened to be the victims, all prosecution of murderers would stop immediately. Any charges would be dropped, and those in prison for killing any unprotected person would all be released, and their records expunged. I'd be outraged! You'd be outraged! Even the docile Harry Reids and Fred Thompsons of this world would be outraged! There would be marching in the streets, leading to riots and civil unrest.

A similar law to the one above was about to be passed in the state of Ohio and some conservative leaders were celebrating as if the second coming of Jesus had just taken place. Victory should be sweet, and defeat should be bitter. But in the world of politics, pro-lifers often celebrate defeat.

One pro-life leader wrote:

> We are so close; I can see the end of abortion from here.
>
> When we stood at the foot of Mount Rushmore we were hundreds of thousands of votes away from our goal. Right now we are 17 votes away from restoring legal protection to every child who's [sic] heart we can hear.... Dr. Jack Willke testified that the Heartbeat Bill will save *95 percent* of the babies who would otherwise be aborted.... Not only will you live to see the end of abortion, you can be a part of it! [192] (emphasis mine)

Asian Americans make up 4.4% of the U.S. population, Native Americans, about .7%.[193] Together, percentage-wise that equals the percentage of people the Ohio "Heartbeat Bill" would not protect. Apparently, saving 95% of those scheduled to die is an end to abortion. It is not clear whether Willke is including the countless hundreds of thousands of others killed through morning-after pills and certain kinds of birth control or not in his 5%. Nevertheless, if you really are against abortion, why not just propose a personhood amendment as was found on the ballot in Mississippi[194] in 2011 or help gather signatures in Ohio so it can be on the ballot there in November, 2012[195]?

Dr. Patrick responded to the Heartbeat Bill with a solemn warning in World Net Daily News called "*A Nice Pro-Life Bill – If There is no God*":

> First, let us examine the bill's exceptions. Abortions are permitted for the health and life of the mother.... If the physician commits an abortion without documenting whether the child has a heartbeat, he hasn't even committed a crime, according to this bill.... Furthermore, this bill specifically exempts the mother from prosecution. Why does the bill exempt accomplices? In Justice Black-

---

192 World Net Daily, http://www.wnd.com/2011/09/344369/

193 http://en.wikipedia.org/wiki/Race_and_ethnicity_in_the_United_States

194 http://www.goddiscussion.com/71480/american-family-association-commits-over-100000-to-mississippi-personhood-amendment-campaign/

195 http://www.personhoodohio.com/ph/help.asp

> mun's Roe v. Wade decision, he criticizes such hypocrisy...."It has already been pointed out ... that in Texas the woman is not a principal or an accomplice with respect to an abortion upon her. If the fetus is a person, why is the woman not a principal or an accomplice?[196]

It is evident that the language of some leaders does not line up with God's standard on this issue. If God in His Providence uses a bill like this to save some lives, let us be thankful. But we must not celebrate prematurely. The full term delivery of a personhood amendment to the Supreme Court such as the one found on the ballot in Mississippi would have seemed worthy of greater support. The amendment gained 45% at the polls, even though it had the audacity to outlaw pills and other weapons that are used to kill babies, too.[197]

William Wilberforce fought to have every slave in England released; he carved out no exceptions for rape, incest, condition of the slave owner, or the age of the slave. He won on principle, not pragmatism.

Do We Mean It When We Say We Are Pro-Life?

Rush Limbaugh had instituted "caller abortions", a publicity stunt where he used the sucking sound of a vacuum cleaner on his radio program, pretending to "abort" callers to his show. Of course, the pro-child-killing left was outraged and not a few folks on the right as well. Limbaugh's successful effort was to show that the thought of fake abortions was for many people more offensive than the actual taking of lives.

I have to admit, inspired by Limbaugh, I almost pulled a "stunt" when I was active in the anti-abortion movement in the early 1990s.

My plan was to call for *collie* abortions on a particular date and time just outside Planned Parenthood of Greater Iowa. I don't know if there was a law against me doing abortions on dogs but it would not have mattered a bit. Just the plan itself would have probably gotten me arrested. (By the way, I never would have done it; I love dogs more than some people love their unborn children.) But can you imagine the howling if I had said I was going to do it and gave the time and place? Many in this Disney Generation would have been more outraged at the killing of a little unborn puppy than they were over the 70 human beings slaughtered each week inside the

---

196 http://www.wnd.com/2011/09/346797

197 CBS News,11/8/2011, Mississippi Personhood Amendment Fails at Polls

walls just a few feet away. This would have even angered many who call themselves pro-life. (I'm pretty sure this story is raising the blood pressure of not a few readers even now.)

Proposal: All New Yorkers Become Organ Donors[198]

You know you are on to a scam when a proposal redefines basic language. New York State Assemblyman Richard Brodsky suggested in 2010 that everyone should be considered an organ donor unless they choose to opt out.

This shouldn't come as any surprise, however. Organ donation has never been about informed consent. I doubt if most people who give permission to have their organs removed realize they are authorizing the removal of their organs while they are still alive. Many people think that if they die in the parking lot of a hospital they can have their vital organs removed and given to someone else. They cannot. It is too late. Most organs (the cornea might be one exception, for example) must be taken from your body while you are still breathing and your heart is still beating. And that used to mean you're alive.

There were no legal organ donations of vital organs in the U.S. until after the AMA changed its definition of death in 1973[199] from the previous definitions of irreversible cessation of respiration and circulation (for the jargon-impaired like myself, that means your heart stopped and you stopped breathing, and no one could revive or resuscitate you). These, of course, are Biblically-based definitions of death.

Several awful consequences accompanied this new legal phrase called "brain death".

First, there is no settled criterion on determining or defining brain death 39 years later. Each one is full of exceptions, caveats, hedges and contingencies. If they could tell you what it is that is keeping the heart beating, and lungs breathing, then they would be onto something (it is called in the Bible, "life.")

Second, only a new definition of death could justify the removal of vital organs. So, "he's dead now, we can take his organs" could be said legally, if not sincerely. This death was by decree, not by science or rationality. And sometime patients do fully recover after being declared brain

---

198 http://www.dailypaul.com/133109

199 Ironically, the same year that gave us nationwide "legalized" killing of preborn babies.

dead, if some family member is nearby when the declaration is made and fights for their lives.[200]

Third, declaring people dead while they were still breathing and their hearts were still beating would more easily justify the removal of life support mechanisms. Instead of letting someone die (which is arguably justifiable in some cases) you would simply remove machines from people who were "already dead". If the person is already "dead" under the new definition, there is no reason to dispute whether they are dead under the old one. Now, some want to take organs from unwilling "donors". What was questionably "informed consent" may soon become "presumed consent."

Fourth, the definitions of brain death are deliberately skewed to lean towards a finding of brain death. For example, as described in a Critical Care Nurse Journal,[201] medical personnel are given a checklist to determine whether a person is dead. It is implied that the patient must fail all of the tests or alas, they must be treated as still alive. But, when one moves to the bottom of the checklist, you find this statement under "Other confirmatory tests". (for example, the EEG, cerebral angiography or brain scans) which are "*Useful in situations where clinical exam is equivocal or a full examination cannot be performed*" In other words, if some of the other tests indicate someone is alive, you keep trying until you get some that confirm your preconceived notion that they are dead. It is important to note that, for example, "Texas law does not mandate any particular test for the diagnosis of brain death."[202]

The same article also demonstrates the importance of making these decisions *without delay*:

> It is also imperative that the process be carried out proficiently and in a timely manner. Prolonging the process unnecessarily or giving inaccurate information can result in undue grief for patients' families and can delay the process of organ donation.[203]

I suppose it might be assumed that these definitions would be somewhat uniform across the land or at least across states. You would be assuming wrongly. The journal basically says that individual hospitals can

---

[200] MSNBC News, 3/24/2008, Online Edition

[201] http://ccn.aacnjournals.org/content/24/5/50/F2.large.jpg

[202] Robert Fine (2005) *From Quinlan to Schiavo: medical, ethical, and legal issues in severe brain injury*, Baylor University

[203] http://ccn.aacnjournals.org/content/24/5/50.full

wing it, depending on who is working that day, and how much experience they have, and how the budget is looking at that month. I'm not kidding:

> In the United States, principles of making a diagnosis of brain death are guided by the Uniform Determination of Death Act. Although this document sets the standards for using brain-based criteria to diagnose death, it does not specify the elements to be used in making the diagnosis. However, both individual experts and organizations, such as the American Academy of Neurology, have published guidelines for brain death protocols. Consequently, although *fairly* consistent criteria are used to diagnose brain death, *variability exists* across states and practice settings as a result of local legislation and *institutional policy. Individual hospital practice may also vary, depending on available resources and physicians' experience.*[204] (emphasis mine)

Terri Schiavo

These changes have had one other sorrowful result. The line between death and life has been blurred in the eyes of the public. After a young brain-damaged woman named Terri Schiavo was dying of thirst because her adulterous husband convinced the courts that her feeding tube[205] should be taken from her, many journalists, even medical personnel defended what was done to this poor woman because she was "brain dead" anyway. It needs to be stated plainly that Schiavo was breathing on her own and her heart was beating just fine.

Even though the watershed Schiavo case was in the news daily for months, Ron Paul was completely uninformed about the case. He claimed "this debate deals with the passive treatment of the critically and terminally ill." But Schiavo was neither critically, nor terminally ill.[206]

Shamefully, Discovery still has a story on their children's site completely distorting the case:

> Terri Schiavo was the subject of a national debate about the ethics of life support. Schiavo was in a coma for 15 years, beginning in

---

[204] Ibid.

[205] A straw is essentially a feeding-tube.

[206] http://caffeinatedthoughts.com/2010/12/ron-pauls-questionable-pro-life-principles/

> 1995. She was kept alive on a life support system. Doctors had told Schiavo's husband that she was brain dead with no hope of recovery. He wanted to have her life support systems removed. Her parents did not agree with this decision. In 2005, Schiavo's husband and her parents were involved in a long, public legal battle to decide whether or not she should be kept on life support. Schiavo was removed from life support on March 18, 2005, and died shortly thereafter.[207]

This is completely wrong. There was no life support system, even though the article uses the phrase five times! No doctor told Schiavo that his wife was brain dead. Notice that even those who accept the notion of "brain death" still said she "died shortly there*after*".

"Death with dignity" is a false doctrine and has nothing to do with Christian nursing. It is the mantra of the euthanasia movement that would put to death anybody too sick to "take care of", especially those that might have long term pain or suffering. The killing of Terri Schiavo raised so many questions with ethical, legal and political ramifications.

I recognize that for millions of Americans, the ethics of organ transplants have never been seriously contemplated. Let this be the day you start. I also know that you ought not to take my word for it. I recommend thorough research on the redefinition of death since the early 1970s, now called "brain death." I am confident that you will find that even among those who promote and defend vital organ transplants, the definitions of death are fuzzy and intended to advance the agenda of organ transplantation without first considering the ramifications of the new definition.

Even as families in the U.S. of have gotten smaller and smaller, dependence on the next generation for our retirement has grown, so that we have created an unsustainable situation. The post-war Baby Boom has been followed by a Baby Bust. As the number of Baby Boomers retiring is going up (the first batch started retiring in about 2010), the actual number of workers who pay into Social Security is going down.

Governor Rick Perry of Texas was excoriated for correctly calling Social Security a Ponzi scheme, primarily because it was claimed that he was abandoning those already dependent on it:

> "People who are on Social Security today, men and women who are receiving those benefits today, are individuals at my age that

[207] http://curiosity.discovery.com/question/who-terri-schiavo

> are in line pretty quick to get them, they don't need to worry about anything. But I think the Republican candidates are talking about ways to transition this program, and it is a monstrous lie. It is a Ponzi scheme to tell our kids that are 25 or 30 years old today, "You're paying into a program that's going to be there." Anybody that's for the status quo with Social Security today is involved with a monstrous lie to our kids, and it's not right."[208]

Perry was right. Admitting that a program is a Ponzi scheme does not mean a politician will abandon those who were first duped and whose very lives may depend on keeping the promises. It does mean we no longer try to fix the problem by making more people dependent on a program doomed to eventually fail.

Evaluating the Pro-Life Record of Mitt Romney

Former Governor of Massachusetts, Mitt Romney, claims to have made a dramatic change of position on abortion. I would think this to be a good thing, if I believed it to be true. Certainly people can change their viewpoints, even right before an election. Because people believed Ronald Reagan truly changed his position on abortion, he was not called a flip-flopper. I grant candidates the right to change their minds and hope the new positions are sincere, my conscience is not bound to get behind one who "converts" on a position at the eleventh hour before an election. (However, those who quickly accepted the very late position changes of Perry and Gingrich owe Mitt Romney an apology if they earlier claimed that the Romney change from pro-abortion to pro-life was because he was running for president).

There are at least two major problems with Romney's claim, however. First, he says he has *always* been pro-life and he never admits he was "pro-choice", let alone ever, ever, ever admits that he was pro-abortion.

> I was always personally opposed to abortion, as I think almost everyone in this nation is.[209]

---

[208] http://www.politifact.com/truth-o-meter/statements/2011/sep/12/rick-perry/rick-perry-says-social-security-ponzi-scheme/

[209] http://www.msnbc.msn.com/id/22273924

We are in naïve and big trouble if we accept the fiction that almost everyone in the nation is against abortion. Just who is having these million to a-million-and-a-half "surgical" abortions every year? Not to mention those family members who helped pay for the abortions or in some other way supported them. And what all about those who march in favor of the right to kill; are all of those people personally opposed to abortion? Who are we kidding? Why are we afraid to admit the truth?

Romney continued: "I didn't call myself pro-choice, but my position was effectively pro-choice.[210]" So, what is the difference between effectively pro-choice and really pro-choice? Babies die either way. What if he is only effectively pro-life now, but not really pro-life? He must have some reason for refusing to admit the truth, though for the life of unborn children, I don't know what it is. He actually slipped once and admitted that he had been pro-choice,[211] but continues to disavow even that admission.[212]

The second reason Romney's conversion on this issue is not credible is that his *official position* is that he favors abortions in cases of rape and incest.[213] Imagine if similar positions were held by politicians in the past who were faced with great social evils. Would it have been acceptable to say...

I am pro-life and believe that gas-chambers should be limited to only Jewish shopkeepers and their families.

I am pro-freedom and believe that slavery should be limited to only blacks of inferior intelligence or those with the darkest skins.

I am vehemently against experimenting on children, except for those with ADHD or Autism Spectrum Disorder.

Of course not! And in the same way, we should only vote for or support candidates who understand that *every* innocent life bears the image of God and cannot be destroyed.

---

[210] Ibid.

[211] http://political-transcript-wire.vlex.com/vid/candidates-participate-hosted-abc-64090414

[212] *American Spectator* (3/10/2010) W. James Antle III, Mitt Romney, Pro-Choice? Who Me?

[213] http://www.nationalreview.com/corner/269984/my-pro-life-pledge-mitt-romney

Chapter Sixteen

Counterfeit Marriage

Who ought to decide whether two men or two women can marry each other? Even Christians who believe homosexuality is a sin[214] make conflicting statements over 1) Where jurisdiction lies on the issue of marriage and 2) What should be done about it. These are actually two different questions.

When people say a court has stepped out of its jurisdiction, and the people should get to decide the question instead, they are only half right. Indeed, no court has a right to redefine marriage. But neither do the people have such a right.

A large number of states have held referendums on the issue of marriage in recent years; not a single one has voted to overturn Biblical marriage. Not one. So one could argue referendums or initiatives are the best way to decide this. But what happens when the first state votes *for* gay marriage? Should we then say it was good for the people to decide? Will we shrug our shoulders and say "Oh well, the people decided"? Would we seriously argue that no court could strike down such a decision by the people? Or that the legislators should let the people's decision stand? If a courageous U.S. president were to ignore the courts on this issue, would you not applaud that president?

[214] Homosexual behavior is not an unpardonable sin. The hateful Westboro Baptist Church protesters who protest at military funerals do not seem to understand the grace of God. There is hope for anyone who turns to Christ (including members of Westboro Baptist Church).

The point in this is that no one has "the right" to change what God has ordained: Not the people, not the judges, not the legislators, not the Obama White House. Nobody.

So do we just throw our hands up in the air and give up? Do we throw in the towel? Of course not. Quite the opposite is true. I am not suggesting that because God has ruled on the matter, what men do is irrelevant. Just as no one has the right to engage in mischief by decree, we have the right to use all just power to thwart the efforts to impose policies that would destroy our nation and incur God's Judgment.

We should certainly oust the Justices who give us these diabolical laws, as Iowa did under the leadership of Bob Vander Plaats. In other states, impeachment should begin against unjust judges. Replace legislators and governors who won't stand firm against this onslaught of evil. Petition. Vote. Protest.

What should a governor do when a court strikes down his state's marriage laws? Governor Chet Culver of Iowa ordered marriage licenses issued to same sex couples, just like Mitt Romney of Massachusetts did after a similar ruling in his state. Neither of these men had the courage to stand against the overreaching actions of courts. As the battle rages, I believe there are three fundamental arguments we dare not abandon.

First, *we must not waive the Biblical argument for marriage,* as some have done. Argument from tradition is not a winner. Traditions can be changed. God is the author of marriage. He defines its boundaries. Marriage exists because God made it so at the beginning of creation: "For this cause shall a man leave his father and mother and cleave to his wife." Not only did God himself invent and institute marriage between a man and wife, but he also mentions fathers and mothers from the very beginning, before they existed. This is the natural order. It's not that a man and man should not be married – it is that they *cannot* be married. We can perform all kinds of ceremonies over the two of them and issue them a license and even uphold the act with a Supreme Court decision. It will not make it a marriage. It will simply make all of us more to blind to reality.

We who oppose the efforts to institutionalize the perverse notion of two men or two women getting married are often asked how such a thing could possibly hurt our own marriages. It is true that a strong Christian marriage can withstand any outside interference. Any culture, however, suffers when counterfeit currency is accepted. "Gay Marriage" is a counterfeit. Fake $20 bills affect me even if I only use the real, because in such a scenario, true money is debased or devalued in the society. Likewise, the true meaning of marriage is lost when the counterfeit is allowed to flourish.

We will lose the argument if we don't go back to first things. Utilitarian arguments are bound to fail us, as they have most assuredly done for the unborn child. All the gory pictures, ultrasounds and offers of adoptive parents have failed to stem the tide of bloodshed because we have been afraid to mention God's Name in debate. We have been afraid to call sin, "sin".

Second, *we must repent of our hypocrisy* and recognize that we ourselves have created this monstrous situation. Every act of adultery, fornication, pornography and unbiblical divorce shows contempt for God's Law. Living together outside marriage is to ignore God's law. The strange Westboro Baptist Church bunch are sometimes quick to say that God hates homosexuals, but in arrogance forget that God hates all of our sins, and that our natural condition is to be under His wrath. God hates divorce. God does in His grace sometimes deliver homosexuals, but the devastating results of divorce and remarriage cannot be undone even when forgiveness is given. Every time a Christian politician or public figures is caught up in a sexual scandal our credibility is weakened. Until we admit our own sins, we won't get far arguing against the sins of others.

Nevertheless, there is still a difference between disobedience of an eternal law and whole-hearted denial that such a law exists. Unlawful behavior destroys lives; lawlessness destroys whole nations. Anarchy shall surely follow if we do not turn back to God. Even our own sins must not tempt to us to give in to those who would destroy the very notion of sin. Let God be true, and every man a liar.

Third, *we must not fall for the argument that the government should have no say in upholding marriage*. Ron Paul and Glenn Beck are trying to pull a bait and switch. They claim that licensing and record-keeping of weddings is relatively recent (Okay, 500 years[215] is over half the lifetime of Western Culture, but who is keeping track?). But they are conflating the sanctioning of a wedding with the recognition of a marriage, which are two different things. How one got married was largely irrelevant as to whether states recognized marriages as a legal entity. They always have. The welfare of children, the protection of property rights for couples, and the determination of paternity and other issues pertaining to the family all require that the state protect the family, which is defined as persons related

[215] New York Times (11/26/2007) Stephanie Coontz, Taking Marriage Private

by blood, adoption or marriage. Marriage is not just a private institution, it is a public one. Therefore, the duty to defend marriage lies upon the state.

The chaos of American marriage only outwardly resembles the Biblical meaning. Soon, what remains of the family will be redefined as well, and for the same reasons. If there is no Biblical standard, everything else is up for grabs. All children could be defined as wards of the state. Or a neighbor could sue to have your children be brought into their own "family" because they could raise them better. If the people or the state defines these things by their own whims, like the citizens of Babel, there will be no stopping their madness, save the intervening judgment of God or an outpouring of grace.

We must not be so naïve, however, as to think that homosexual marriage will be the cause of our destruction. It is the symptom of destruction already near completion. Any other culture in the history of the world would have laughed-to-scorn the notion that two men could marry each other. It could only be contemplated when marriage is accepted without the lifetime commitment, without the desire for children, without the loyalty of exclusive sexual relations, without the distinction in roles for husband and wife, and without the responsibility to pass on moral values to the next generation. In short, homosexuals would not want marriage as defined by God in the Bible. They only want the imaginary one, created by human invention.

How did we get to this place? Stephen Baskerville of Patrick Henry College observes:

> Homosexuals did not destroy marriage, heterosexuals did. The demand for same-sex marriage is a symptom, not a cause, of the deterioration of marriage. By far the most direct threat to the family is heterosexual divorce.[216]

It is the decline of marriage, not an ascendancy of reason that has brought us here. Baskerville lays the fault at the practice of no-fault divorce. Anytime a couple gets divorced because "they don't love each other" a new false foundation for marriage has been laid down, because most people think marital love is primarily sensual or emotional, rather than right behavior and attitude. The same would be true for such things as incompatibility, or divorce for the sake of children. The latter reason ironically mirrors the reason some couples give for staying together.

---

[216] http://www.amconmag.com/blog/divorced_from_reality

Passing a Marriage Amendment May Not Be Enough

It has become clear in recent years that feminist proponents of homosexual marriage in America aren't about to let a little thing called a constitutional amendment slow down their assault upon the world as God made it.

Suppose we pass the Marriage Amendment (HJ 56) that Senator David Vitter of Louisiana sponsored:

> SECTION 1. Marriage in the United States shall consist only of the union of a man and a woman. Neither this Constitution or the constitution of any State, nor state or federal law, shall be construed to require that marital status or the legal incidents thereof be conferred upon unmarried couples or groups.

Stephen Baskerville, writing for The *American Conservative* pointed out that what is happening across the pond is likely to happen here:

> Britain's Gender Recognition Act allows transsexuals to falsify their birth certificates retroactively to indicate they were born the gender of their choice. "The practical effect C9 will inevitably be same-sex 'marriage'," writes Melanie Phillips in the Daily Mail. "Marriage as a union between a man and a woman will be destroyed, because 'man' and 'woman' will no longer mean anything other than whether someone feels like a man or a woman.[217]

Though this sounds pessimistic, it may become reality. Nevertheless, I am not going the route of libertarian-infatuated Glenn Beck and giving up, or conceding the point that this whole debate is irrelevant. What would we do then? Suggest a constitutional amendment defining male and female? The founders of our country recognized that certain things are self-evident. But those who are hell-bent on throwing off God's standards are willing to redefine reality in order to promote their agenda. Law can no more save a country than it can save an individual. These are first of all moral issues, and only secondarily, legal issues.

Marriage, as I have pointed out elsewhere, is a God-ordained institution. The abandonment of the standards of God's Word and a dearth of true

---

[217] Ibid.

gospel preaching, have doomed our nation to godless laws. And it is only a revival that will rescue us from the judgment of God.

Application in the Voting Booth

Professor Baskerville added this lament: "No American politician of national stature has seriously challenged unilateral divorce".

Perhaps he doesn't consider Mike Huckabee of "national stature", but former Governor Mike Huckabee of Arkansas has continued to speak out against no-fault divorce.[218]

> I think America has got to sort of brace itself and say, "How good is this?" For example, on the issue of marriage, no-fault divorce became the vogue in the early '60s. When states first introduced it, then everybody got on the bandwagon, and the result is now one in two marriages virtually ends in divorce in the country.
>
> Divorce is one of the key predictors of poverty for a child growing up in a home that's broken. Without making any judgments about the value or rightness or wrongness of it, it's an economic fact that when children are involved in a divorce they are more likely to end up spending part of their childhood in poverty than if they have a two-parent household.

In an article entitled "Ark. Governor Embraces Covenant Marriage: Movement Seeks to Make it Harder to Get Divorced" Huckabee's credentials on this perspective were legitimized.[219]

At the state level we should be looking for candidates who will strengthen laws protecting marriage and discouraging divorce. But let's not be fooled. Electing the right leaders won't get the job done by itself. There must be a revival of not only marriage according to Biblical standards, but this must come because people are responding to the gospel of Jesus Christ. Otherwise, we can only slow down the symptom of "homosexual marriage", which stems from our failure to uphold God's standards in our own marriages.

---

218 Washington Post, Interview with Mike Huckabee, May 23, 2006

219 http://www.msnbc.msn.com/id/6440961/ns/us_news/

SECTION FOUR

GETTING THERE FROM HERE

Chapter Seventeen

Character Counts

> Moreover thou shalt provide out of all the people able men, such as fear God, men of truth, hating covetousness.
>
> Exodus 18:21

Due to the scandals which swirled about President William Jefferson Clinton and his impeachment, the American people were forced to answer the question "Does character count?" To some it seemed silly to judge a man's fitness to be a president based upon peccadilloes in his personal life. People always lie about sex we were told, so it did not matter that as a matter of law and fact, Clinton had lied *under oath*. Does how a man lives in his personal life have any bearing on how that man will lead the people?

The Bible is not silent on the issues of qualifications for government officials. When Moses was overburdened with the responsibility of judging all the cases brought before him, his father-in-law Jethro, under the shining Providence of God, suggested that he appoint capable men to help him. In Chapter 14 we dealt with whether or not someone's religion was fair game in deciding who to vote for (it is). Now we deal with those qualifications in particular.

Such as Fear God

Before the U.S. Constitution was ratified, atheists could not serve in the civil realm in most states, because they could not honestly take the oath of office, which required belief in God.[220] Maryland required "a declaration of a belief in the Christian religion." The North Carolina Constitution of 1776 also required that

> No person, who shall deny the being of God or the truth of the Protestant religion, or the divine authority of the Old or New Testaments...shall be capable of holding any office or place of trust or profit in the civil department within this State.[221]

It should be also noted that North Carolina, like many other states, forbade a practicing member of the clergy to serve in civil office as well, for the prevailing thought was that his ministry would be corrupted if he tried to be a pastor and governor *at the same time*:

> That no clergyman, or preacher of the gospel, of any denomination, shall be capable of being a member of either the Senate, House of Commons, or Council of State, *while he continues in the exercise of pastoral function*.[222] (emphasis mine)

By the early 1800s, nearly all of the provisions of the U.S. Constitution were either applied to the states or adopted by the states, including Article 6 which abolished religious tests.

In light of the ban on the religious test for holding office, is it right for Christians to consider whether a candidate fears God or not? Of course it is. The ban only forbids a legal religious test for holding office; it does not keep voters from using this to make their own decisions. Some have argued that keeping the spirit of the injunction requires individuals to block religion from their evaluations. But that is like saying that in keeping with the spirit of the 1st Amendment parents must allow their children to swear, or that in the spirit of the 2nd Amendment all businesses must allow guns on their premises.

A religious test recognizes that men who take oaths in God's name will be held to a higher accountability than just their own notions, or even fear of being caught by other men in violating the oath of office.

How will the fear of God make governors more able to carry out their duties? First, it will make them rule justly (1Sa 23:3). It will also keep

---

[220] http://undergod.procon.org/view.resource.php?resourceID=69

[221] Ibid.

[222] Ibid.

them from ruling with an iron fist or with cruelty (Neh. 5:15),[223] make them personally generous (Acts 10:2), give them respect for the disabled and the aged (Lv. 19:14, 32) and help them to see the plight of the poor and the immigrant (Lv. 25:35f).

Fearing God means that the leader will not be swayed by the ever-changing whims of a fickle electorate. He will strive to obey the commandments of God in his personal life. The Scriptures speak of righteousness and holiness. The world speaks of ethics and morality. What are the differences between the two characteristics? The latter speak of one's outward behavior only and usually only in relation to fellow men. Christians recognize the Bible requires an inward righteousness as a gift of grace. It demands a right relation to God. Of course, no one claims to be able to read the heart of another. But still, one's actions and words can display what is in the heart.

Few people today speak in terms of expecting their leaders to be righteous. No doubt in part, this is because we think in terms of self-righteousness. Character is usually horizontal in nature, and is understood by the world as having nothing to do with God. Leaders should be honest, trustworthy and faithful, yes. But how that leader relates to his Creator is often seen as out of bounds in the evaluation of those seeking office.

As I demonstrated in Chapter 2, any leader in this life will be a sinner, but God's grace in the heart of a truly converted man will restrain his sin, until that day when all will be made right. The Bible describes many leaders who were holy and righteous.

Men of Truth

An able leader will not find himself caught up in lies because he changes his story at every campaign stop. My stepfather, Dick Strauss, reminded me as a teenager that if I told the truth, I'd never have to remember what I said. One of the great blessings of the electronic age is the difficulty life can prove to be for candidates who want to lie. They will be detected. But will we hold them to account when they lie?

Another great benefit to our current system is that the primary season is spread out enough so that candidates can be vetted by the average Joe[224]

[223] See Matthew Poole, *Commentary*, Volume 1, Encyclopedia Puritannica, p. 891

[224] Samuel Joseph Wurzelbacher (aka Joe the Plumber) provoked Barack Obama into admitting that "*I think when you spread the wealth around, it's good for*

on the street. He will ask questions that the press refuses to ask due to bias in favor of a candidate or fear that the candidate will cut off access to that journalist. The Iowa Caucuses and New Hampshire Primary seem especially favorable for the winnowing process, but other smaller states would likely work as well. We need not be dependent on debates or speeches which tend to be highly controlled and often irrelevant. In the day of recording devices and blogging, it also allows these interested citizens be reporters, bringing out a candidate's strengths and weaknesses for the whole world to see.

Access to the internet has made learning about a candidate's views, public persona, and voting record quite simple in our day, so there isn't much excuse to go in the voting booth ignorant about the candidates. Fallen men will hide their flaws and their records if they can get away with it. This is sadly to be expected. We can certainly apply Proverbs 18:17 which teaches that one man's story may seem right until another comes along and questions him. Joseph wanted proof or verification of the claims his brothers made concerning his father and younger brother, perhaps because they had dealt treacherously with him in the past (Gen. 42:16-20).

While debates are often full of nonsense—more resembling a game show than a serious discussion of differences—they do provide an opportunity to check the integrity of the candidates. In 2008, Mitt Romney said he never accused John McCain of supporting amnesty for illegal aliens, until he was shown his own campaign television ad that used those very words. He then suggested on ABC News that he had not seen the ad, which was not helpful because the campaign ad ends with these words: "I am Mitt Romney, and I approved this message."[225]

Ron Paul faced a similar problem of credibility when a number of newsletters published by him over a 10-year period were found to contain many racist, anti-Semitic remarks, as well as many conspiracy theories. In 2008, Paul said that he hadn't read the articles, that it was the job of the editor. Later it was discovered that many of the publications named him as the editor. But even if he did not write them, he is responsible for them, because he received millions of dollars in donations through them. Who puts out thousands of letters with such things in them and never gets questioned about them by the readers?

---

everybody" when the then-candidate was being filmed during a campaign stop in his neighborhood.

[225] http://spectator.org/blog/2008/01/06/romneys-newest-problem

Hating Covetousness

> Thou shalt not covet thy neighbour's house; thou shalt not covet thy neighbour's wife, or his manservant, or his maidservant, or his ox, or his ass, or anything that is thy neighbour's.
>
> Exodus 20:17

William Penn wrote:

> God, in the choice of magistrates, made it part of their qualification to hate covetousness; foreseeing the mischief that would follow to that society or government where covetous men were in power; that self would bias them, and they would seek their own ends at the cost of the public.[226]

The Tenth Commandment forbids coveting. It is an unlawful attitude towards anything belonging to our neighbors. This one command deals with our hearts. Sins against this command include greed and envy. The leaders we must choose should not enamored with material wealth. That does not mean they can't be wealthy, but they should hold onto that wealth with a loose grip.

Envy rots the bones (Prov. 14:30). It may be worse than greed, for it is not focused on one's own wealth, but focused on the wealth of others. And it is not mere jealousy, a desire to have what belongs to others. It is a hatred for those whom God has granted wealth or success. Envy pushes an ever more and more progressive tax system, and drives much of the discussion about economics today. It is a plague that affects both political parties.

While the following passage was fitted for the Kings of Israel, many of the ideas are pertinent to the rise of men to the presidency. Notice that the king must himself be ruled by the laws he imposes on others. Also, he is not to use his political office for personal gain.

> One from among thy brethren shalt thou set king over thee: thou mayest not set a stranger over thee, which is not thy brother. But he shall not multiply horses to himself, nor cause the people to return to Egypt, to the end that he should multiply horses: forasmuch as the LORD hath said unto you, Ye shall henceforth return no more that way. Neither shall he multiply wives to himself, that his heart

[226] Penn, William, *No Cross No Crown*

> turn not away: neither shall he greatly multiply to himself silver and gold. And it shall be, when he sitteth upon the throne of his kingdom, that he shall write him a copy of this law in a book out of that which is before the priests the Levites: And it shall be with him, and he shall read therein all the days of his life: that he may learn to fear the LORD his God, to keep all the words of this law and these statutes, to do them: That his heart be not lifted up above his brethren, and that he turn not aside from the commandment, to the right hand, or to the left: to the end that he may prolong his days in his kingdom, he, and his children, in the midst of Israel.
>
> Deuteronomy 17:15b-20

Popularity of Mordecai

Other virtues gain the commendation of God. Mordecai, whom God providentially raised up to rescue the Jews from the hand of Haman, was also raised up to the second highest office in the land:

> Mordecai the Jew was next unto king Ahasuerus, and great among the Jews, and accepted of the multitude of his brethren, seeking the wealth of his people, and speaking peace to all his seed.
>
> Esther 10:3

Two relevant observations are in order. First, Mordecai was popular among the people. Had the land of the Medes and Persians been democratic, Mordecai would have been chief contender for the Jewish Party's nomination. Second, the unselfishness of this newly appointed leader was seen in his concern first and foremost with the welfare of his people. Saints were probably praying for both Ahasuerus and Mordecai, for God also granted the land peace (1Ti. 2:2).

We're no different than the average guy. We wouldn't marry someone we don't like. I don't think we would even let somebody clip one hair on our heads if we didn't like them. Do we vote for people we don't like? No, we don't. Candidates won't get elected, unless people like them. Arriving at this conclusion doesn't mean a candidate should *try* to be liked. We don't like that. Government leaders, especially in a democracy, are frequently tempted to pander and seek more than all else, popularity. The reason is simple: they want to be re-elected.

> Now about that time Herod the king stretched forth his hands to vex certain of the church. And he killed James the brother of John with the sword. And because he saw it pleased the Jews, he proceeded further to take Peter also.
>
> Acts 12:1-3

Is a concern for character just a recent trend in American politics? George Washington wrote,

> A good moral character is the first essential in a man.... In every nomination to office I have endeavored as far as my knowledge extended or information could be obtained to make fitness of character my primary object.[227]

President Washington, two days after his recess appointment of Cyrus Griffin to the federal bench, defended his choice, first speaking of his availability, then concluding with this thought:

> This circumstance, added to the knowledge of his having been a regular student of law, having filled an important office in the Union in the line of it, and being besides a man of competent abilities, and of pure character, weighed with me in the choice.[228]

Of course, we have not always had leaders in our country who displayed good character. Mark Levin, an attorney with the Landmark Legal Foundation has demonstrated in his book *Men in Black* that several Supreme Court Justices were of questionable fitness for office based upon their bad character.[229]

---

[227] http://www.archive.org/stream/writingsofgeorge10washuoft/writingsofgeorge10washuoft_djvu.txt

[228] Ibid.

[229] Levin, op. cit.

May I Vote For One Who is Not a Christian?

> One from among thy brethren shalt thou set king over thee: thou mayest not set a stranger over thee, which is not thy brother.
>
> Deuteronomy 17:15b

Though it may be argued that this passage applies only to ancient Israel and the required appointment of ethnic or national Jews, the text at the head of the chapter requires that civil leaders must fear God and kiss the Son. The Bible also teaches that there is no fear of God before the unbeliever's eyes (Romans 3:18, Psalm 36:1).

When it comes to this question, Christians are sometimes challenged with a quote from Martin Luther which usually goes like this: "I would rather be ruled by a wise Turk[230], than a foolish (or stupid) Christian."

I would like to make several observations about this quote.

First, there is strong reason to believe this has been falsely attributed to Martin Luther[231] for it is contrary to much of what Luther wrote about the rule of Turks.[232] Second, I am not suggesting that all Christians are qualified to hold public office. They are not. Third, let us look at a genuine quote from Luther, who was arguing that the clergy should not take up arms:

> I say this not because I would teach that worldly rulers ought not to be Christians, or that a Christian cannot bear the sword and serve God in temporal government. Would God they were all Christians, or that no one could be a prince unless he were a Christian! Things would be better than they now are and the Turk would not be so powerful.[233]

As an early reformer, Luther recognized that the gospel was severely restricted in lands ruled by Muslims, especially Turkey. He wrote:

---

230 A Muslim

231 http://how2fish.blogspot.com/2007/12/governed-by-wise-turk.html

232 http://web.archive.org/web/20071231154836/http://cranach.worldmagblog.com/cranach/archives/2007/02/draftthe_wise_t.html

233 http://www.archive.org/stream/worksofmartinlut009285mbp/worksofmartinlut009285mbp_djvu.txt

> For although some praise his [the Turk's] government because he allows everyone to believe what he will so long as he remains the temporal lord, yet this praise is not true, for he does not allow Christians to come together in public, and no one can openly confess Christ or preach or teach against Mohammed.
>
> For it is misery enough to be compelled to suffer the Turk as overlord and to endure his government; but willingly to put oneself under it, or to desire it, when one need not and is not compelled – the man who does that ought to be shown the sin he is committing and how terribly he is going on.[234]

Noah Webster also wrote:

> In selecting men for office, let principle be your guide. Regard not the particular sect or denomination of the candidate—look to his character as a man of known principle, of tried integrity, and undoubted ability for the office. It is alleged by men of loose principles, or defective views of the subject, that religion and morality are not necessary or important qualifications for political stations. But the Scriptures teach a different doctrine.[235]
>
> When you become entitled to exercise the right of voting for public officers, let it be impressed on your mind that God commands you to choose for rulers, "just men who will rule in the fear of God." The preservation of government depends on the faithful discharge of this duty; if the citizens neglect their duty and place unprincipled men in office, the government will soon be corrupted; laws will be made, not for the public good so much as for selfish or local purposes; corrupt or incompetent men will be appointed to execute the laws; the public revenues will be squandered on unworthy men; and the rights of the citizens will be violated or disregarded. If a republican government fails to secure public prosperity and happiness, it must be because the citizens neglect the divine commands, and elect bad men to make and administer the laws.[236]

---

[234] Ibid.

[235] Noah Webster, *Letters to a Young Gentleman Commencing His Education*

[236] Noah Webster. *History of the United States: to which is prefixed a brief historical* ... Wilcox, Dickerman.

Lesser of Two Evils

"Shall we do evil, that good may come?" the apostle Paul asks.

No. God condemns such thinking. We have many ways of expressing this lie. "The ends justify the means" is just one. In politics, we violate this Scripture when we argue that we can (and even should!) vote for the lesser of two evils; yet this is exactly what D. James Kennedy seemed to advocate:

> Suppose I know a candidate is for the pro-choice position.[237] My response is that I cannot support that person. Period. That's because I believe this one issue trumps all others. Even if a pro-abortion-rights politician claims to be a Christian, I cannot support him or her in good conscience. (However, left with a choice between one pro-choice candidate and another, one could argue for voting for the lesser of two evils).[238]

One can only make that argument if he is willing to disobey the prohibition against doing evil. Voting for a lesser evil is still voting for an evil. This is not a demand for perfection, but recognizing minimum qualifications. Would you let your children play on a playground where only two or three known child molesters are allowed to hang out? Would you recommend a babysitter who treated all of her own children wonderfully, except for the one she kept chained up in the attic?

Suppose two candidates are running for political office. One runs on a platform of seeking to abolish the Seventh Commandment in government policy. The other candidate defends clear violations of the Sixth Commandment. If we accepted the humanist mindset where man is the measure of all things, we might sadly be tempted to make such a choice. Reasoning within ourselves or amongst ourselves, we might try to pit one commandment against the other, and justify supporting one rebel over another. But again, a Christian is not bound to make such a choice. We can abstain.

Now suppose that terrorists held you and your mother hostage. They placed you in a room and insisted at gunpoint that you choose either button

[237] This whole passage is awkward because Kennedy is bent on using language acceptable to those who want to kill children. See my section on language in chapter 15.

[238] D. James Kennedy and Newcombe, op. cit., p. 58. Kennedy passed away before the book was published so it is possible that some of these words were added later by Newcombe or editors.

A or button B. Button A would kill your mother instantly. If you choose Button B the terrorists have said they will torture your mother for one hour before killing her. Is the correct answer A or B? The correct answer is "none of the above." You cannot do evil (kill your mother) that good may come (she be relieved of torture).[239]

> For if the truth of God hath more abounded through my lie unto his glory; why yet am I also judged as a sinner? And not rather, (as we be slanderously reported, and as some affirm that we say,) Let us do evil, that good may come? whose damnation is just.
>
> Romans 3:7-8

Application in the Voting Booth

First, while an unbeliever may have gifts, and a believer may have weaknesses, why would a believer seek to be ruled by someone who was not ruled by Christ?

> Be ye not unequally yoked together with unbelievers: for what fellowship hath righteousness with unrighteousness? and what communion hath light with darkness?
>
> II Corinthians 6:14

Second, I'll take an honest hayseed over a pettifogger every time. That doesn't mean I want a simpleton in the White House, but good character can hide a lot of other flaws. If a candidate shows tendencies toward dishonesty, what good does it do if his positions on issues or his record seems favorable?

Third, I should look elsewhere if a candidate seeks the good of certain favored groups or divides the country up into parts, trying to play one off of the other. A good leader will seek the good of *all* the people.

Fourth, it would be better not to vote, if I am given only bad choices. Who would deliberately pick one poison over another, when given the choice of not choosing at all?

---

[239] I am not suggesting the situation ethics "lifeboat game". "Neither" is the correct answer in the scenario I proposed.

Chapter Eighteen

I'll Scratch Your Back, You Scratch Mine

"Rudy Giuliani is, without question, an *acceptable* candidate"

That was broadcaster and former presidential candidate Pat Robertson's not-so-ringing endorsement of Mayor Giuliani for president in 2007. It was roughly equivalent to having Bill Cosby announce that "You may find it tastes a little like rust, but I still would recommend Jell-O brand gelatin, if no other dessert is available" or Michael Jordan bellowing "I can directly attribute the blisters on my feet to wearing Nikes, but nevertheless, they are in some cases better than sandals, so I say, 'just think about doing it.'"

> Do we begin again to commend ourselves? or need we, as some others, epistles of commendation to you, or letters of commendation from you? Ye are our epistle written in our hearts, known and read of all men: Forasmuch as ye are manifestly declared to be the epistle of Christ ministered by us, written not with ink, but with the Spirit of the living God; not in tables of stone, but in fleshy tables of the heart.
>
> II Corinthians 3:1-3

An endorsement resembles a recommendation: This guy is a lot like me. If you trust me, you can trust her. I can support this candidate; you can too.

It is true that a commender rarely agrees with everything the recipient of that endorsement believes, does or says.[240] However, if it does not mean that you agree with them on *the most important things*, an endorsement doesn't mean anything at all.

Endorsements actually show you more about the endorser than the endorsed. For example, what does it tell you about someone who would endorse a Republican candidate who thinks it is principally okay to kill some unborn babies, but who would never endorse someone who thinks it is okay to promote high tax rates. It tells you that money is more important than life itself to that endorser. If they are running for office, too, then shun them like they have the plague (because they do).

Can we for a moment look at the reality? The endorsement cycle seems like a giant game of back-scratching. The idea is simple. A future presidential candidate says "I'll support you. If you win, I would expect that you will support me in your state when I am running for president." (Nobody actually says it this crassly, however.) Nothing is inherently wrong or surprising about this. It seems logical that a favor is returned for a favor. It also seems reasonable that you would endorse somebody whose views are similar to your own and that the similarity would likely result in a reciprocal endorsement. Of course, there are no guarantees. Sometimes the endorser never becomes the endorsee, as Connecticut Senator Joe Lieberman so painfully discovered in 2004.

In 2000, former Democratic vice-president and presidential candidate Al Gore picked Connecticut Senator Lieberman to be his running mate. In a very close election, the Gore/Lieberman ticket lost to the George Bush/ Dick Cheney team. Now, fast forward to December 2003, when Lieberman was himself running for president. Gore announced on television that he was endorsing Lieberman's competitor, rival northeastern Governor, Howard Dean of Vermont. Ouch! No courtesy call. No email. No "Dear Joe" letter. It is certainly fair to ask why Lieberman was Gore's choice to be a heartbeat from the presidency in 2000, but not worthy of his endorsement when the moderate Connecticut Democrat himself campaigned for president in 2004. Lieberman apparently agreed:[241]

---

[240] I wouldn't expect that Governor Huckabee agrees with every controversial idea I've put in this book, for example.

[241] CNN Politics, Democrats Attack Gore's Decision by Howard Dean, 9/12/2003

> Lieberman said he spoke by phone with Gore for about four or five minutes Tuesday morning—a phone call he said came "too late."
>
> "I don't have anything to say today about Al Gore's sense of loyalty," said Lieberman, who had waited to announce his candidacy until after Gore said he would not run in 2004. "I have no regrets about the loyalty that I had to him."
>
> But he said he was caught off-guard.
>
> "I was surprised about the decision. I was surprised that Al Gore didn't notify me before I learned about it from the media—that would have been the right thing to do....
>
> Lieberman also said political endorsements "don't pick presidents"....
>
> He added that it's "less likely now" that Gore could play a key role in any future Lieberman administration.

That Lieberman would say "political endorsements don't pick presidents" sounds like sour grapes, but when he uses the phrase "less likely now" you gotta laugh and know that he really means "not in a million elections". Funny guy, that Joe Lieberman!

Though I doubt the average voter cares too many whits about endorsements, I'm not suggesting that they cannot or do not help at all. In fact, for the potential voter and Christian, it can tell you more than the candidate had perhaps hoped for. Candidates who profess to be pro-life but endorse candidates who are not, have some serious explaining to do. These are not private encouragements to run for office given by one friend to another. They are not simple positive statements made about politician on some specific issue. (I can certainly commend Giuliani for his handling of the crisis in New York on 9/11 or Barack Obama for going after Osama Bin Laden. I can do this without endorsing their candidacies.) What I am talking about is the formal giving of endorsements of candidates *in their person*.

For example, Texas Governor, Rick Perry endorsed Rudy Giuliani for president in 2008 when there were still plenty of other pro-life candidates running. Because of party politics, he will probably never have to explain this[242].

The same is true of former Pennsylvania Senator, Rick Santorum, who along with George W. Bush supported pro-abortion Senator Arlen Specter over pro-life congressman Pat Toomey in 2004. The explanation Santorum gives now is that he obtained a promise from Specter that Specter would not hold up any pro-life nominees for the Supreme Court. But this does not explain Santorum's endorsements and PAC money donations to Susan Collins, Lisa Murkowski and Lincoln Chafee, for example.

When Meg Whitman, former CEO of eBay, ran for governor of California in 2010, former Massachusetts Governor Mitt Romney endorsed her candidacy during the primary season. Whitman believes the taxpayer should be willing to pay the doctor bills for every woman in California who wants to kill her unborn son or daughter:

> My view is that if we are going to be pro-choice, that people do have the ability to have an abortion if they think it is the right thing for them, subject to the rules that we just described, that it needs to be available to all women, and whether you are rich or poor, you need to be able to access that right. And it's unfair to women who cannot afford an abortion, and that's why I support public funding.[243]

In other words, since it's a right, no one should be denied one because of lack of money. (I wonder if she supports the 2nd Amendment by handing out taxpayer money to everybody who can't afford a gun.)

Perhaps one could argue that there was no Republican pro-life candidate running for governor. But why must Romney endorse any candidate at all, then? Why didn't he offer up seed money to some pro-life candidate willing to run for Governor of California? Whitman didn't need Romney's

---

[242] Sadly, a candidate must do some serious explaining if he endorses a like-minded candidate of the other party, but as long as a guy is in your party, you are rarely called to account for supporting them, no matter how awful their record is.

[243] http://www.flashreport.org/commentary0b.php?postID=2009101507025849

PAC money; she spent more of her own money than any candidate has ever spent on a gubernatorial campaign in U.S. history.

Putting party over principle, presidential candidate and former U.S. Speaker of the House, Newt Gingrich, also endorsed Meg Whitman, as well as the Margaret Sanger Award winner, Dierdre "Dede" Scozzafava in the highly publicized 23rd District U.S. House race in New York. Doug Hoffman, ran on the Conservative Party ticket and was pro-life.[244] As it turns out, Bill Owens, the Democrat won. The whole ordeal reinforces my thesis: Endorsements tell more about the candidate doing the endorsing than the candidate being endorsed.

Secondary Separation

The Bible calls for Christians to separate themselves from those under church discipline. A question that has been debated for some time is whether we must separate from those who refuse to honor that sanction, hence a secondary separation.

Boycotts can be viewed in the same way. Suppose you are boycotting a company because it advertises on a particularly offensive program. Should you extend that boycott to cover grocery stores that carry that product? At some point it is easy to see the absurdity of taking this too far.

The same logic applies to endorsements, for example. Some people, like myself, refuse to vote for any candidate who does not support the protection of every unborn child. Should we also refuse to vote for candidates who endorse other candidates who are not 100% pro-life? Though I consider it reasonable to consider the endorsements by candidates in the broader evaluation of their candidacy, it does not reach the level of absolutely quashing my ability to vote for that candidate. You can see how this could also get absurd if you ask the question, "Can I vote for the candidate who endorses a candidate who endorses a candidate who is not 100% pro-life?"

Let's not kid ourselves, however. We should treat the examination of a candidate's views and record on these issues with a life or death attitude. And that includes examining the endorsements they make.

---

[244] http://www.lifenews.com/2009/09/28/state-4459

Application in the Voting Booth

While it may not be the determining factor in deciding who to vote for, we should look closely at who our candidate has endorsed in the past, which is much more important than who is endorsing our candidate now. It may tell you what kind of nominations this person will make for his or her cabinet or for judicial appointments.

Chapter Nineteen

I Just Voted, But Who's Counting?

Every vote "counts". This has been the rallying cry of both major parties since the legally contested election of 2000 between Vice-President Al Gore and Governor George W. Bush of Texas. While the final decision seemed to come down to about 300 votes in favor of Bush out of millions cast in Florida, the whole contested election should make the Christian rethink where their faith is placed.

May I remind you that disputes over the final total were not really limited to whether or not "hanging" or "pregnant" chads should be counted. Yes, the 2000 election was so close someone had to decide if a ballot that was not *completely* punched through should count. Other questions were raised. Were all of Pat Buchanan's votes really intended for him, or did the ballot-makers conspire to make them deliberately ambiguous? Again, should counties that were not in dispute be counted again? And don't forget the military votes. What if a vote arrived late, should it be counted anyway since it wasn't the soldier's fault he or she was half way around the globe defending the country? All of these things were fought over, not to mention the claims of ballot-box stuffing or intimidation at polling places. Other voters were even given false information in phone calls about their voting locations or times.

Does any sane person think that if a national election would come down to a handful of votes, we would really know with any certainty which candidate really got the most votes? It would be impossible to know, if the word "impossible" means anything. This is why we have the rule of law. Someone has to decide. Perhaps in excruciatingly close elections like this we should resort to the flip of a coin.[245] At least it wouldn't be left up to the decision of fallen, partisan sinners. Law should rule over anarchy.

What is a vote?

I have wrestled for over a year to discover a Biblical definition of a vote. It is difficult because no people group in Scripture, as far as I can tell, had direct elections to appoint kings or governors. I conclude that your vote as a Christian is the simple expression of your opinion, preference, belief or desire that God appoint a particular person to rule over you. More than anything, it is a prayer or an act of faith. Think of the voting booth as a prayer closet. When I was younger, I remember that my mother would rather give up her vote than tell a single soul who she voted for. There was a lesson in there somewhere, I think.

In our arrogance, we have convinced ourselves that voting is some duty that God has given to us to pick the leader of the free world. But remember, it is God who picks our leaders.

The Bible spends a lot more time telling us how citizens should live under Caesar's rule, and how Caesar should rule over the people, than how to elect a new Caesar. So, in spite of this book's title, the importance of voting (in and of itself) can be over-rated. This is a reminder that it is God who sets up kings.

Does God Require That I Vote?

Every presidential election season, we are told that in order to please God, we must vote. Is it really true? During the 2008 presidential election Barack Obama beat John McCain by 8,538,559 votes.[246] Let's be honest. Over 8½ million Obama voters could have stayed home[247] and their candidate would still have won. On the other hand, if you would have preferred McCain over Obama but stayed home, your vote would have made no difference, unless you persuaded 8.5 million voters who also sat it out to join you in the voting booth. If you are trying to make a difference, it is worse than this. One could argue that the 58 million votes cast for McCain were wasted votes since they did not change a thing.

---

[245] Proverbs 16:33 says, "The lot is cast into the lap; but the whole disposing thereof is of the LORD."

[246] http://www.cnn.com/ELECTION/2008/results/president

[247] I acknowledge that this is technically imprecise because of how the electoral college works, but this does not affect my point.

The American electoral college system does create a slightly larger potential for an election decided by one vote. Instead of choosing our president by adding up all the votes cast in the country, a president is actually chosen by having 51[248] separate elections, with each state having a total value based upon the number of Senators and U.S. House members it has, according to the last census. Simply put, each candidate gets the electoral votes it earns from winning individual states.

Hypothetically, eleven people alone could decide who becomes the president of the United States. Let me play the fool for just a moment. If only one person showed up to vote in the following 11 states, and all of them voted for candidate "X", then candidate "X" would be made president, even if every single eligible voter showed up to vote and voted for candidate "Y" in the remaining 39 states.

State[249]	Number of Electoral Votes for 2012
California	55
Texas	38
Florida	29
New York	29
Illinois	20
Pennsylvania	20
Ohio	18
Georgia	16
Michigan	16
North Carolina	15
New Jersey	14
Total For These States	270
Total Needed to Elect	270

Realistically, even in a state with a small population such as Wyoming or Alaska the odds that your one vote will "count" are about as likely as

[248] The District of Columbia also gets 3 electoral votes.

[249] http://en.wikipedia.org/wiki/Electoral_College_(United_States)

you getting hit by lightning *and* winning the million-dollar lottery on the same day.

So, are Christians bound to vote? Wayne Grudem thinks we *must* vote:

> I believe that every Christian citizen who lives in a democracy has, at the very least, a minimal obligation to be well-informed and to vote for candidates and policies that are most consistent with biblical principles.[250]

Billy Graham says it is our "God-given obligation" to vote:

> If everyone stayed home from the polls and neglected to vote...our system of government soon would come to an end.[251]

D. James Kennedy said we *have to* vote:

> I must say this to you: it is a sin not to vote.... Jesus Christ said this: "render therefore unto Caesar the things that are Caesar's." This means that we are to render to the state whatever it is our responsibility as citizens of the state to render. And certainly, in this nation, that includes at the very minimum that we should vote.[252]

John Lofton's lonely voice disagrees with the previous Christian leaders:

> Don't start with the presupposition that we have to all be involved in politics, or as Dr. James Dobson said, "we have a God-given responsibility to vote." What is he talking about? First of all, there's no voting in the Bible.[253]

Rendering unto Caesar what is Caesar's only requires that we pay taxes and obey the laws. The coins in front of the disciples were minted by Caesar and bore his inscription or image, therefore money minted or printed by Caesar belongs to Caesar, according to Jesus. Sadly, there is a sort of legalism that has been placed upon Christians to go beyond this in

---

[250] Grudem, op. cit. (2010) p. 74

[251] http://www.billygraham.org/articlepage.asp?articleid=4628

[252] Kennedy and Newcombe, op. cit., p. 32

[253] Gregg Jackson and Steve Deace, op. cit.

our loyalty to our country. It has come to the point where many Christians would feel they have committed a great sin if they failed to vote in every election. This is to put a burden upon ourselves that did not come from God. Our government itself puts no such obligation upon us. It is a privilege to vote, yes; but it is not an obligation to vote.

How Elections Are Really Decided

Obviously, the greater the number of voters in a particular election, the less power and influence derives from a single vote, so that your vote in a mayoral election in a small town is much more likely to matter than one cast for president.

While a single vote usually doesn't determine the winner of elections, they are actually determined by those who influence large numbers of people to vote in a certain way—the actions of the influencers[254] count. This is true whether it is talk show hosts, authors or activists who make the news. Nevertheless, it is decisions by the candidates themselves which have the greatest effect on the outcome of elections. John McCain may have lost the 2008 election when, in the middle of the campaign, he decided to go back to Washington and vote *for* TARP, the bailout legislation that was wildly unpopular among the electorate at the time.

Why Vote Then?

First, a vote can be a witness to what is right. When there are clear differences between candidates, for instance, even casting a vote for "the loser" is an expression of your values. The overall vote total not only determines who wins, but how great a mandate the winner has been given to rule under the platform for which he campaigned. So while our individual vote may not count for much, collectively, like-minded people (as Christians are called to be, see Romans 15:5f) can sound a trumpet for the sake of righteousness.

[254] This is a good time to point out that I reject elaborate conspiracy theories. For some of you, that proves I must be part of the *big* conspiracy.

Chapter Twenty

Move to the Center? Nuts!

Though the GOP presidential nominee Barry Goldwater became a social moderate in later years, when he was nominated by the GOP in 1964 he sounded more like Alan Keyes than Alan Colmes:

> Those who elevate the state and downgrade the citizen must ultimately see a world which in earthly power can be substituted for Divine Will, and this Nation was founded upon the rejection of that notion and upon the acceptance of God as the author of freedom.[255]

At the time, Goldwater also supported prayer in public schools.[256]

Pat Buchanan's failed run at the White House was at the center of a firestorm when he emphasized "culture wars" in his Republican Convention speech in 1992:

> Friends, this election is about more than who gets what. It is about who we are. It is about what we believe and what we stand for as Americans. There is a religious war going on in this country. It is a cultural war, as critical to the kind of nation we shall be as the Cold War itself. For this war is for the soul of America. And in that struggle for the soul of America, Clinton & Clinton are

---

[255] http://www.washingtonpost.com/wp-srv/politics/daily/may98/goldwater-speech.htm

[256] http://www.claremont.org/publications/crb/id.1237/article_detail.asp

> on the other side, and George Bush is on our side. And so to the Buchanan Brigades out there, we have to come home and stand beside George Bush.[257]

It would be a caricature to take this one small section of Buchanan's speech, label it the "culture wars" speech, and act as though that is all he spoke about. It was not. He also addressed military issues, the legacies of Ronald Reagan and George H. W. Bush in winning the Cold War, and a contemporary topic in the news: the L.A. riots. Some social moderates in the GOP, however, blamed the divisiveness of this speech for the Republican loss to Bill Clinton in the November 1992 elections. Battles within the Republican Party over social issues seem to be much more significant than the fight against the Democrats.

The conventional wisdom is wrong that wise presidential candidates run to the base during the primary and to the center in the general election. The theory, in actual practice, has been proven wrong so many times to the detriment of the Republicans that it is secretly being promoted by Democrats. When the GOP falls for it, they lose. My theory is that the closer the two candidates are perceived to be on the political spectrum by the general public, the more likely it is that the Democrat will win. I disagree with those that say social conservatives must downplay their true views in order to win.

Let's briefly examine how the conventional wisdom has worked out since 1972.

In 1972, although Nixon may have governed somewhat as a moderate, his landslide victory was due to George McGovern being so readily perceived as a liberal.

In 1976, Ford ran as a moderate and lost to the moderately perceived "born again" Jimmy Carter.

By 1980, it became obvious that Carter's conservatism was a fraud and Ronald Reagan, who defines conservatism, won easily.

In 1984, the Democrats had not learned their lesson and put up another liberal, Walter Mondale. Another landslide victory for the GOP.

In 1988, George H.W. Bush ran on Reagan's coattails as a conservative and easily beat another northeast liberal, Michael Dukakis.

By 1992, however, Bush was now seen as a moderate, after breaking the "no new taxes" pledge and lost to another Southern Democrat, William Jefferson Clinton, who said the era of big government was over.

---

[257] http://www.americanrhetoric.com/speeches/patrickbuchanan1992rnc.htm

By 1996, the successes of Newt Gingrich and the first Republican-led GOP House in 40 plus years made Clinton seem as one who could reach across the aisle and get things done. Bob Dole had an opportunity to contrast himself with Clinton, but much like John McCain, did not do so, and the Democrat won.

In 2000, it is widely believed that George W. Bush followed the conventional wisdom by de-emphasizing social issues in the general election campaign and narrowly escaped losing to Al Gore, who also tried to play himself as a moderate.

In 2004, President Bush, learning from his father's loss and seeing the Democrats repeat their earlier mistakes, ran to the right while Kerry, the northeast liberal, ran to the left. Bush won quite handily.

2008 actually demonstrates my theory the most easily. Until Sarah Palin was added to the ticket, McCain failed to really distinguish himself on any issues with Barack Obama and was floundering. After firebrand Palin was added, McCain caught up with Obama. Only after "reining in" Palin and voting with Obama on TARP, did the perception that they weren't that much different set in, almost guaranteeing the loss for McCain.

At any rate, it is not easy to separate out those who are socially conservative from those that are fiscally conservative. They are almost always the same people. In spite of the claim that the Tea Party was only about smaller government and lower taxes, most of the successful new candidates from that movement were in fact also social conservatives, including Nikki Haley and Susana Martinez (Governors of South Carolina and New Mexico, respectively), and Rand Paul, Senator from Kentucky.

Analysis of the data shows that those who are most pro-life and pro-family are the most reliable conservatives on taxes and spending, as well.[258]

Vows and Oaths

Politicians have a reputation of making promises they can't, won't or don't keep. An old "Born Loser" comic strip I saw years ago illustrated how a tolerance for promise-breaking can backfire on a candidate.

Mr. Smith asked Mr. Jones if he would vote for him. Mr. Jones replied that he could not, for he had already promised to vote for Mr. Johnson. Mr. Smith attempted to charm Jones by suggesting that "promising is one

[258] See Andrew E. Busch (2012) *Social Conservatives and Economic Conservatives, Society*, pp. 13-23

thing, doing is another." "In that case," Mr. Jones replied, "I promise to vote for you."

Of course, voter booth backlash is the ultimate revenge for offended taxpayers. The more unflinching the campaign promise, the worse it is when the office-seeker reneges on it. Ironically, it was not the signing of Grover Nordquist's no-new-taxes pledge that would undo President George H.W. Bush's reelection campaign, it was his infamous, convention-emphasized, nationally televised, chant-inspiring phrase, "Read my lips—no new taxes!" President Bush will probably go to his grave regretting those six words. Sadly, many presidential campaign promises are broken before anyone breaks a sweat at the inaugural ball.

In recent election cycles, Republican candidates have been asked to sign an increasing number of pledges to keep their campaign promises in certain areas. Rick Santorum defended this practice in a USA Today editorial, after he vowed before God that he would keep the 14 points of a pledge developed by the Iowa-based FAMiLY Leader.

> At a time when voters have grown skeptical about politicians and candidates who run on a certain platform only to backtrack once elected, signing a pledge is a good way to strengthen our political promises….the pledges we see today are oaths to voters.[259]

This is the problem. The oath that Santorum took, was not made to just voters, it was made before God.

Santorum went on to say:

> To me, in a time when our nation's problems are so vast and so deep, a candidate should be able to meet that serious responsibility with something more than just promises…. I know I speak for my fellow candidates who have signed these pledges in saying it is an honor to be able to do so, because that is what a pledge is: an oath to honor our word. It shouldn't be a lot to ask for in a candidate.

The practice came to a head in 2011, when GOP hopefuls were asked to sign promises to protect unborn children, uphold the right to carry a gun, and not to raise taxes, among others. None of the candidates who signed the pledges would say they do it because their own word is not to

[259] USA Today, Why I Sign Pledges by Rick Santorum, *7/13/2011*

be trusted. No, it's always the other guys' failures to keep their promises that have made the voters skeptical.

The Susan B Anthony List (SBAL) pro-life organization also asked candidates to sign a pledge. When asked whether a candidate's past positions were a concern, the spokesman for the organization said its "goal was simply to get all of the presidential candidates to sign the pledge."[260]

Though the words "oath" and "vow" are frequently used interchangeably, sometimes a distinction is made between the two. Generally an oath is a promise or pledge of honesty made to men and witnessed by God with an attached calling for a curse upon oneself if you fail to keep the promise or tell a lie. A vow is made to God, and sometimes witnessed by men.[261] Weddings usually involve taking a vow, though now it is frequently only seen as a pledge made to your spouse-to-be:

> "Do you promise to love, comfort, honor and keep her for better or worse, for richer or poorer, in sickness and in health, and forsaking all others, be faithful only to her so long as you both shall live?"

Historically, witnesses in a trial took an oath called a "swearing in", and were asked "Do you swear to tell the truth, the whole truth, and nothing but the truth, so help you God?" This was accompanied by the raising of the right hand. As a result of secularism in the U.S., placing the left hand on the Bible and concluding with the phrase "so help me God" have virtually disappeared from American courtrooms.

The President of the United States is required to take "the oath of office" as follows: "I do solemnly swear (or affirm) that I will faithfully execute the Office of President of the United States and will to the best of my ability, preserve, protect and defend the Constitution of the United States."

---

[260] Des Moines Register, *Iowa Christian Conservatives Split on Gingrich's Right-to-Life Record* by Jennifer Jacobs, *11/28/2011*

[261] http://www.creeds.net/Westminster/c22.htm

Enough with Meaningless Vows and Pledges Already!

Jesus addressed frivolous oaths:

> Again, ye have heard that it hath been said by them of old time, Thou shalt not forswear thyself, but shalt perform unto the Lord thine oaths: But I say unto you, Swear not at all; neither by heaven; for it is God's throne: Nor by the earth; for it is his footstool: neither by Jerusalem; for it is the city of the great King. Neither shalt thou swear by thy head, because thou canst not make one hair white or black. *But let your communication be, Yea, Yea; Nay, nay: for whatsoever is more than these cometh of evil.* (emphasis mine)
>
> Matthew 5:33-37

This echoes the wisdom of Solomon found in Ecclesiastes 5:2-7 as it pertains to vows:

> Be not *rash* with thy mouth, and let not thine heart be *hasty* to utter any thing before God: for God is in heaven, and thou upon earth: therefore *let thy words be few*....When thou vowest a vow unto God, defer not to pay it; for he hath no pleasure in fools: pay that which thou hast vowed. *Better is it that thou shouldest not vow, than that thou shouldest vow and not pay*. Suffer not thy mouth to cause thy flesh to sin; neither say thou before the angel, that it was an error: wherefore should God be angry at thy voice, and destroy the work of thine hands?

One vow offered and signed by some of candidates was 50 times longer than the presidential oath of office and marriage vows combined. It was vague, complicated and open-ended; and unnecessarily bound the conscience.

Don't misunderstand me, I don't believe the Scripture passages cited above forbid making vows. The New Testament describes vows and oaths that Jesus and the disciples made. But using them to attract voters during a campaign season seems tawdry and ostentatious.

I also don't have a problem with political organizations sending out surveys to candidates asking them for their positions on issues and then publishing the results. But having candidates make vows to God is coercive and makes a mockery of making vows. Why do we believe politicians will keep these vows with any more faithfulness than their wedding vows or the oath they will take to defend the Constitution?

Chapter Twenty-One

I Don't Get These New-Fangled Voting Machines

We've had a problem at least since the 2000 elections, when supposedly a vote for Pat Buchanan was really a vote for Al Gore. But putting in high-tech voting machines doesn't seem to be helping. We need someone to put out voter guides telling us how to get our votes to register for the right person, for Newt Gingrich once said that "a vote for Santorum is a vote for Romney."

Back in 2008, I was told by Romney supporters that "a vote for Huckabee was a vote for McCain" This whole thing is leaving me with lots of questions about the 2012 presidential race. If I get off my couch and vote for Newt, who gets that vote, Nancy Pelosi? So to get my vote to register for Santorum, do I really have to vote for Romney, the guy he endorsed in 2008? What if I desire to vote for Rick Perry, must I vote for Rudy Giuliani, even though he never got in this time (and barely got in last time)?

Who does my vote count for if I want to vote for Speaker Gingrich? Jon Huntsman? Finally, if I want Romney to be president, who do I vote for again? Mike Huckabee? I get so confused.

It will get worse this fall, if we have any third-party candidates. I can hear it now: A vote for Ron Paul (or some other third party candidate[262]) is a vote for Barack Obama. I've got a great idea. Let's agree that our votes will count for the people we voted for.

---

[262] Talk show host Michael Medved calls them losertarians.

I Don't Buy What They Are Selling

Suppose three candidates are running for president, whether in a primary or a general election. The conventional wisdom is:

- Candidate "A" is to be loathed and feared.
- Candidate "B" is a good candidate (but who I believe is only barely qualified, if it all).
- Candidate "C" is the best candidate (but who supposedly cannot win)

I intend to vote for "C". The problem is that "C" is running as an independent or in a third party. The last time out around that party got only 71 votes.

So, the same folks who told me *I must vote* now tell me I must vote for the nearly unqualified candidate in order to stop the terrible candidate, implying that *I* am responsible if the bad guy wins. I am also told that I am wasting my vote, because candidate "C" can't win. By that definition, once the winner is decided, all votes for the non-winner can be shown to have been wasted votes, since only one candidate can win: the winner. There is only one system that will guarantee you never waste your vote by voting for a non-winner. It is called a one-party system—like they had in the old Soviet Union.

Otherwise, forget how your neighbor will vote. Ignore the polls, which often turn out to be false prophets that will lead you astray and cause you to vote for the wrong candidate. I suggest you vote as if your vote is the only one in the world that matters. Vote as if you were appointing the person to office. Vote as if Christ were with you in the voting booth—because He is. Then, your conscience will be clear and clean.

CONCLUSION

Starting From Scratch

> "Always vote for principle, though you may vote alone, and you may cherish the sweetest reflection that your vote is never lost."
> John Quincy Adams

I am not the same person who started this book over 15 months ago. I am less confident in men, more confident in God. I am now more concerned about the specific temptations Christian politicians *and* voters face, than I am the disasters our country faces. It is much more important to me that Christians recognize they are a holy nation than whether historical documents or the court system says the U.S. is a Christian nation. This does not mean that Christians shouldn't do politics; it is that politics shouldn't do them in.

There is never an easy way to say "Your mom is dead." Whether it is easy or not though, I must still tell you that most of what we have believed about politics is *dead* wrong. This sounds pessimistic, I know. But if I am correct, it is time for Christians to bury these rotting corpses and move on. Embracing corpses is not healthy.

For the Christian, death is never the end anyway, it is just the beginning. We do not grieve as others do.[263] Because we believe in the resurrection of the dead, we know that the passing of the old makes way for the new.[264] Unless a grain of wheat falls into the ground and dies, it remains alone. But if it dies, it shall bring forth fruit.[265]

Mixing politics and religion is a necessary evil, and the issues can become complicated. My final effort here is to express things that we have

---

[263] I Thessalonians 4:13

[264] II Corinthians 5:17

[265] John 12:24

looked at in depth with a clearer statement of the principles involved. There are nine.

Number One: Sinners Are Voting for Sinners

Because every man is a sinner, we can be sure that our favorite candidate is one, too. Any candidate who doesn't fail us as a candidate will likely disappoint us as a public official. That doesn't mean we shouldn't expect our leaders to be honest and just leaders, but rather that those looking for "Mr. Perfect" should know that the entire pool of potential candidates is made up of sinners.

Even the kings of the Old Testament who were pleasing in God's eyes often failed in major ways because they were sinners. For example, they failed to tear down the idols of the people's imaginations. This was true from the time of David until Hezekiah began to reign in Judah.

Therefore, the Christian should be humble when he criticizes the flaws of the other guy's candidates. We should be thankful for small victories in the advance of righteousness, for there will be no heaven on earth until Christ returns.

Candidates aren't the only sinners. Voters are sinners, too. One of the downsides of democratically elected officials is that they tend to be beholden to the whims of sinners. We should be surprised they don't pander even more than they do. It is often said that nations get the leaders they deserve. It can be worse than that. We often get the leaders we voted for. Thankfully, "He hath not dealt with us after our sins; nor rewarded us according to our iniquities." (Ps. 103:10).

Of course, how we view sin has a great impact on how we view the role of government.

Number Two: Our Political Process is Seriously Flawed

Winston Churchill opined that the democratic system of picking our own leaders may be the worst system in the world, except for all of the rest. We have a system that encourages public officials to vote for, or sign into law, bills that are laced with poison. With our emphasis on positive thinking, candidates who seek higher office often brag about what they have done, and lie about what their opponent has done. Most presidential candidates egotistically suggest that they are the only one who can "save us" from the abyss. Finally, in a democracy, even Christian rulers are tempted to put pleasing people as a higher priority than pleasing God.

Because Christ goes before us, we can even use a flawed system and expect the blessing of God when we do what is right and vote on principle. We should encourage candidates to stand boldly and always tell the truth, even if it hurts their own candidacies. Neither they—nor we—should think that they are our last hope.

Number Three: For the Christian, Only Candidates That Are 100% Pro-Life Need Apply

Believing in abortion exceptions suggests that some lives are expendable. This is a violation of the Sixth Commandment and the fundamental duty leaders have to protect life. The Golden Rule requires that we consider what we would want others to do if we were the ones society described as worthless eaters. If a leader won't protect your life, he isn't likely to protect your freedom or your property.

Many Americans prove that they are sheep, following whoever has the courage to lead them (even if he or she leads them down the wrong path). Polls show that they waver on the issue of abortion. They might well follow if a truly pro-life leader emerges.

Number Four: Government, in General, Has Become an Idol

When we expect governors to take care of us, ultimately protect us, or teach us what is right or wrong, we have put them in the place of God. Neither good governors nor good laws change the hearts of people who refuse to serve God. We have replaced evangelism with campaigning, the Law of God with polls, and the power of the gospel with the power of politics. We have prioritized saving the planet over saving the inhabitants of the planet (our neighbors), and we fear those who want to control our bodies with socialized medicine more than fearing the One who is able to throw both body and soul into hell.

In the Hollywood political flick, *Primary Colors*, Adrian Lester plays Henry Burton, a young and idealistic political worker who wants to support a candidate with integrity. Instead he finds himself in the middle of a presidential team for a philandering presidential candidate who holds all the right political views, but exudes dishonesty at every level. Although Burton threatens to leave the campaign several times because of the outrageous behavior of others in the "war room", he ends up staying on lest he miss the opportunity to have a positive influence on the candidate and his staff.

I found myself weeping at the conclusion of the movie, not because the conniving candidate wins, but because Burton is right there at the inaugural ball, joining hands with others on the winning team, but losing his integrity.

This story was sad because it illustrates too often what happens to the Christian who compromises for the sake of influence and before he realizes it, has become the one who has *been* influenced, as Godfrey said earlier. Setting aside integrity for the purposes of influence means having neither. It would be better to be an outsider like John the Baptist who shared the gospel with a profligate king and lost his head, than to compromise in order to get in office, and soon find that all of our hoped for influence has disappeared.

Number Five: Some of Us Are Too Patriotic

I lament the likelihood that this conclusion might be the most offensive in the book. I am not suggesting that we join the blame-America first crowd or those who would burn the U.S. flag. On the contrary, we have much to be thankful for in our country.

I *am* calling the Christian to a separation of hope and state. This world is not our permanent home. We must not join others who have grown dependent on the government, while at the same time throwing off the Law of God.

Right now, we are One Nation, Under God's Judgment. Our coins still say "In God We Trust", but we trust more in our political ingenuity than our prayer-answering God. When a politician says "God bless America," too often it sounds like a promise claimed rather than a plea for mercy from the hand of a just God.

If the land is to be preserved, it will only be because of the grace of God, not because we are a chosen people, nor because we have gotten more involved with politics.

Number Six: High Taxes Concern Us More Than High Places

When Christians vote for candidates who have a record of lowering taxes but who refuse to protect innocent life[266], we have sold the lives of our neighbors for a pittance. We are doing as the worshippers of Moloch, who offered up their own children on an altar in order to benefit themselves.

Number Seven: Voting is Free

We are free to vote our own consciences, without answering to pollsters or the opinions of others. We are not bound to pick who we think the winner will be and vote for them. We are only bound to please Christ, who is in the voting booth before we get there. Concerning ourselves with voting strategies usually means we are being manipulated.

We are free to vote for our own brothers and sisters in Christ. We can do this without guilt. We are not violating the law. It is quite alright that we use the high standards God has given us for judging candidates. We are not bigots for doing so.

We are free to vote for a third party or independent candidate. We are not responsible for the outcome if the worst of three or more candidates wins when we voted for the best qualified candidate. We are not bound to trust any man nor disclose our vote to any other person. The vote is really a test, not of our own wisdom in figuring out what a candidate will do, or how our vote will affect the election, but it *is* a test of our obedience to God.

We are free not to vote. Sometimes there may be no candidates who qualify. Or we may have no confidence that any of the candidates will do what is right or make a difference. That is okay. Perhaps we have other responsibilities that are more pressing or beneficial to the kingdom of God. Sadly, many of us have a false guilt over not voting, but miss opportunities on a regular basis to share about Jesus, or apply God's moral law in our discussions about the issues of the day.

---

[266] Proverbs 16:33 says, "The lot is cast into the lap; but the whole disposing thereof is of the LORD."

Number Eight: Anarchy is Worse than Tyranny

Don't become a rebel. You will do as much harm in the long run as any big-government liberal. Pray for quietness and peace, not for revolution. Kindly share the gospel with your unbelieving neighbor. Don't ask the government for more and more favors, but don't disarm its ability to protect us from havoc-wreakers within and enemies without. There is evil in this world.

If we focus on the slights we receive in this world—as if the "culture wars" were fought by filling out petitions and complaining about "Happy Holidays" signs at Target—we will have forgotten that the world hates us and contributed to the cultural decline ourselves by focusing on the small things and ignoring the big ones. We should not strain at a gnat and swallow a camel.

Number Nine: All Things for Our Good

Develop a gratefulness that surpasses your troubles. In comparison to any other time in history or any other place on earth, the average U.S. citizen lives like royalty. We live in luxury and drive in comfort. We have the freedom to share the gospel and publicly attend the church of our choice. God has not treated us as our sins deserve (Ps. 103:10).

For the moment at least, we have it pretty good. If God chooses to allow us hard times, that will be for our good, as well. Maybe we need toughening up for a coming persecution that we must endure. We've likely become too attached to this passing world, at any rate. We've put the state of the state over the state of the church.

Face it. We are very unlikely to ever get the ideal candidate for president that we would want. For the Christian, it is of great comfort to know that the leaders of this world are chosen by God. All things work together for our good, even when our favorite candidate gets 5% in the voting booth and the one who wins the election is bent on opposing everything we believe. Christ was in the voting booth before us. He promises that his every decision is made on our behalf. He gave us George W. Bush and Barack Obama, and he will give us exactly what we need this next election.

When we go into the voting booth, we need not be confident that our vote will "count" in the eyes of men, but rather that it counts with God.

I leave you with another thought from John Quincy Adams:

> Duty is ours; results are God's.

Has politics and all that goes with it just about worn you out? Then let me offer you some real hope and change:

> Humble yourselves therefore under the mighty hand of God, that he may exalt you in due time: Casting all your care upon him; for he careth for you.
>
> I Peter 5:6f

> Come unto me, all ye that labour and are heavy laden, and I will give you rest. Take my yoke upon you, and learn of me; for I am meek and lowly in heart: and ye shall find rest unto your souls.
>
> Matthew 11:28f

> But they that wait upon the LORD shall renew their strength; they shall mount up with wings as eagles; they shall run, and not be weary; and they shall walk, and not faint.
>
> Isaiah 40:31

Appendix 1

Making Insurance Companies Cover Pre-Existing Medical Conditions

Failure to embrace some new social programs can be considered unrealistic, foolish or downright heartless. Take the generally accepted idea that insurance companies should have to cover those with pre-existing conditions. Who could be against that? The prevailing view is that only heartless Barbarians and Neanderthals wanting to take us back to the stone ages could oppose it. Even Mitt Romney included this requirement in MassCare, as Obama did in Obamacare. Former Arkansas Governor Mike Huckabee, on the other hand, believes this will cause a kind of domino effect, with each new tip-over bringing about more loss of freedom.[267] Adding this mandate inevitably leads to complete socialized medicine.

Here is how it would work:

Loss of Freedom #1: Requiring coverage of pre-existing conditions means some customers will certainly cost the company much more than the customer could ever pay in (Huckabee compares it to getting a vehicle insured after it is already wrecked or insuring a house that has already burned down).

Loss of Freedom #2: The only way to make up for the loss from #1 is to raise rates higher on everybody else (few want that option since premiums in many places are well over $10,000 per year already) or require everybody to pay for insurance whether they want it or not, especially the young and healthy.

---

[267] http://www.valuesvotersummit.org/2010archive

Loss of Freedom #3: The only way that mandating purchase will work is to fine people more than the cost of insurance premiums. Nobody has done that yet, but simple laws of economics will eventually require it. Otherwise, many people will just pay the fine and wait until they are sick to get insurance, as Huckabee points out.

Loss of Freedom #4: Higher costs will mean some companies quit offering insurance to its employees, which means more insurance companies like Principal Financial Group of Des Moines, Iowa will get out of the insurance industry altogether. In turn, less competition means higher prices and even less options for customers.

Loss of Freedom #5: The Domino Effect will continue to destroy the health system. For example, when some companies try to exclude certain conditions this often results in more government regulation (as in Massachusetts) but because even governments recognize limits on what companies can do, the bureaucrats eventually pinch on the other end, resulting in rationed care. This will happen more and more as the whole system moves towards a single payer of medical bills, the U.S. Federal Government, which is already staggering under the weight of trillions of dollars of debt.

Loss of Freedom #6: Another way governments try to "help" customers is limit the amount doctors and hospitals can charge for services (reducing reimbursement rates). But reducing costs in this way often leads doctors to go out of business as well. Although insurance companies also cap costs or limit coverage, demand for this coverage drives the free insurance market to make them available (as long as the government doesn't interfere).

Loss of Freedom #7: Huckabee knows that a single-payer system (socialized medicine) cannot allow individuals to pay for their own medical care. It goes against the envy-driven mentality behind the whole notion of universal health care. It just wouldn't be fair if "people with money" could use their own filthy lucre to buy medical treatment while everybody else was dependent on the government. Getting treatment outside the system will be seen as bribing a public official. Socialism not only eventually kills the free market, the free market destroys socialism. It is a fight to the death. One system or the other must prevail, they cannot both survive.

Some Solutions: Too many states now forbid companies from offering catastrophic insurance. One reason insurance is so expensive is because it is paying for minor procedures and services which become more expensive every time another group has to approve it. Also having a third-party pay (even insurance itself) means that consumers don't care what things cost as long as somebody else has to pay for it. And of course, insurance companies and doctors take advantage of this. Allowing competition from state-to-state would help end this counterproductive practice.[268] Regulations must be reduced, not increased.

None of this means people with pre-existing conditions should just be allowed to die. Charitable Hospitals should be able to completely write off care given to those who can't afford it. Families, churches, individual Christians and caring neighbors should be helping people as well as community fund-raising groups.

Reducing the bureaucracy and dependency on third party payers will drastically reduce the cost of medicine overall.

[268] Adapted from http://caffeinatedthoughts.com/2010/10/governor-mike-huckabee-touches-the-new-third-rail-of-politics-insurance-coverage-mandates/

Appendix 2

I See Dead People

By Paul deParrie

I recently read that on the day President Bush signed the Partial-Birth Abortion Ban Act into law, the sun let off an explosion unlike any recorded in history. Some prophetic-types even sent out pictures of the flaming corona saying it looked like a baby. Interpretations abounded.

I see something in those flames, too. I see dead people. More precisely, I see dead babies—and I feel responsible.

Back in 1993, I was the editor-in-chief for Life Advocate magazine. One of our reporters had secreted a copy of a medical paper by Martin Haskell which he presented at the annual meeting of the National Abortion Federation (NAF) in September of 1992. In it was described, in very clinical terms, Haskell's newly-developed Dilation and Extraction or D&X abortion procedure—now popularly called "partial-birth abortion."

It was a block-buster article. We were the only news organ that we were aware of with the information. We prepared the article, but during our staff meeting Andrew Burnett, our publisher, said he was concerned. He wondered if, by publishing the article about the gruesome-appearing type of abortion, anti-abortion work might be damaged because "The Movement" might refocus its efforts away from the millions of invisible babies being killed in the U.S. every year. He was worried that The Movement might be toward this small number of egregious and visible abortions. He wondered if people would forget about the cruelty of the ordinary suction aspiration abortions or even other late-term procedures which, in fact, are far more cruel than the D&X. He wondered if the pockets of "pro-life" people would be picked clean for a war against a single procedure, while the killers marched on slogging through the blood of the innocents.

Well, we eventually chose to run the story in the February 1993 issue of the Life Advocate. The dreaded results were not long in coming. National Right to Life (NRTL) contacted us and wanted to use our story and our four-panel artist's rendering of the procedure—the one you have all, no doubt, seen.

Then it was off to the races. NRTL and its state affiliates, along with many other "pro-life" organizations, began hyping the story and telling their mailing lists that they (for a price, of course) could help stop this gruesome procedure—"partial-birth abortion", they dubbed it.

Ah, yes! It was the fundraisers' dream—for both sides of the war. The "pro-life" forces crafted utterly useless laws banning the procedure and pled for money to promote and defend in court these purposeless statutes. "We can save lives and curb this cruel practice," they bleated. However, none of the laws would stop a single abortion because there were already several other procedures—some more truly cruel and torturous than D&X—available to be used by the child killers.

In addition, the shrill shriek of the pro-aborts was heard throughout the land. "This is just the beginning of losing our abortion rights," they cried disingenuously while raking in the cash.

Both sides knew precisely what they were doing. "Pro-life" leaders knew that the ban wouldn't stop any abortions. The opposition leaders knew that banning a single procedure would not end "abortion rights." The money, though, was good for both.

Nor were the politicians adverse wallowing in the pig sty. Even normally pro-abort office-holders could vote for the ban and gain a few "pro-life" votes—and possibly campaign support from pragmatic right-to-life organizations. The standard for "pro-life" organizations giving to candidates was not whether they opposed abortion itself, but whether they would vote for the D&X ban.

The whole scene went downhill fast. I originally tried to console myself that raising the "partial-birth abortion" issue would cause the public to have more discussion about their half-hearted support for child killing. I hoped that the pro-abort defense of D&X would shock the public mind and reveal the truly crass, bloody, inhuman "face of pro-choice America." Instead, it eventually just made people more callused toward the barbaric killing. "Well, any kind of surgery looks gruesome," they took to saying.

Of course, after ten years and millions spent by The Movement, Bush finally signed the ban. Whoopie-do! Now Bush gets to pretend that he is a "pro-life" hero. Naturally, the fight has to go on in the courts for years, so "Keep those cards and letters—and money—coming, folks, and don't let the pro-aborts snatch our victory away!" (I predict the ban will lose in court.) The pro-aborts will raise millions for the same.

Ten years and everybody makes out like bandits. For another ten years everyone will continue to gain—everybody but the babies.

Nowadays I tend to imagine the millions, possibly tens of millions, of dollars raised by "our side" for this fruitless exercise. I imagine if that money had been used to hire professional sidewalk counselors to talk to abortion-bound mothers outside the clinics. I imagine mobile ultrasound vans outside clinics. I imagine some of that money going to the attorneys to defend the rights of the counselors and picketers at the clinics. I imagine if that money had been used to provide medical services for those who changed their minds. I imagine, over ten years, thousands of babies alive today, tens of thousands of babies alive today, who are not with us now. I weep for them.

Jesus told us to feed the hungry. He told us to feed the hungry that were right in front of our face—not start a movement that would eventually feed hungry people in the future. When we invest our time, energy and money to save babies, it should be directed as much as possible at babies who are dying today, not those who may (or may not) be aborted in 2050. Yet, the D&X ban (aside from being ineffective) is precisely 180 degrees out from that principle. Over the last ten years, The Movement has spent untold millions to pass a law which pretends to save babies, while the human presence at the abortuaries has dropped to near zero in most of the nation.

My 1993 decision to run that article helped to dilute the activist, anti-abortion movement probably far more than the federal Freedom of Access to Clinic Entrances (FACE) law and all the lawsuits. The attention of the anti-abortion activist was successfully diverted from the clinic doors where killing was going on every day to funding a "winnable" piece of fluff legislation called the Partial-Birth Abortion Act.

I had a part in that, and I am sorry. Sure, I could assuage my conscience saying that someone else would have eventually published it and started this whole mess, but that is simply dishonest. I was the one who decided to go to print.

So, if you wonder why I still go out to the clinics and the streets and the churches with my big, graphic signs trying to convince women to stop killing their babies, it is because I see something.

I see dead babies.
Paul deParrie was editor of Life Advocate magazine.[269]

[269] Used by permission.

Appendix 3

An Honorable Society[270]

By Mike Ericson, Pastor
Trinity Presbyterian Reformed Church, Johnston, Iowa
(From a sermon preached on 1/29/2012)

> Honour thy father and thy mother: that thy days may be long upon the land which the LORD thy God giveth thee.
>
> Exodus 20:12

The law of God is holy, it is righteous, it is good. The LORD has given his law, not only to show forth our iniquity even as a schoolmaster, driving us and drawing us unto Christ, but also as it reveals his holy will unto us: How we are to live, how we in Christ are to walk, the fruit we are to bear, and how we are to show our love to God in simple, straightforward obedience. We have not the strength of our own to do these things, but only by the Spirit of God.

We come now to the Fifth Commandment. In the second giving of the law:

> Honour thy father and thy mother, as the LORD thy God hath commanded thee; that thy days may be prolonged, and that it may go well with thee, in the land which the LORD thy God giveth thee.
>
> Deuteronomy 5:16

[270] Used by permission. Transcript Adapted for Print. You may listen to the complete sermon here: http://www.presbyterianreformed.org/player.php?id=300608201662

These Ten Commandments are summary, principial statements regarding God's will for us, even our sanctification. And as a summary, each one of these as they are related together in our love for God and our love for our neighbor, stands as a theme or a category covering many aspects, and here the Fifth Commandment speaks of our relations, one with another. Not just relation between child and parent or our relatives, as aunts or uncles, or families, but also all of the relations in a society: the relations we have here in our ecclesiastical society, the household of faith, the family of God; and the relations we have in our civil society, between our president, and our judges. This commandment speaks to us about those honorable relations in a society, in the various key governments or structures in the society: the family, the church or the commonwealth (or the state). An honorable society, so that it may go well with you; that it may go well with you in your households, your church or the land in which you live. Walking honorably, and treating one another with honor.

Let me speak to you this morning about godly societies and this relation of honor in them. We are all in relations of various sorts, whether in families, in a church, or in a land in civil governments.

The first thing we would address then is the scope of the commandment. Second, is the general duty to honor. Third, the blessing and the promise associated with this commandment.

What does the Fifth Commandment cover, what does it speak about, its scope or its breadth? We notice here that the archetype or prime root from which this commandment draws and speaks is the authority of father and mother. Question: "Who are they that have the first and natural right to honor and respect?" Answer: "natural parents, fathers and mothers."[271] This is the natural state of things. For after Adam and Eve, all have had an earthly mother and earthly father, even those who come into a family by adoption.

The root or picture that is drawn from in this commandment is to show that relation and authority in natural parents, but also a picture or archetype of that kind of relation throughout society. Father is that image of authority over a child. This image is applied also to church relations and it's applied to governmental relations.

The Westminster Larger Catechism asks in Question 124: "Who are meant by father and mother in the Fifth Commandment? Answer: By father and mother, in the Fifth Commandment, are meant, not only natural parents, but all superiors in age and gifts; and especially such as, by God's

---

[271] Fisher's Catechism, Question and Answer #17

ordinance, are over us in place of authority, whether in family, church or commonwealth."

They did not make this up. They are not stretching beyond the commandment. This is not some popish twisting of Scripture to say, "I am to be your father." Rather, it is searching the Scripture and discovering people that are not the natural father are called father or treated as such.

For example, Paul gives Timothy these instructions:

> Rebuke not an elder, but intreat him as a father; and the younger men as brethren; The elder women as mothers; the younger as sisters, with all purity.
>
> I Timothy 5:1, 2

Now I think there the term "elder" is related especially to the phrase "elder women" and is referring here to age, someone who is older than you. He doesn't just merely say treat them with respect, or honor, or a certain dignity, but tells Timothy what? Those that are your elders, you treat as your father. Honor thy father. And Timothy (young people) those women that are elder, you are to treat as mothers. You see how he takes his exhortation and places it in the framework of these duties, of what he owes. Now, age is the distinction here. They are superior in age. And so the Larger Catechism is quite in accord with Scripture. Honor thy father and thy mother. You are to treat those who are superior in age with honor and respect, not disdain. That is quite a reverse from our culture, isn't it? The Scriptures tell us the gray head is a covering of honor. It is a visible sign of that distinction of age. In our culture, gray hair is a sign of shame, but this is not so according to the Word of God.

The same is true regarding the government. And I think this is what you find, for example, when Christ enters Jerusalem, in Mark's gospel, where they cry out "blessed be the kingdom of our father, David." All of these people who were crying out "Blessed be the kingdom" were not all of natural descent from David, so I think very clearly there they are referring to King David. There is that relationship between them. The scope of this commandment is not narrowly focused upon the family, but also upon our relations with other people.

There's a danger of a leveling society, in which we will not acknowledge father, mother, children, or that there is a distinction in our associations or relations.... You see a leveling society, just that, wants to level everything. No recognition of difference in age. No recognition of difference in station. No recognition of difference of authority. No recognition of difference of gifts. The society that would be blessed that it may go well with them will recognize these relations and differences, as it were, in authority, or gifts, or age, and so on. When everyone receives a trophy, there's no honoring of gifts or achievement. And we live in a society that is bent upon leveling everything.

We have schools that are afraid to even give children grades! Everything's leveled. Everyone gets an excellent. Everyone's done well. We find the disaster of these things, for example, in the 1500's in the Peasant Revolts, in which, because of a twisted understanding of the Gospel, they thought that in society, therefore, everything was to be leveled. No authorities. No rulers. No difference in wealth. No difference in gifts.

Today that movement is "occupy this" and "occupy that". Everything is leveled, leading to a resentment of gifts and a resentment of authority. A resentment of the fact that they may have to pay back loans that they took out to try to reach themselves those very things they resent in others. This is not to suggest that there are no abuses in our society.

You find leveling in communism, although it's a twisted lie, because things are not really level in communism. You have the rulers that are very wealthy with all power and the ruled thinking that somehow there are no rulers.

One of the interesting phenomena in our culture now is the internet. It's one of the great leveling devices. There were uprisings, for example, in the Middle East, where Facebook was instrumental. Now I'm not speaking against the internet. I didn't invent it; I'm not speaking against it. There's much good that can be done there. But there's also a danger that we as Christian's need to be careful about. And that is because it tends to be faceless and almost personless, it is a great leveling agent. Now some of that can be a good thing in the sense that just your average person can get his ideas out there. I'm not suggesting that's a bad thing. But you see how it is so easy to be disrespectful on a blog or to be disrespected. And we find people have, at times, little respect for age or station. Everything's leveled. And everybody's ideas—because of pride at times—are considered to be the best there ever were. And there's a lot of disrespect. And we must watch for this in all our relations, be it in the commonwealth or in the church or in the home. (You saw Korah's problem with the idea that God had placed some people in authority in Numbers 16.)

We find a promise appended to this commandment: "That thy days may be long upon the land which the Lord, thy God, giveth thee." And so when the Apostle Paul speaks to children, he gives them that exhortation in Ephesians 6:2, "Honor thy father and mother which is the first commandment with promise".

Obedience to this commandment has a special promise given to it: so that things might go well in our land. That it might go well in our homes. That it might go well in our churches. That it might go well in our civil society. Even as the first four commandments, especially the first three, have those duties that are focused even more centrally, immediately unto God, so now, the Fifth Commandment focuses on our duties, one to another. And so that in our societies, that it may go well, we find that promise.

One asks, what is the fruit and consequence of the conscientious performance of these relative duties, even treating those who aren't living very honorably with the respect due unto their station and so on and so forth? Hereby outward peace and concord will be better maintained between man and man and likewise the members of Christ's body will be knit more closely to one another in love. For there to be peace in the home, in the household, for there to be peace and prosperity in the land, peace in the church among the brethren, we are to give honor to whom honor is due and to live honorably. This touches all our relations.

God has ordained a structure in our lives and our relations. He has determined, as we read in Acts, the bounds of their habitation, the bounds of your habitation. I am not saying you cannot improve your station to a certain degree; but this is a recognition that God has placed some to be kings, and no matter how hard you try or work in certain situations, you will not be king. And you do not need to, nor can you, tear the king down just because you're not king. Likewise, God has made some very wealthy and they were born into that, many of them. We cannot resent that. This is to resent God himself. God has placed you where you are.

I remember at times in my early days in seminary there were some women that took classes and they were very resentful that they were women. Because, at least in a Bible-believing denomination, they realized that they were never going to be pastors. God has made you who you are and placed you where you are within a general structure. And we submit unto God. Scriptures refers to Him, in that sense, as the father of all mankind, as their Creator. And we will give them the respect that is due unto them, not beyond reason, not outside of their station, but we will give them the respect and honor that is due unto them because God is God and we live under Him. By God's grace, let us seek to honor Him first and foremost.

Appendix 4

One Hour Well Spent

Outline of Sermon Preached by Pastor George McDearmon[272]

Why Should I Pray for the Nations?

I. Because God Has Sovereignly Determined That Mankind Live in Nations

II. Because God Has Established Governing Authorities

III. Because God is the Sovereign Lord Over All Nations - Because He Can Do Whatever He Wishes with Them (II Chronicles 20:6, Jeremiah 10:6, John 19:10)

IV. Because God Has Directed Us to Do So (I Timothy 2)

How Should I Pray for the Nations?

I. That Our Leaders Would Be Men of Virtue and Integrity: Character is Determinate - What a Leader Does is a Fruit of What He Is (Proverbs 16:12; 29:2; 8:15f)

II. That Our Leader Would Have Wise Counselors - (Proverbs 20:18; 20:28; 24:6)

III. That Our Government Would Do Its God-Given Job (Administrate Justice, Proverbs 20:8, 18; 21:15, Romans 13:1-7)

IV. That Our Citizens Would Live Righteously (Proverbs 28:2,4) "The More Sin, The More Government"

---

[272] http://www.sermonaudio.com/play.asp?ID=9604104930&sourceID=blbcsa

V. That There Would Be an Awakening of True Biblical Religion. (I Timothy 2:1f)

Index